LIBRARY OF NEW TESTAMENT STUDIES
471

Formerly the Journal for the Study of the New Testament Supplement Series

Editor
Mark Goodacre

WOMEN IN THE GREETINGS OF ROMANS 16.1-16

A Study of Mutuality and Women's Ministry in the Letter to the Romans

SUSAN MATHEW

BLOOMSBURY

LONDON · NEW DELHI · NEW YORK · SYDNEY

Bloomsbury T&T Clark
An imprint of Bloomsbury Publishing Plc

50 Bedford Square   175 Fifth Avenue
London   New York
WC1B 3DP   NY 10010
UK   USA

www.bloomsbury.com

First published 2013

British Library Cataloguing-in-Publication Data
A catalogue record for this books is available from the British Library.

ISBN: HB: 978-0-567-42944-5

Typeset by Free Range Book Design & Production
Printed and bound in Great Britain

Dedicated to
my husband Mathew and
children Josh, Abhishek, Ashish and Jyothish

CONTENTS

PREFACE

This book represents a minor revision of my doctoral thesis accepted by the University of Durham, UK in 2010. I wish to thank Prof. Mark S. Goodacre, who read and accepted this work for publication in the Library of the New Testament Studies, Dominic Mattos, the Commissioning Editor, and the whole editorial team at Bloomsbury Publishing.

I would like to express my appreciation and heartfelt gratitude to many people who, in various ways, helped me to complete this research.

My supervisor, Prof. John M. G. Barclay, the Lightfoot Professor of Divinity, deserves a special word of thanks for his valid suggestions, insightful comments, constant encouragement and careful supervision of my thesis. Moreover, I thank him for his whole-hearted support for the project that was begun along with my research to help the children affected with cerebral palsy at my home town in India. I also remember his and Diana Barclay's rich hospitality on various occasions. My special thanks to Dr. Stephen Barton, my second supervisor for his timely help and encouragement. I express my gratitude to my examiners, Dr. Paul Ellingworth (Aberdeen University) and Dr. W. R. Telford (Durham University) for their constructive comments and suggestions.

I would like to express my thanks to all who have helped me financially at the various stages of development of this work. My special thanks are due to: Dr. Robert Song for kindly arranging a PGR Scholarship from Durham University in the first year; the scholarship committee in the Department of Theology and Religion for offering timely financial support; Langham Partnership International for providing a scholarship from the second year till the completion of my research. This research could not have been possible without the financial assistance from Langham. I consider it a privilege to be a Langham scholar. I am grateful for the support, prayer and fellowship I had from fellow scholars who represent different nations. My special thanks are due to the Scholars Directors, Dr. Howard Peskett and Dr. Ian Shaw. I am grateful to the staff at Ustinov College – especially to Theresa McKinven, the Vice-Principal, and Ms. Brenda Ryder, Student Support Officer – for their timely support during my research. I am very much indebted to the British Council for choosing me as the winner of the Shine International Award 2010 (North East).

The practical assistance from the staff of the Department of Theology and Religion was incalculable. To the members of Tyndale House, Cambridge, I want to thank you for providing a space for me in your library, where I prepared the final draft of my thesis. I express my thanks to my friend Ben

Blackwell for proofreading my thesis before the first submission and Adam Earl, who has carried out meticulous work before the publication of my book. My special thanks are due to the following persons and institutions: to Dr. Mark and Ruth Bonnington at Kings Church, Durham; Rev. Alan and Sandra Bell at Emmanuel Church, Durham; the Trustees of CANDLE (Caring and Addressing the Needs of Differently-Abled Lives through Education) FOR INDIA charity; NHS and Children's Community Centre, Chester-Le-Street and St. Hild's School, for supporting my youngest son Jyothish, who is affected with cerebral palsy; to Stuart and Rachel for being good family friends; to Katia and Christophe for kindly giving their car as a gift; Prince and Lucy and Sunderland Pentecostal Fellowship; K.T. Koshy and New Castle Christian Fellowship for their love and support; and our friends from Kerala all over the UK who extended fellowship and hospitality on various occasions; to the students and colleagues at Faith Theological Seminary, Kerala, India and my mother church in Kerala for upholding me and my family in prayer.

I am grateful to my parents for their love, prayer and support, especially my Dad for being a model in Christian life and ministry, and to my sisters and their families and my brother for their love and support. I cherish the fond memories of my Mom who went to be with the Lord when I was twelve years old, whose love, advice and discipline still guide the paths of my life. To Dr. Mathew C. Vargheese, my companion in life and ministry, who whole-heartedly supported my project and to our children Josh, Abhishek, Ashish and Jyothish for being with me patiently in every step of my work.

Above all, thanks be to God who enabled me to complete this research. 'For from him and through him and to him are all things. To him be the glory forever. Amen' (Rom. 11.36).

Susan Mathew, Manakala, Kerala, June 2012

ABBREVIATIONS

Abbreviations of ancient literature follow the *SBL Handbook of Style* (2004) wherever possible. In addition, the following abbreviations are used:

AB	*Anchor Bible*
ABD	*Anchor Bible Dictionary*
AGJU	*Arbeiten zur Geschichte des antiken Judentums und des Urchristentums*
AJP	*American Journal of Philology*
BCE	Before the Common Era
BDAG	Bauer, W., W. F. Arndt, F. W. Gingrich, and F. W. Danker, *Greek–English Lexicon of the New Testament and Other Early Christian Literature*. 3rd ed. Chicago, 2000
BJS	*Brown Judaic Studies*
BRev	*Bible Review*
BT	*The Bible Translator*
BWANT	Beiträge zur Wissenschaft vom Alten (und Neuen) Testament
CBQ	*Catholic Biblical Quarterly*
CD	*Damascus Document*
CE	Common Era
CFTL	Clark's Foreign Theological Library
CRINT	Compendia rerum iudaicarum ad Novum Testamentum
DPL	*Dictionary of Paul and His Letters*
EBib	*Etudes Bibliques*
EDNT	*Exegetical Dictionary of the New Testament*, ed. H. Balz, G. Schneider. ET. Grand Rapids, 1990–93
EKKNT	Evangelisch-katholischer Kommentar zum Neuen Testament
ETR	*Etudes théologiques et religieuses*
EvQ	*Evangelical Quarterly*
ExpTim	*Expository Times*
GR	*Greece and Rome*
HTR	*Harvard Theological Review*
HTS	*Harvard Theological Studies*
ICC	International Critical Commentary
IJT	*Indian Journal of Theology*
JAAR	*Journal of the American Academy of Religion*

JAC	Jahrbuch für Antike und Christentum
JB	Jerome Bible
JBL	Journal of Biblical Literature
JETS	Journal of the Evangelical Theological Society
JJS	Journal of Jewish Studies
JRS	Journal of Roman Studies
JSJ	Journal of the Study of the Judaism in the Persian, Hellenistic, and Roman Periods
JSNT	Journal for the Study of the New Testament
JSNTSup	Journal for the Study of the New Testament: Supplement Series
JSOT	Journal for the Study of the Old Testament
JTS	Journal of Theological Studies
KEK	Kritisch-exegetischer Kommentar über das Neue Testament
KJV	King James Version
LSJ	Liddell, H. G., R. Scott, and H. S. Jones, A Greek–English Lexicon, 9th ed. with revised supplement. Oxford, 1996
LTJ	Lutheran Theological Journal
LXX	Septuagint
MM	Moulton, J. H. and G. Milligan, The Vocabulary of the Greek Testament. London, 1930. Reprint, Peabody, 1997
MSS	Manuscripts
NCBC	New Critical Bible Commentary
New Docs	New Documents Illustrating Early Christianity: A Review of the Greek Inscriptions and Papyri. Edited by G. H. R. Horsley and S. Llewelyn. North Ryde, NSW, 1981–
NovT	Novum Testamentum
NovTSup	Novum Testamentum Supplements
NTAbh	Neutestamentliche Abhandlungen
NTD	Das Neue Testament Deutsch
NTS	New Testament Studies
PCPSSV	Proceedings of the Cambridge Philological Society, Supplement Volume
QD	Quaestiones disputatae
RBen	Revue bénédictine
REB	Revised English Bible
ResQ	Restoration Quarterly
SBL	Society of Biblical Literature
SBLDS	Society of Biblical Literature Dissertation series
SBT	Studies in Biblical Theology
SE	Studia Evangelica
SNTS	Society for New Testament Studies
SNTSMS	Society for New Testament Studies Monograph Series

SNTW	Studies of the New Testament and Its World
SVF	*Stoicorum Veterum Fragmenta*
TDNT	*Theological Dictionary of the New Testament.* Edited by G. Kittel and G. Friedrich. Translated by G. W. Bromiley. 10 vols. Grand Rapids, 1964–76
TGI	*Theologie und Glaube*
THKNT	*Theologischer Handkommentar zum Neuen Testament*
TJ	*Trinity Journal*
TynBul	*Tyndale Bulletin*
VC	*Vigiliae Christianae*
WBC	Word Biblical Commentary
WMANT	Wissenschaftliche Monographien zum Alten und Neuen Testament
WW	*Word and World*
ZNW	*Zeitschrift für die neutestamentlische Wissenschaft und die Kunde der älteren Kirche*

Papyri

P. Amh.	*The Amherst Papyri, Being an Account of the Greek Papyri in the Collection of the Right Hon. Lord Amherst of Hackney, F.S.A. at Didlington Hall, Norfolk*, ed. B.P. Grenfell and A.S. Hunt. London
BGU	*Aegyptische Urkunden aus den Königlichen* (later *Staatlichen*) *Museen zu Berlin, Griechische Urkunden.* Berlin
P. Cair. Zen	*Zenon Papyri, Catalogue général des antiquités égyptiennes du Musée du Caire*, ed. C. C. Edgar. Cairo
P. Fay.	*Fayum Towns and their Papyri*, ed. B. P. Grenfell, A. S. Hunt, and D. G. Hogarth. London 1900
P. Giess.	*Griechische Papyri im Museum des oberhessischen Geschichtsveriens zu Giessen*, ed. O. Eger et al. 3 vols. Leipzig/Berlin, 1910–22
P. Giss.	*Griechische Papyri im Museum des oberhessische Geschichtsvereins zu Giessen*, ed. O. Eger, E. Kornemann and P. M. Meyer. Leipzig-Berlin 1910–12
PGM	*Papyri graecae magicae*, ed. K. Preisendanz. 2 vols. Leipzig, 1928–31
P. Hamb.	*Griechische Papyrusurkunden der Hamburger Staats- und Universitätsbibliothek*
P. Iand.	*Papyri Iandanae*, ed. C. Kalbfleisch et al. Leipzig
P. Mert.	*A Descriptive Catalogue of the Greek Papyri in the Collection of Wilfred Merton*
P. Oslo.	*Papyri Osloenses.* Oslo

P. Oxy.	*The Oxyrhynchus Papyri*. Published by the Egypt Exploration Society in Graeco-Roman Memoirs. London
P. Princ.	*Papyri in the Princeton University Collections*
P. Ryl.	*Catalogue of the Greek and Latin Papyri in the John Rylands Library,* Manchester
PSI	*Papiri greci e latin*
P. Tebt.	*The Tebtunis Papyri*. London

Inscriptions

CII, CIJ	*Corpus Inscriptionum Iudicarum*, ed. J.-B. Frey. 2 vols. Pontificio Istituto Di Archeologia Cristiana,1936–52
CIL	*Corpus Inscriptionum Latinarum*
CPJ	*Corpus Papyrorum Judaicarum*, 3 vols
EG	*Epigrafia greca*, ed. M. Guarducci. 4 vols. Rome, 1967–78
I Eph.	*Die Inschriften von Ephesos*. 8 vols. Bonn, 1979–84
IG	*Inscriptiones Graecae*, Berlin
IGR, IGRR	*Incriptiones Graecae ad res Romanas pertinentes*, ed. R. Cagnat et al. 3 vols. Paris, 1906–27. Reprint, Chicago, 1975
IKilikiaBM 1	*Journeys in Rough Cilicia, 1962–63*, ed. G. E. Bean and T. B. Mitford. DenkscheWien 85. Vienna, 1965
MAMA	*Monumenta Asiae Minoris Antiqua*. 10 vols. Manchester, then London, 1928–93
SEG	*Supplementum Epigraphicum Graecum 1–11*, ed. J. J. E. Hondius et al., 1923–. 12–25, ed. A. G. Woodhead et al., Leiden, –1971.

Josephus

Ag.Ap.	*The Life Against Apion*
Ant.	*Antiquitates Judaicae (Jewish Antiquities)*
J.W.	Jewish War

Philo

De Somn	*De Somniis*
In Flacc	*In Flaccum*
Leg. Ad. Gaius	*Legatio ad Gaium*
Leg.Alleg.	*Legum Allegoriae*

Mishnah

m.Git	Gittin
m.Sota	Sota
m.Yebam	Yebamot
m.Yoma	Yoma

Babylonian Talmud

b.Pesah	Talmud Pesahim
b.Qidd	Qiddushin

Tosefta

t. Meg	Megillah
t. Zeb	Zebahim

Jerusalem Talmud

1 Clem	*1 Clement*
Herm.Man	Shepherd of Hermas, *Mandate*
y. Ber	Berakhot

Cleobulus *Epig.*	*Epigrammata*
Periander *Ep.*	*Epistulae*
Pittacus *Epig.*	*Epigramma*
T. Sim	*Testament of Simon*
T. Zeb	*Testament of Zebulun*
Thales *Epig.ded.*	*Epigramma dedicatrium*
Theognis *Eleg.*	*Elegiae*

Unless otherwise noted, the translations of the ancient texts in this thesis follow, where available, the renderings of LCL. The translations of New Testament texts are my own unless otherwise stated.

CHAPTER 1

INTRODUCTION

1.1. Purpose of study

Despite the apparent restrictions on women in the worship and ministry of the church elsewhere (1 Cor. 14.34-35; cf. 1 Tim. 2.11-12), the Pauline greetings in Rom. 16.1-16 affirm the mutuality of men and women in Christian ministry.[1] Romans 16.1-16 contains a list of persons who were actively engaged in the ministry of the church; Paul greets them and acknowledges their ministry. No less than ten women are mentioned and Paul acknowledges their ministry in a similar way to his acknowledgement of the men.

What is the significance of the greetings in Rom. 16.1-16 for our understanding of the role of women in Christian leadership and ministry? How do we account for Paul's positive approach to the role of women's ministry in the church? What can we say about the women mentioned in Rom. 16.1-16 and their leadership roles? What models of mutuality are implied in this passage, and how do they relate to the notion of mutual interdependence explained elsewhere in Romans and Paul's other letters?

1.2. The issues raised

The form of greeting in Romans 16 is different from other letters, and the second person plural aorist imperative ἀσπάσασθε is used sixteen times. Paul instructs his recipients to greet both individuals and groups, an instruction rarely found outside Romans. The second person use of ἀσπάσασθε throughout Rom. 16.1-16 is significant because it suggests that people should form closer bonds with each other and strengthen their relationships. Paul directs the greetings to the members of the church, and all members of the Roman church are assumed to participate in greeting one another. The exhortation in Rom. 16.16 to 'greet one another with a holy kiss' (ἀσπάσασθε ἀλλήλους

---

1   Although the simple definition of 'mutuality' is 'relationships of reciprocal care', a richer and deeper definition can be deduced on the basis of Paul's exposition of mutual relations in Romans 12–16. See section 1.7.

ἐν φιλήματι ἁγίῳ) can be interpreted as a summation of Rom. 16.1-16 and as a practice intended to include the entire church community.

It is also significant that the greetings that acknowledge the toil, hard work, and ministry of specific women are descriptively linked with Christ, Paul, and the wider church. Most of the women in Rom. 16.1-16 appear to hold a prominent position amongst the other individuals in the list indicating, by implication, their active participation in ministry and the preference Paul has given them as his associates. The descriptive phrases in Rom. 16.1-16 are employed with far greater frequency than in other Pauline letters and serve to emphasise the strong commendation attached to Rom. 16.1-16. Moreover, by acknowledging his relationship with specific people in the Roman church, Paul is strengthening the individual relationships within the community.

When viewed in light of the entire letter, the greetings in Rom. 16.1-16 become even more relevant to the letter's purpose of creating unity and love among the Roman Christians. The letter should not simply be interpreted as a political move by Paul to boost his credibility within the church;[2] the verbal echoes and thematic links in Romans show that Paul is tactically conveying the need for togetherness in the community.

The three major focal points of this study discuss the leadership roles of women in the Pauline churches as observed in Rom. 16.1-16, the disposition of the mutuality reflected in the greetings to men and women, and the way in which the greetings to men and women in Rom. 16.1-16 relate to the ethos of mutualism in Romans 12–15. We can break these focal points down into the following questions:

1 What are the special characteristics of the greetings in Romans 16?
2 What can we know about these women and their leadership roles?
3 By what criteria are their ministries acknowledged by Paul?
4 What are the peculiarities of the form of greetings and the descriptive phrases in Rom. 16.1-16?
5 How does the relational language modify the greetings?
6 What models of mutuality are implied in this passage with its exhortations to mutual greeting?
7 How do these greetings relate to the notion of mutuality and love in Romans 12–13 and mutual recognition in Romans 14–15?

These questions will be answered by a detailed analysis of the function of the greetings in Rom. 16.1-16 and by analysis of the greetings as a continuation of Paul's exhortation throughout Romans to cultivate positive mutual relations (chs. 12–15).

---

2   For further discussion on Paul's reasons for writing Romans, see A. J. M. Wedderburn, *The Reasons for Romans*, J. Riches (ed.) (SNTW; T&T Clark: Edinburgh, 1988), 97f.

1.3. Romans 16: an integral part of the letter to the Romans

Although there is a consensus among scholars about the Pauline authorship of
Romans, scholars are divided in their opinion about the authenticity and origin
of Romans 16. Questions asking whether Romans 16 is an entirely separate
letter, or whether it was actually a letter intended for the Ephesians, have been
accompanied by much discussion.[3] Moreover, the variations in the manuscript
evidence, the silence of many of the fathers about chs. 15 and 16, the different
positions of the doxology, and the individuals addressed in Romans 16 have
been at the forefront of scholarly discussion about Romans. The textual history
of Romans shows that there are three basic forms of the letter: a fourteen-chapter
form, a fifteen-chapter form (1.1–15.33 with ch. 16 intended for the Ephesians
rather than the Roman church), and a sixteen-chapter form (this form includes
the doxology and is attested in modern editions of the Greek New Testament and
many existing manuscripts. However, the text is not uniform due to the presence
and position of the benedictions found at the end of ch. 16).[4]

There are two issues concerning the Ephesian hypothesis: first, whether the
Ephesian material constitutes a complete letter or is actually only part of a
larger one;[5] second, whether this Ephesian material was related to Romans as
a result of Paul's composition and circulation, or whether it was added by later
redactional work.[6]

However, the textual evidence proves that Romans 16 is addressed to
Rome.[7] The content of Romans 16 complements the wider purpose of the

---

3   Scholars like J. B. Lightfoot, F. J. A. Hort, Eduard Riggenbach, Donatien de Bruyne,
and Peter Corssen of the late nineteenth and early twentieth centuries studied the fundamental
issues of the textual tradition of Romans. Their studies are important to understand the textual
traditions although their conclusions are open to debate. See J. B. Lightfoot (ed.), *Biblical Essays*
(New York: Macmillan, 1904), 285–374; F. J. A. Hort, 'On the End of the Epistles to the Romans',
Journal of Philology 3 (1871), 51–80; E. Riggenbach, 'Die Textgeschichte der Doxologie Röm.
16, 25–27 im Zusammenhang mit den übrigen, den Schluss des Römerbriefs betreffenden,
textkritischen Fragen', *Neue Jahrbüchen für deutsche Theologie* 1 (1892), 526–605; D. de Bruyne,
'Les deux derniers chapitres de la lettre aux Romains', *RBen* 25 (1908), 423–30; P. Corssen, 'Zur
Überlieferungsgeschichte des Römerbriefes', *ZNW* 10 (1909), 1–45. See also H. Gamble, *The
Textual History of the Letter to the Romans: A Study in Textual and Literary Criticism* (Studies and
Documents 42; Grand Rapids: Eerdmans, 1977), 15.

4   See Gamble, *Textual History*, 16–35.

5   T. W. Manson, 'St. Paul's Letter to the Romans – and Others', in K. P. Donfried (ed.),
The Romans Debate, revised and expanded edition (Peabody: Hendrickson, 1991), 3–15. Cf. H.
Koester, 'Ephesos in Early Christian Literature', in H. Koester (ed.), *Ephesos: Metropolis of Asia*
(Pennsylvania: Trinity Press, 1995), 119–40, at 122, 123. Koester assumes that Romans 16 was
a letter to Ephesus. The greetings to Paul's fellow workers and personal acquaintances show that
they must have been located in Ephesus rather than in Rome.

6   Gamble, *Textual History*, 41. See also J. Ziesler, *Paul's Letter to the Romans* (TPI;
London: SCM, 1989), 20.

7   P. Lampe, 'The Roman Christians of Romans 16', in K. P. Donfried (ed.), *The Romans
Debate* (Peabody: Hendrickson, 1991), 217. Lampe denies the possibility of P[46] supporting the
hypothesis that Paul's original letter included only chs. 1–15.

letter.[8] The greetings in Romans 16 function to create bonds between Paul's personal friends and the Roman church, between the Roman church and Paul himself, and between the individual members of the ethnically and socially diverse Roman church.[9] The greetings are sent to the Roman church as a whole, and thus all the members of the church are included in the mutual greetings (which are intended to create love and unity among them). The style and structure of the Pauline epistolary conclusions show that without the sixteenth chapter, 'the 15 chapter text lacks an epistolary conclusion and the unusual aspects of some elements in chapter 16 find cogent explanation only on the assumption of its Roman address'.[10]

1.4. The women named in Romans 16

Romans 16 opens with a letter of recommendation for Phoebe (Rom. 16.1-2), and is followed by specific greetings (16.3-15), the general exhortation of greeting one another with a holy kiss (16.16), hortatory remarks (16.17-20), the grace benediction (16.21b), the greetings from Paul's associates (16.21-23), and a second grace benediction (16.24). This study focuses on the material in 16.1-16: the letter of introduction for Phoebe and the greetings to twenty-six individuals (with twenty-four identified by name) – nine of which are women. The women named in Romans 16 are Phoebe (ἀδελφή, διάκονος, and προστάτις); Prisca (co-worker); Junia (fellow-prisoner, outstanding among the apostles); Mary, Tryphoena and Tryphosa, Persis (hard-working members); Julia; Nereus' sister; and Rufus' mother (a mother to Paul). Because the women mentioned in the list have favourable descriptions that echo Paul's descriptions of his male associates (and even of Paul himself), I will argue that these women held influential positions in the church and were responsible for the leadership of Christian communities.

In recent years, discussion concerning Rom. 16.1-16 has included two main issues: first, the specific connotation of the titles used for the women; second, their social roles in relation to the Pauline mission and the Roman church in particular. To locate my study within this discussion, I will briefly review previous research pertaining to the roles of the women mentioned in Rom. 16.1-16, their relationship with Paul, and their work for the church.

---

8   Scholars are divided in their opinion regarding the authenticity of 16.16-20: one group suggests a Pauline postscript (Moo [D. J. Moo, The _Epistle to the Romans_ (Grand Rapids: Eerdmans, 1996), 929], Fitzmyer [J. A. Fitzmyer, _Romans: A New Translation with Introduction and Commentary_ (AB 33; New York: Doubleday, 1993), 745]), while the other explains the distinct features as due to non-Pauline interpolation (Jewett [R. Jewett, _Christian Tolerance: Paul's Message to the Modern Church_ (Philadelphia: Westminster, 1982), 17–23], Ollrog [W.-H. Ollrog, _Paulus und seine Mitarbeiter_ (WMANT 50; Neurkirchen: Neukirchener, 1979), 226–34]). For more discussion see R. Jewett, _Romans_ (Minneapolis: Fortress, 2007), 986–96. See also Lampe, 'Roman Christians', 221.

9   For more discussion on the greetings, see chapter 2.

10   Gamble, _Textual History_, 127.

1.4.1. Phoebe

The main debates about Phoebe concern her potential role in the Roman church, her position as διάκονος of the church of Cenchreae, and her status implied by the title προστάτις. The interpretation of διάκονος ranges from the provision of practical help to recognised leadership in the church of Cenchreae. Likewise, προστάτις ranges from helper to benefactor in meaning.[11]

Regarding her expected mission to the Romans, Jewett proposes that Phoebe's relation with the Roman church was to be the patroness of the Spanish mission (Jewett proposes that the Spanish mission is the focus of Romans). He considers Phoebe an upper-class benefactor, and suggests her responsibility is to create a 'logistical base' for the Spanish mission.[12] He also argues that the greetings following the recommendation for Phoebe (16.3-16) suggest that the individuals mentioned 'are being recruited as advisers and supporters of Paul and Phoebe'.[13]

I think that Jewett's interpretation of Phoebe's role as ambassador for the Spanish mission, with the individuals in 16.3-16 as recruits to support her, is highly reductionist. Romans is a letter permeated with Paul's theological contributions to the community's mutual behaviour, and the greetings in 16.1-16 commend the aforementioned individuals' partnership in both Paul's own missional endeavours and the wider Christian mission as a whole. Moreover, I doubt whether Phoebe is a wealthy and upper-class benefactor as Jewett proposes, since wealth may not have been an essential prerequisite for being a patron in the early church.[14] Paul's requests for Phoebe (16.1-2) seem open-ended, but Jewett misapprehends this when he interprets them solely in terms of the Spanish mission. Paul's recommendation of Phoebe raises the question of her relationship with Paul as a colleague: was she inferior or superior to Paul? Whelan suggests that the relation between Paul and Phoebe implies some sort of mutual obligation. He suggests Romans 16 shows Paul 'exploiting this network of "clients" on behalf of Phoebe introducing her to his network of connections and thereby reciprocating her benefactions to him and his church'.[15] Whelan's suggestion of the mutual obligation

11   Cranfield and Käsemann suggest the role of informal service and helper. See C. E. B. Cranfield, *A Critical and Exegetical Commentary on the Epistle to the Romans*, 2 vols. (Edinburgh: T&T Clark, 1979), 781; E. Käsemann, *Commentary on Romans* (Grand Rapids: Eerdmans, 1980), 410.

12   Jewett, *Romans*, 90. See also R. Jewett, 'Paul, Phoebe, and Spanish Mission', in J. Neusner et al. (eds.), *The Social World of Formative Christianity and Judaism: Essays in Tribute to Howard Clark Kee* (Philadelphia: Fortress, 1988), 144–64; Jewett, *Romans*, 89–91, 941–48.

13   Jewett, *Romans*, 948.

14   Meggitt suggests that it is not plausible to infer that the individuals mentioned by Paul in his letters are mentioned due to the fact that they are 'elite or prosperous in the society'. J. Meggitt, *Paul, Poverty and Survival* (SNTW; Edinburgh: T&T Clark, 1998), 134.

15   C. F. Whelan, 'Amica Pauli: The Role of Phoebe in the Early Church', *JSNT* 49 (1993), 67–85, at 84. There is a sense of mutual indebtedness between Paul and Phoebe; Phoebe is the patron of Paul and Paul is reciprocating her actions. Whelan suggests Phoebe is sent to the

between Paul and Phoebe is significant to my thesis; however, I would go further and suggest that the mutual obligation is not confined to Phoebe but is extended to all the individuals and groups greeted. Romans 16.3-16, apart from commending different individuals' work, reveals a rhetorical strategy to apply Paul's theological and ethical admonitions of mutual relations in the previous chapters (12–15). By calling on the mutual relations within the wider community, Paul probably wants to bring to light the mutual obligation required between Phoebe and the wider church community as well as between Phoebe and himself.

According to Cotter, 'Phoebe's role as benefactress and guardian is evidence of the financial independence possible for many women in the Imperial period. She also may have been able to act as guardian due to influential people among her family members and friends. Such exercise of power is completely conventional.'[16] Cotter's claim that Phoebe's role as benefactress would be seen as a societal norm carries important implications for my research. During my interpretation of the passage I will take into account the socio-historical context of the passage by analysing women's leadership and participatory roles in the religious, political, and cultural spheres of the Greco-Roman world.

The social and theological role of Phoebe has been a topic of interest in recent years,[17] and many commentators have also highlighted the role of Phoebe in relation to the Pauline mission.[18] Although the relationship between Phoebe and Paul has been the object of focus in previous studies, the mutuality in her social and ecclesial leadership has been given lesser attention. I will examine the structure of the passage, the titles used, and Paul's requests on Phoebe's behalf. I will highlight both her social and theological roles, as well as the mutuality in her relationship with Paul and the wider community.[19]

Ephesian church, while I suggest that Phoebe is sent to the church in Rome and that Romans 16 is an integral part of the letter to the Romans. See also J. C. Campbell, *Phoebe: Patron and Emissary* (Paul's Social Network: Brothers and Sisters in Faith; Minnesota: Liturgical Press, 2009).

16   W. Cotter, 'Women's Authority Roles in Paul's Churches: Countercultural or Conventional', *NovT* 36 (1994), 350–72, at 369.

17   A. D. Clarke, 'Jew and Greek, Slave and Free, Male and Female: Paul's Theology of Ethnic, Social and Gender Inclusiveness in Romans 16', in Peter Oakes (ed.), *Rome in the Bible and the Early Church* (Grand Rapids: Baker Academic, 2002), 103–25, at 117. E. E. Ellis, 'Paul and his Co- workers', *DPL*, 183–89, at 185. E. E. Ellis, 'Paul and his Co-Workers', *NTS* 17 (1977), 437–52, at 442; E. S. Fiorenza, *In Memory of Her: A Feminist Theological Reconstruction of Christian Origins* (London: SCM, 1995); E. S. Fiorenza, 'Missionaries, Apostles, Co-workers: Romans 16 and the Reconstruction of Women's Early Christian History', *WW* 6 (1986), 420–33, at 426; see S. Croft, 'Text Messages: The Ministry of Women and Romans 16', *Anvil* 21 (2004), 87–94, at 89; D. C. Arichea, 'Who was Phoebe? Translating *Diakonos* in Romans 16:1', *BT* 39 (1988), 401–409, at 409; J. M. Bassler, 'Phoebe', in Carol Meyers (ed.), *Women in Scripture* (Grand Rapids: Eerdmans, 2000), 134–35, at 135.

18   Cranfield, *Romans*, 2:781; Käsemann, *Romans*, 410; J. D. G. Dunn, *Romans 9–16* (WBC; Texas: Word Books, 1988), 886, 887; Fitzmyer, *Romans*, 729–30; Jewett, *Romans*, 945.

19   See below chapter 4; 4.2.

1.4.2. Prisca

Prisca is greeted with her husband Aquila, and Prisca's name precedes her husband's. This has led to major debates about the social status of Prisca and whether she took responsibility for leading the church that met in her house.

The social status of Prisca and Aquila has been widely debated. On the one hand, scholars suggest that they are of 'relatively high status because of their patronage of Paul, frequent travels, and the capacity to own property in Corinth, Ephesus, and Rome, large enough for house churches'.[20] On the other hand, the basis of Aquila's trade and travel costs might suggest that they are not of high status.[21] Although Meggitt is right that the criteria suggesting high status (hospitality and references to travel) 'are not sustainable grounds for regarding an individual as wealthy',[22] presumably they were relatively wealthy. It is unusual, when mentioning a married couple, for the female's name to be given precedence; Winter argues that placing a wife's name ahead of the husband's 'would indicate that the wife was either of a higher rank or higher social status than he'.[23] This might indicate her role in the church, her personal contribution, and her relationship to Paul and his mission, which is evident in the title 'my co-workers'. As Jewett suggests, this usage is unique to Paul and reveals a 'distinctive Pauline approach to missional collegiality, referring both to himself and to others with this egalitarian term'.[24] I think it is possible that mutuality is the best model to follow in the ministerial partnership. The greeting formula ἀσπάσασθε is combined with a thanksgiving formula εὐχαριστῶ in order to express indebtedness, not only from Paul, but from all the Gentile churches (πᾶσαι αἱ ἐκκλησίαι τῶν ἐθνῶν); consequently, this implies mutuality between Paul and Prisca as well as Paul, Prisca, and other Gentile churches.

Fiorenza argues for Prisca's house church leadership since the house church 'provided space for the preaching of the word, for worship, as well as for social and eucharistic table sharing'.[25] Fiorenza suggests that the house churches presuppose that some wealthy citizens have joined the Christian movement who could provide space and economic resources for the community. Paul's rhetoric in greeting Prisca describes an aspect of mutuality embedded in her

20   Jewett, *Romans*, 956; G. Theissen, *The Social Setting of Pauline Christianity: Essays on Corinth* (Edinburgh: T&T Clark, 1982), 90; W. Meeks, *The First Urban Christians* (New Haven: Yale University Press, 1983), 59.

21   P. Lampe, *From Paul to Valentinus: Christians at Rome in the First Two Centuries* (Minneapolis: Fortress Press, 2003), 195. Lampe suggests that a lower status is possible due to Aquila's trade, and also because the cost of travel is still affordable for lower-class people.

22   Meggitt, *Paul, Poverty and Survival*, 134, 135. Meggitt argues that hospitality is not indicative of elite status since the desire of one to give to others is a matter of goodwill rather than wealth.

23   B. W. Winter, *Roman Wives, Roman Widows: The Appearance of New Women and the Pauline Communities* (Grand Rapids: Eerdmans, 2003), 180. See also R. MacMullen, 'Women in Public in the Roman Empire', *Historia* 29 (1980), 208–18, at 209.

24   Jewett, *Romans*, 957.

25   Fiorenza, *In Memory of Her*, 175.

leadership roles as he appreciates and acknowledges her contribution to the Pauline mission.

1.4.3. Junia

The current debates about Junia, who is greeted with Andronicus, centre on Junia's gender (was the individual actually male ['Junias'] or female ['Junia']), whether she is an insider of the apostolic circle or an outsider, and whether she was Joanna of the Jerusalem church. The argument about the name was founded on the question of whether a woman could be an apostle in the church. Those who agree that Junia was a woman further differentiate between whether she exercised leadership among the apostles or not.

More recently, Epp has argued that Junia was a woman apostle because Paul would not have referred to them as 'outstanding among the apostles' unless he found the qualities of apostleship in them.[26] Although there is no evidence that they witnessed the resurrected Jesus, Epp points to the fact that 'they were "in Christ" before he [Paul] was and they were in prison with Paul and therefore had suffered as he had for his apostleship'.[27]

However, Burer and Wallace argue that Junia was 'well known to the apostles' rather than being 'outstanding' among them.[28] In a recent article titled 'Did Paul call Andronicus an Apostle in Romans 16.7?' Hutter argues, 'The lexical-grammatical evidence makes it possible, the evidence from the context is inconclusive, and the historical evidence makes the non-inclusive interpretation more probable.'[29] Belleville has examined computer databases of Hellenistic Greek literary works, papyri, inscriptions, and artefacts, before concluding (like Epp) that Junia was a feminine name and held notability among the apostles.[30] Cervin discussed the Latin names and their method of transcription into Greek, and demonstrated that, from the nature of the name, and the nature of transcribing Latin names into Greek, Junia is indeed a feminine name.[31] Thorley discusses the arguments for 'Junia' on linguistic grounds.[32] Winter deals with women in the civic context, exploring the possibility of comparing Junia Theodora with Phoebe and Junia.[33]

---

26   E. J. Epp, *Junia: The First Woman Apostle* (Minneapolis: Fortress, 2005), 69, 70.

27   Epp, *Junia*, 69, 70.

28   M. H. Burer and D. B. Wallace, 'Was Junia Really an Apostle? A Re-examination of Rom 16:7', *NTS* 47 (2001), 76–91.

29   D. Hutter, 'Did Paul call Andronicus an Apostle in Romans 16:7?', *JETS* (2009), 747–78, at 778.

30   L. Belleville, Ἰουνιαν ... ἐπίσημοι ἐν τοῖς ἀποστόλοις: A Re-examination of Romans 16:7 in Light of Primary Source Materials', *NTS* 51 (2005), 231–49.

31   R. S. Cervin, 'A Note Regarding the Name "Junias" in Romans 16:7', *NTS* 40 (1994), 464–70.

32   J. Thorley, 'Junia, a Woman Apostle', *NovT* 38 (1996), 18–26.

33   Winter, *Roman Wives, Roman Widows*, 193–204. See pp. 84, 85.

Bauckham opts for a sound-equivalence theory for the names Joanna and Junia;[34] he builds his argument on the presuppositions that Junia and Andronicus were among the founders of the Jerusalem Christian community, and that Paul's description of Junia as 'prominent among the apostles' references her prominence among women followers of Jesus.[35]

Although her role is discussed in the above studies, Paul's purpose of including Junia in the list of greetings, and describing her with specific implications for the Roman church, have not been significantly considered. I will build on Paul's descriptions that imply why she is remarkable to the Roman church, and observe mutuality between the description of Junia's leadership role and her partnership in Christian mission.

1.4.4. Other women members of the greeting list

The same descriptive phrase (κοπιάω [to labour], Rom. 16.6, 12) is used to describe four other women in the greeting list: Mary, Tryphoena, Tryphosa, and Persis. πολλὰ ἐκοπίασεν εἰς ὑμᾶς describes Mary (v. 6); πολλὰ ἐκοπίασεν ἐν Κυρίῳ denotes Persis (v. 12); κοπιώσας ἐν Κυρίῳ depicts Tryphoena and Tryphosa (v. 12). Dunn argues that the term does not denote a leadership function, as in 1 Thess. 5.17, because Paul merely recognises devoted work on behalf of the church (1 Cor. 16.16; 1 Thess. 5.12).[36] But again, their roles within larger relationships of mutuality need to be considered.

Paul states that Rufus' mother was also a 'mother of mine' (16.13). Though it is unclear what Paul really meant by this, it could be inferred that she might have helped him in a specific situation or ministered to him regularly at some point in his labours.[37] Nereus' sister and Julia are mentioned in a cluster of names in v. 15 without any designation. The inclusion in the greeting list implies some sort of recognition of their participation in ministry and Paul's mutual obligation to them (although this mutual obligation is not specified).

The unusually long greeting list in Romans 16 (including its acknowledgements and greetings for a number of women related to Paul and the Roman church) causes us to ask what Paul's purpose was in greeting these particular women along with the other male members of the Roman church. *Prima facie*, these women presumably assumed leadership roles alongside Paul or his male associates mentioned in Romans 16 (or perhaps even alongside others mentioned with similar descriptive phrases in Paul's other epistles). The concept of mutuality is easily lost when focusing on Romans 16 alone, but I would like to revive it by examining Paul's exhortations in the previous chapters. Paul S. Minear gives a passing reference to this in his discussion of Phoebe: 'Would she be able to present more fully and directly the reasons for

---

34   R. Bauckham, *The Gospel Women: Studies of the Named Women in the Gospels* (Grand Rapids: Eerdmans, 2002), 181–94.

35   Bauckham, *Gospel Women*, 184.

36   Dunn, *Romans 9–16*, 894.

37   T. R. Schreiner, *Romans* (Grand Rapids: Baker Academic, 1998), 793.

mutual acceptance which Paul had set forth in earlier sections of the letter?'[38] It is crucial to find out how these women's leadership roles are embedded in relationships of mutuality. I will look at the mutual relations between Paul and the women, and also between the other people mentioned in the passage. The leadership roles of these specific women, within the contexts of Pauline church leadership and relational mutuality, have not been discussed until now.

1.5. Women's leadership in Pauline churches

Women in Pauline church leadership have been a focus of much attention due to the incompatible statements Paul makes about the role of women in the church: especially the prohibition and restriction on their participation in church activities, veiling, and silence in the church (1 Corinthians 11; 14). Other epistles witness Paul appreciating women for their hard work and toil for him and the church, so there seems to be a question of inconsistency in Pauline views on women. I would like to list some of the positive and negative affirmations of women's roles in recent studies that relate to hierarchical, feminist, and egalitarian models in relational and leadership spheres. Although an extensive analysis of different views is impossible due to limitations of space, they are important as a backdrop for my research. What fascinates me is whether a model of mutuality is pertinent and practical in properly functioning gender roles.

Fiorenza suggests that the history of the early Christian movement includes the egalitarian leadership of women.[39] She comments, 'women and men in the Christian community are not defined by their sexual procreative capacities or by their religious, cultural or social gender roles, but by their discipleship and empowering with the Spirit'.[40] She regards Gal. 3.28 as a 'communal Christian self-definition' rather than 'a statement about the baptized individual'; the differences of religion, class, race, nationality, and gender are irrelevant because all are baptised and are one in Christ.[41] She propounds a 'feminist Christian spirituality' and 'discipleship of equals',[42] and also comments on two major objections: 'the church of women does not share in the fullness of the church' and 'the charge of "reverse sexism" and the appeal to "mutuality

---

38   P. S. Minear, *The Obedience of Faith: The Purposes of Paul in the Epistle to the Romans* (SBT 2/19; London: SCM, 1971), 24.

39   Fiorenza, *In Memory of Her*, 140. In 1993, Fiorenza published a work titled *Discipleship of Equals: A Critical Feminist Ekklesia-logy of Liberation*, in which she shares her vision about the world of justice and well-being against the powers of patriarchal oppression and dehumanisation. E. S. Fiorenza, *Discipleship of Equals: A Critical Feminist Ekklesia-logy of Liberation* (New York: Cross Road, 1993). Luise Schotroff visions a liberated womanhood in relation to God rather than affirming equality with men. Luise Schotroff, *Lydia's Impatient Sisters: A Feminist Social History of Early Christianity*, trans. Barbara and Martin Rumscheidt (Louisville: John Knox, 1995).

40   Fiorenza, *In Memory of Her*, 212, 213.

41   Fiorenza, *In Memory of Her*, 213.

42   Fiorenza, *In Memory of Her*, 344.

with men" whenever we gather together as the *ekklesia* of women in her name'.[43] She addresses the second objection by stating that 'women in turn have to reclaim their spiritual powers and to exorcise their possession by male idolatry before mutuality is possible'.[44] I will attempt to define the relationship between men and women in a model of mutuality that is not divorced from the egalitarian model but entails it. The egalitarian model seems to be a static phenomenon, whereas mutuality is dynamic.

The negative statements regarding women's participation in worship and church pose a problem since, in Rom. 16.1-16, Paul appreciates women in the church and acknowledges their leadership roles. Wire argues that 'the women prophets in Corinth's church have a place in the group Paul is addressing, some role in the rhetorical situation'.[45] According to Wire, 1 Corinthians mostly concerns women directly or indirectly, and is directed to one party in Corinth: 'the Corinthian Prophets'.[46] She tries to reconstruct the authority of the women prophets in the Corinthian community, and suggests that Paul feels threatened by them. Interestingly, these issues do not arise in Romans.

Although women's exercise of power throughout the Imperial period was conventional, Cotter argues that:

> the women in Paul's letters who show themselves to be leaders in these communities appeared to fit into cultural norms acceptable in Roman culture. But the reality of their involvement due to the character of the assembly as God's *ekklesia* endowed the leadership with a countercultural equality with the men members of the community.[47]

In the context of the Christian church, Cotter's finding is very significant since Romans calls for mutuality in the role of women in the *basileia* of God.

In some respects, this form of mutuality differs from the inclusive type. Clarke suggests a 'theology of inclusiveness' is present in the greetings of Romans 16 along with other Pauline letters (Gal. 3.28; 1 Cor. 12.13; Col. 3.11; cf. Eph. 2.13-16). The greetings presented in Romans 16 'transcend all ethnic, social and gender barriers'.[48] 'Inclusiveness' appears to entail an egalitarian perspective – unity and equality; however, I will argue that the model of mutuality entails inclusivism but still appreciates diversity and dynamism.

---

43 Fiorenza, *In Memory of Her*, 347.

44 Fiorenza, *In Memory of Her*, 347. C. Heyward and Mary Grey argue for the concept of relationality in their feminist approaches, which is significant as it has redemptive and healing power. C. Heyward, *The Redemption of God: The Theology of Mutual Relation* (Washington, DC: University Press of America, 1982), 152; Mary Grey, *Redeeming the Dream: Feminism Redemption and Christian Tradition* (London: SPCK, 1989); see also K. Ehrensperger, *That We May Be Mutually Encouraged: Feminism and the New Perspective in Pauline Studies* (London: T&T Clark, 2004), 117–20.

45 A. Wire, *The Corinthian Women Prophets: A Reconstruction through Paul's Rhetoric* (Minneapolis: Fortress Press, 1990), 9.

46 Wire, *The Corinthian Women Prophets*, 9.

47 Cotter, 'Women's Authority Roles in Paul's Churches', 372.

48 Clarke, 'Jew and Greek', 103–25.

Martin describes an extreme hierarchical model of the relationship between men and women in a chapter entitled 'Prophylactic Veils'. In this chapter, Martin deals with the veiling of women in public worship and female subordination. The text seems to condone the subordination of women, which is an apparent contradiction of Paul's acknowledgement of equality between men and women in the Lord. Paul's citation of the baptismal formula that 'in Christ there is neither male nor female' (Gal. 3.27-28) is acknowledged as a retention of the ancient notion that the eschatological human being will be androgynous, having overcome the polarity of the male/female dichotomy.[49] He suggests that veiling situates women in their proper position in the ordered hierarchy of society, which also means that they are not intended to be passive but must participate in their covering. The veil was the sign of a woman's own authority as well as a sign of weakness and relative powerlessness. Because women's bodies are different from men's, and were assumed to be inferior, after the resurrection femininity was thought to be swallowed up by masculinity. Martin suggests that Paul could not consider the female form to be equal to masculinity due to this hierarchy of physiology.[50] Martin's attempt to present the different ideological expressions of body in ancient times is interesting, but the question remains as to what extent Paul was really influenced by the body ideology of contemporary times. I think that too many details from this background could eclipse the actual focus of the text, and, consequently, pose a danger of reading these details into the text.

In *Women in their Place: Paul and the Corinthian Discourse and Sanctuary Place*, Økland examines the hierarchy of spaces that control the relationship between men and women.[51] She analyses not only 1 Corinthians, but also a wider set of texts and argues for an ancient discourse of gender and sanctuary space. 'Paul's exhortations concerning women's ritual roles and ritual clothing in 1 Cor. 11-14 structure and gender the Christian gathering as a particular kind of space constructed through ritual, a "sanctuary space".'[52] The author holds the view that the gendered power relationships are maintained by hierarchical measures. In 1 Cor. 11.2-16, Paul's argument is about hierarchy, creation and head coverings, and hair style and nature; Paul seems to be suggesting, through an organised hierarchy within the passages, that there should be a clear difference between male and female.[53] Women cannot teach, and thus serve as mediators of *logos* between God and men (1 Cor. 14.36), because they can only be receivers of knowledge. This makes sense within a hierarchical worldview where women occupy the place at the bottom of the cosmological hierarchy and men are located higher up and closer to the surface of the *logos*.

---

49   D. B. Martin, *The Corinthian Body* (New Haven: Yale University Press, 1995), 229; for detailed discussion see 229–49.

50   Martin, *Corinthian Body*, 248, 249.

51   J. Økland, *Women in their Place: Paul and the Corinthian Discourse of Gender and Sanctuary Space* (JSNTSup 269; London: T&T Clark International, 2004).

52   Økland, *Women in their Place*, 1.

53   See Økland, *Women in their Place*, 137–43.

However, Watson argues that the appropriate criterion for judging the texts is through the reality of *agape*. He argues that *agape* is the inner Trinitarian love opened up to human participation in Jesus and his Spirit. If *agape* is the beginning and end of Christian faith and living, then it is *agape* that must provide the final criterion for Christian reflection on sexuality and gender.[54] Christian women and men are not free from *eros*, but they practise a qualitatively different love whose origin and pattern is the divine love to which they are constantly redirected in worship, preaching, and sacrament, and mutual fellowship with one another.[55]

Paul envisions a community of togetherness in which men and women together participate in the grace of God and the fellowship of the Holy Spirit. Watson refers to the 'belonging together' of *agape* in Paul's vision in 1 Corinthians 13. Watson refers to 'patriarchy' as the project of male self-definition 'apart from woman', and feminism as the other extreme of female self-definition 'apart from man'. He emphasises that 'belonging together' does not represent a *via media* between the two extremes of patriarchy and feminism.[56] Watson's view of belonging together through love is useful for my study as it echoes Paul's exhortation to mutualism in Rom. 16.1-16 and the promotion of community relationships. Watson bases his argument on 1 Corinthians 13; however, in Romans the language of mutuality ('one another') is repeated more frequently. Moreover, Paul seems to make a special effort to commend this type of relationship to the Romans.

In this study I will explore whether it is possible to reconstruct Paul's gender vision within his communitarian ethic. I will propose that a balanced mutual ethic is engendered by the *basileia* of God. In relation to this, I will explore the impact of the greetings in Rom. 16.1-16 on Paul's differing notions about the participation of women in Christian ministry. I will also discuss how far the body metaphor in Romans 12, and the up-building metaphor in Romans 14 and 15, influences gender roles and relationships in Christian ministry and church leadership.

1.6. Greetings as a letter form

Greeting is a distinct literary form found in the closing of a letter. The two types of greetings Paul used in his letter closings are: (1) *informational* (information regarding greetings) and (2) *instructional* (instruction to greet others). Among Pauline greetings in letter closings, the greetings in Romans have special significance as they have an instructional mandate. There are three types of greetings corresponding to the three persons of the verb: the first-person form, the second-person form, and the third-person form. The first and third-person

---

54 F. Watson, *Agape, Eros, Gender: Towards a Pauline Sexual Ethic* (Cambridge: Cambridge University Press, 2000), ix.

55 Watson, *Agape, Eros, Gender*, ix.

56 Watson, *Agape, Eros, Gender*, 5.

greetings can be put together under the banner of informational greeting, which is information of greeting by the sender to the addressee (ἀσπάζομαι; ἀσπάζονται), whereas the second-person greeting can be called instructional greeting (ἀσπάσασθε), that is, instruction to the recipient to greet others. How do greeting individuals and groups operate to influence wider relational communitarian ethics? This question promotes the starting point of this research. The impact of the greetings on Pauline exhortations (Romans 12–15) and vice versa is another possibility for new research.

In his work *The Textual History of Romans*, Gamble deals with Romans 16 and the Pauline conclusions.[57] He highlights the commendatory character of the descriptive phrases, and notes that the imperative form of the greeting verb represents a direct personal greeting from the writer (in this case Paul) to the recipients.[58] Gamble argues that greeting with a kiss is 'a sign of fellowship within the community, of the community with the Apostle, and indeed of one community with others'.[59]

In *Neglected Endings* Weima deals with the forms, variations, and hermeneutical significance of the closing conventions in Pauline letters,[60] and notes that the greetings have an important role in establishing and maintaining relationships. Weima suggests that 'the second person type of greeting involves the congregation in passing on his greeting to others' and expressed 'a stronger sense of public commendation for those individuals being specifically greeted by the apostle'.[61] He suggests that the greeting in Romans is unique because it contains more greetings, has two greeting lists (16.3-16; 21-23), has a commendatory element in the first list, and, finally, because 'the kiss greetings were not an expression of farewell but a challenge by the apostle to the readers to let peace and harmony characterize their relations with each other'.[62]

In an article entitled 'Greetings as a New Testament Form', Mullins deals with the elements of greeting, the types of greeting, and the elaborating phrases. According to Mullins, the second-person type of greeting is an 'indirect salutation':

> The writer of the letter indicates that the addressee is to greet someone for him. In this way the writer of the letter becomes the principal and the addressee becomes his agent in establishing a communication with a third party who is not intended to be among the immediate readership of the letter.[63]

---

57   Gamble, *Textual History*, 84–95.
58   Gamble, *Textual History*, 93.
59   Gamble, *Textual History*, 76.
60   J. A. D. Weima, *Neglected Endings: The Significance of the Pauline Letter Closings* (JSNTSup 101; Sheffield: Sheffield Academic Press, 1994).
61   Weima, *Neglected Endings*, 108.
62   Weima, *Neglected Endings*, 117.
63   T. Y. Mullins, 'Greeting as a New Testament Form', *JBL* 87 (1968), 418–26, at 420.

It implies at least 'a fair cordiality between the writer and the person greeted' and the second-person type of greeting implies close relationships and 'friendly bonds'.[64]

Considering the previous arguments as the bases of my research, I would like to develop their views on the second-person greeting. What is the social dynamic in the greeting with the verb ἀσπάσασθε? Is ἀσπάσασθε the same as if Paul were greeting the third party, or the second group greeting the third party? It is significant that greetings in the second-person imperative induce a web of relationships. For example, when one person is being greeted, the whole Roman community joins in the greeting, and vice versa, thus creating a web of mutual greetings. Therefore the Pauline purpose of greetings in the second-person imperative in Romans reaches its climax in Rom. 16.16, where ἀσπάσασθε ἀλλήλους is used. In this study, I will explore the social dynamics extended and enacted in these greetings and the implication of the inclusion of women in the relationships of honour and mutuality they create.

1.7. Mutualism in Paul's communal ethos

Mutualism in this context may be defined as follows: it refers to relationships of reciprocity (i.e. where each has something to contribute to the other) whose purpose is mutual promotion (i.e. where the task of each is to serve the interests of the other). Because of this purpose in mutual service, relationships may not be simultaneously equal: in one serving the other there will be temporary forms of asymmetry. But, crucially, this asymmetry is reversible and constantly reversed: there is never a settled hierarchy in one direction, but continual processes of reciprocal asymmetry in which a relationship of power which is unbalanced at one time or in one respect is continually reversed and unbalanced at another time or in another respect, in a dynamic, non-static, process of mutual promotion.

The theme of mutuality is not an isolated theme in the greetings (Romans 16) but it is the continuation of Paul's exhortations throughout Romans: especially in Romans 12–15. The verbal and thematic links indicate Paul's desire to create love and mutuality among the Roman believers. The terms 'love' (eight times) and 'one another' (eleven times) used in Romans (12–16) imply Pauline emphasis on mutuality.[65] The body metaphor and the term 'one another' (Romans 12, 13), and Paul's exhortation to welcome one another as Christ has welcomed (Romans 14, 15), clearly impact the greetings (Romans 16).

It is likely that Paul assumes the paradigm of mutuality in Romans 12–15 as the model to be employed when he urges Roman believers to greet certain men and women, and also one another (Rom. 16.1-16). The women are described

---

64   Mullins, 'Greeting as a New Testament Form', 420.
65   Love: Rom. 12.9; 13.10a, 10b; 14.15; 15.30; 13.8a, b, 9; and 'one another': Rom. 12.5, 10a, b, 16; 13.8; 14.13, 19; 15.5, 6, 14; 16.16.

with significant roles that indicate their leadership; moreover, Paul's rhetoric of greetings implies their leadership within the structures of mutualism. Therefore, in dealing with Romans 12–15, it will be important to look at the Pauline ethos of mutuality both in general and in particular.

1.7.1. General research

The initial research on the community aspect of Pauline theology was undertaken by Banks,[66] and deals with the community as a family and as a body with unity in diversity among the members. He also mentions the contribution of women in church in various chapters.

Horrell suggests that the ἀδελφός language indicates mutual regard or 'other regarding' morality (Romans 14 and 1 Corinthians 8) in relation to a weaker sibling. Additionally, he deals with solidarity, difference, and other-regard: 'corporate solidarity does not then imply uniformity, not even in the matters of ethical conviction, but implies precisely a community within which differences can remain, because of the generous other-regard which offers a welcome to the other'.[67] Horrell suggests solidarity and 'other-regard' are the two 'metanorms' of Pauline ethics in the model of Christ. Mutual love (φιλαδελφία) is 'the love of siblings', which could be expressed not only in material sharing, but also in hospitality and support to travellers at the local level and throughout the Christian congregations. Like Horrell, I wish to think through Paul's communal ethos by studying a range of texts, but I will focus on a feature he has not fully explored, that is, relationships of mutuality in the Christian community.

1.7.2. Particular research on Romans 12–15 in relation to community building

A lot of research has been done on the question of division in the Roman churches. The different views regarding Romans 12–15 are dealt with in this section as they are important to understand the model of mutuality in Paul's exhortations to the Roman community.

Watson, in his work *Paul, Judaism and Gentiles: A New Perspective*, and in the article 'The Two Roman Congregations: Romans 14.1–15.13', assumes that there were two groups, 'Jewish Christians' and 'Gentile Christians', who were divided: 'Paul's argument does not presuppose a single congregation in which members disagree about law; it presupposes two congregations, separated by mutual hostility and suspicion over questions of the law, which he wishes to bring together into one congregation.'[68] He suggests that 'because

---

66   R. Banks, *Paul's Idea of Community: The Early House Churches in their Historic Setting and the Church as the Body of Christ in the Pauline Corpus* (Exeter: Paternoster Press, 1980). Other works on the body metaphor include G. L. O. R. Yorke, *The Church as the Body of Christ: A Re-examination* (Lanham: University Press of America, 1991); E. Best, *One Body in Christ: A Study of the Relationship of the Church to Christ in the Epistles of the Apostle Paul* (London: SPCK, 1955); Y. S. Kim, *Christ's Body in Corinth: The Politics of a Metaphor* (Minneapolis: Fortress, 2008).

67   D. G. Horrell, *Solidarity and Difference: A Contemporary Reading of Paul's Ethics* (London: T&T Clark International, 2005), 199.

68   F. Watson, 'The Two Roman Congregations', in K. P. Donfried (ed.), *Romans Debate*, 206.

Christ came to save both Jews and Gentiles, Jews are exhorted to join with the Gentiles in common worship'.[69] According to him, 'Rom. 16 confirms the hypothesis about the purpose of Romans derived from 14.1–15.13. The purpose of Romans is to encourage Jewish and Gentile Christians in Rome, divided over the question of the law, to set aside their differences and to worship together.'[70] Although Watson assumes the two congregations come together in worship, the Pauline idea of mutual acceptance between the groups retaining their convictions needs to be developed further.

Barclay's view is significant to my research as I reconstruct the theology of the mutuality that entails otherness, interdependence, personhood, recovery of the community's collegiality, and partnership. In his article 'Do We Undermine the Law?', he suggests that the Gentiles and Jews are divided on the issue of Jewish law and Paul exhorts them to welcome and tolerate fellow believers even if they do not observe such rules. 'The mutual tolerance demanded by Paul in the Roman churches requires that neither side allow their strongly-held convictions to determine the contours of Christian commitment.'[71] The mutual tolerance between the groups enhances mutual welcoming.

Reasoner analyses the context of Romans 14–15 from the historical perspective that the strong and the weak were divided in the matter of vegetarianism: something that fits with first-century Roman society. He analyses Paul's solution to the division in the perspective of the whole letter of Romans, and explains how the righteousness of God given to believers through Christ is related to the believers' obligations. He suggests:

> Obligation as a social force was pervasive throughout Roman society, and Paul defines the obligation of the strong in a way they would not expect – they are to align their eating habits with the 'weak' and support the 'weak' (14.21; 15.1-2) – rather than force the weak to defer to their social status, as would be the norm in Roman society.[72]

What needs to be explored further is how such obligations relate to the model of Christ and are taken up within an ethos of mutuality.

The idea that Rom. 14.1–15.13 is a general paraenesis based on 1 Corinthians 8–10 to deal with a problem that could arise in any community, as Karris suggests,[73] is an issue we will need to discuss. I will argue that Paul

---

69   Watson, 'The Two Roman Congregations', 206.

70   Watson, 'The Two Roman Congregations', 211.

71   J. M. G. Barclay, 'Do we Undermine the Law?: A Study of Romans 14:1–15:6', in J. D. G. Dunn (ed.), *Paul and the Mosaic Law* (Tübingen: Mohr, 1996), 287–308, at 302.

72   M. Reasoner, *The Strong and the Weak: Romans 14:1–15:13 in Context* (SNTSMS 103; Cambridge: Cambridge University Press, 1999), 232.

73   R. J. Karris, 'Romans 14:1–15:13 and the occasion of Romans', in Donfried (ed.) *Romans Debate*, 65–84. Karris analyses Rom. 14.1–15.13 from a history of religions perspective, an exegetical perspective and a paraenetic perspective and suggests, 'there is very little history of religions or exegetical evidence that there were communities of the "weak" and the "strong" in Rome'. Karris, 'Romans 14:1–15:13', 84.

is addressing the actual situation and that the exhortations are relevant to the Roman community.

In the social-scientific treatment of Romans by Esler in his work *Conflict and Identity in Romans*, he argues that Romans 12–15 outlines 'identity descriptors'.[74] He suggests thematic links between the chapters of Romans that 'relate to the attitudes and behaviour appropriate to the members of the Christ movement'; that these may be called '"norms" in a social identity sense or, more particularly, "identity descriptors"'.[75] I wish to explore, however, the ways in which Paul urges the Romans to let their identity be defined and developed in relationships of mutuality.

The aspect of brotherly love is fundamental to mutual relations that Aasgaard, in his work '*My Beloved Brothers and Sisters!*', deals with in regard to Christian siblingship in Paul. In his discussion of Romans 12–15 he argues that Paul emphasises mutual relations in Rom. 12.10. 'Paul here aims at φιλαδελφία as a general and mutual obligation among Christians; the exhortation is directed towards all indiscriminately.'[76] He argues that Paul's strategies in Rom. 14.1–15.13 link the sibling metaphor very closely to the motif of non-judgement: 'A sibling should not be passed judgment on, nor be despised (14.10) ... the appropriate way of judging a sibling is to refrain from judging, and thus avoid destructive consequences, such as the injury or the ultimate ruin of a co-Christian (14.15, 21).'[77]

The peculiarities of the Pauline exhortations (12–15) to the Roman community have been studied from various angles in recent years. The 'other regarding character', the mutual love, and the differentiated motives of the groups (the strong and the weak) have been the focus of research. However, the thread of mutuality that underlies chs. 12–15, and its impact on the greetings in ch. 16, have yet to receive the degree of attention that they deserve.

1.8. The contribution

As we have seen, a variety of research has been done on the greetings, the roles of women (Romans 16), and the Pauline exhortations (Romans 12–15). However, the major focus of this research is on women's leadership roles in the Pauline churches and the relationships of mutuality.

---

74 P. F. Esler, *Conflict and Identity in Romans: The Social Setting of Paul's Letter* (Minneapolis: Fortress, 2003), 308. See also B. Winter, 'Roman Law and Society in Romans 12–15', in P. Oakes (ed.), *Rome in the Bible and the Early Church* (Carlisle: Paternoster Press, 2002), 67–102.

75 Esler, *Conflict and Identity*, 339. He suggests links between 14.1–15.13 and 15.14–16.27 and 12–13, with a theme of love.

76 R. Aasgaard, '*My Beloved Brothers and Sisters!*': *Christian Siblingship in Paul* (JSNTSup 265; London: T&T Clark, 2004), 172.

77 Aasgaard, '*My Beloved Brothers and Sisters!*', 210.

Assuming that Romans 16 is an integral part of the letter, the focus of this research centres on the greetings in Rom. 16.1-16 that indicate the leadership of women in the Pauline churches. The instructional greetings indicate the persons who were to be greeted by the recipients of the letter, and the rhetoric of the passage (i.e. the way the individuals are presented in the greetings list) implies their possession of leadership roles. Moreover, their relationship to Paul denotes their association with him and their partnership in Christian ministry. These types of greeting have the function of increasing mutual relations, not only between Paul and the persons greeted, but also between the persons who do the greeting and those who are being greeted. Moreover, the mutuality in Rom. 16.1-16 seems to be in continuity with earlier themes of love and mutuality (Romans 12 and 13), and also with Paul's commendation to welcome and receive others to counter the division within the Roman community (chs. 14 and 15). The analysis of the mutual relations in Romans 12–15 could help us deduce a model of Pauline mutuality, or 'Pauline love-mutualism', because Paul describes genuine love as the motivation for mutual relations (Rom. 12.9). The extensive use of ἀλλήλους language in Romans 12–16 (out of the fourteen uses of the word throughout Romans, eleven of the uses occur in Romans 12–16) indicates Paul's emphasis on mutual relations among fellow believers and his strategy in bringing it about. It would seem that love-mutualism is something that Paul hopes will hold the community together in the midst of differences and diversities.

1.9. Method and procedure

The method of study will be analytical, exegetical, and rhetorical. The socio-cultural context of the selected passage will be analysed in order to deduce the significance of women's ministry in Paul's greetings. I will also engage in theological analysis of Paul's notion of mutuality. A total view of Paul's communitarian ethic will also be helpful in defining and reconstructing the mutuality model. Based on this model, the thesis will follow the following progression.

The second chapter deals with the rhetorical analysis of greetings. In this chapter the structure of conclusion in Hellenistic letters, Semitic letters in general, and the Pauline letters in particular are studied, and the different types of greetings are also addressed with special attention given to the peculiarities of the greetings in Romans 16.

The third chapter deals with women in leadership in the Greco-Roman world. This chapter focuses on women in the public sphere: law, politics, patronage, and as heads of the household. Women in leadership in the religious sphere are also studied with a focus on their role in Synagogues.

The fourth chapter is the hub of the thesis as it deals with the importance of women in the Pauline mission. The women of Rom. 16.1-16 are analysed in comparison with women in the Roman Empire. The women specifically mentioned with roles in the Pauline churches are discussed in order to place them in the wider sphere of Pauline associates. The descriptions of the roles of the women in Rom. 16.1-16 are also discussed.

The fifth chapter focuses on the theological and ethical analysis of Romans 12–13 by discussing Paul's strategies to bring about mutuality. The body metaphor and the practical implications in bringing about love and mutuality are the centre of attention.

The sixth chapter discusses Paul's strategies in dealing with the contextual issue of the weak and the strong in the Roman church (Romans 14–15). The solution to the problems in the community is by fostering mutual welcome and acceptance through the self-renunciation of one's own interests.

The seventh chapter concludes the study and reconstructs a theology of love-mutualism. The model of mutuality in the greetings is deduced from exegetical analysis of Romans 12–15. The leadership of women within the structures of mutualism, implied in the greetings of Rom. 16.1-16, is a challenge to communitarian ethics as far as Paul's social vision for Christian community is concerned.

CHAPTER 2

THE FORM OF GREETINGS IN THE ROMANS LETTER CLOSING

2.1. Introduction

The epistolary style of the Pauline letters is marked by the presence of four major features/sections: '1) the Opening (sender, recipient, salutation); 2) the Thanksgiving; 3) the Body ([including] transitional formulae, autobiographical statements, concluding paraenesis, apostolic parousia); and 4) the Closing (peace benediction, hortatory section, greeting, autograph, grace benediction).'[1] Although the first three sections are widely discussed by scholars, the final section has not been given much attention. However, Weima notes its significance:

> A Pauline letter closing ... is a carefully constructed unit, shaped and adapted in such a way as to relate it directly to the major concerns of the letter as a whole, and so it provides important clues to understanding the key issues addressed in the body of the letter.[2]

Thus the closing sections of Pauline letters are as important as the other epistolary sections.

Greeting was a 'distinct literary form' found in the closing of a letter.[3] Among the Pauline greetings in the letter closings, the greetings in Romans are especially significant. The two types of greetings Paul used in his letter closings are: *informational* (information regarding greetings) and *instructional* (instruction to greet others).

---

1   Weima, *Neglected Endings*, 11. The relationship between rhetorical analysis and epistolary analysis is much discussed by scholars. S. J. Stowers observes the need 'to compare Christian letters to the whole range of letters and to approach them with a knowledge of ancient epistolary and rhetorical theory' (S. J. Stowers, *Letter Writing in Greco-Roman Antiquity* [Library of Early Christianity 265; Philadelphia: Westminster Press, 1986], 23), whereas J. L. White notes, 'The use of rhetorical techniques, especially in the theological body of St. Paul's letters, indicates that a knowledge of these traditions is quite relevant to the study of early Christian letters' (J. L. White, *Light from Ancient Letters* [Philadelphia: Fortress Press, 1986], 3).
2   Weima, *Neglected Endings*, 22.
3   Mullins, 'Greeting as a New Testament form', 418. He suggests, 'It forms a communication bridge even where there is no specific merchandise to be exchanged' and creates friendship.

The aim of this chapter is to analyse the form of the greetings in the closing section of Romans (16.1-16) since they differ from greetings in other Pauline letter closings. The discussion proceeds against the backdrop of the Hellenistic and Semitic epistolary styles, with which Paul might have been acquainted. This helps us to understand how far the greetings enhance mutual relationships, which is one of the key aspects of Paul's exhortations to the Roman believers (Romans 12–15).

2.2. Letter closing in the Hellenistic letters

In order to understand the Pauline epistolary style, it is important to look at the epistolary theory and practice of the ancient world to which Paul is indebted. The Greek papyrus letters and literary letters of antiquity supply the evidence for this examination.[4] A letter consists of three main parts: salutation, body, and conclusion. Here, the epistolary conventions of letter closing in Hellenistic letters are discussed, with special attention given to the greeting formulae and descriptive phrases.

The final or farewell wish is an essential element in Hellenistic letters.[5] Gamble notes, 'functionally, the final wish marks the definitive conclusion of a letter, much in the manner of the concluding asseveration ("sincerely," etc.) and signature in modern usage'.[6]

---

4   Gamble, *The Textual History,* 57: The papyrus letters are 'described as "non-literary" because they were not intended for "publication"... [in contrast to the] "literary" letters of antiquity, by which we may refer either to letters transmitted through literary tradition or to letters composed in rather sophisticated and artful style'.

5   For more discussion see F. Ziemann, *De Epistularum Graecarum Formulis Sollemnibus Quaestiones Selectae* (Berlin: Haas, 1912), 334–56; F. X. J. Exler, *The Form of the Ancient Greek Letter of the Epistolary Papyri (3rd c. B. C.–3rd c. A. D.): A Study in Greek Epistolography* (Washington, DC: Ares Publishers, 1923), 73–77, 103–107; H. Koskenniemi, *Studien zur Idee und Phraseologie des Griechischen Briefes bis 400 n. Chr.* (Helsinki: Akateeminen Kirjakauppa, 1956), 151–54; Gamble, *Textual History,* 58–59; J. L. White, 'Epistolary Formulas and Clichés in Greek Papyrus Letters', in *SBL Seminar Papers* 2 (Missoula, MT: Scholars, 1978), 289–319, 289–29; 'The Greek Documentary Letter Tradition: Third Century BCE to Third Century CE', *Semeia* 22 (1981), 92–95; 'New Testament Epistolary Literature in the Framework of Ancient Epistolography', *Aufstieg und Niedergang der römischen Welt,* II, 25.2 (Berlin: de Gruyter, 1984), 1730–56, 1733–34; *Light from Ancient Letters,* 198–202. There were letters in which a farewell wish did not occur: business letters (agreements of sale, loans, receipts, contracts, and tenders written in letter form) and other types of letter. F. Francis refers to these types of letter (private, public, secondary, early as well as late) that do not have closing formulas but just stop: e.g. P. Tebt. 34; P. Tebt. 29; P. Tebt. 34; P. Oxy. 1071. See F. O. Francis, 'The Form and Function of the Opening and Closing Paragraphs of James and 1 John', *ZNW* 61 (1970), 110–26, at 125.

6   Gamble, *Textual History,* 58.

The two basic forms of the farewell wish are ἔρρωσο ('Be Strong!', 'farewell', 'good-bye'),[7] or εὐτύχει ('May you prosper');[8] ἔρρωσο occurs more than the other.[9] In the older papyrus letters, the farewell wish is expressed in the verb itself: ἔρρωσο and εὐτύχει. But towards the end of the second century CE the more expansive form ἐρρῶσθαί σε εὔχομαι ('I pray that you may be well') combined a farewell and closing health wish, and was used instead of simpler forms. This form became the standard closing formula in the second and third centuries.[10] The farewell wish functions to bring the letter to a definitive close, and it can also include various elaborations.[11]

Another epistolary convention, the 'health wish', expresses concern about the welfare of the recipient by mentioning the letter writer's own well-being.[12] The basic form of the health wish varies with historical periods as reflected in the Greek papyrus letters. The ancient Latin letters were different from the Greek letters and had the *formula valetudinis* as a fixed form of health wish. However, the location of this formula was not fixed, and it could appear in the opening or closing sections: sometimes in both.[13] In contrast to this, the Greek health wish had different forms depending on its location in the letter. Exler notes that the form of the Greek health wish, in a letter's opening, has the basic

---

7   The present passive imperative of ῥώννυμι (to be strong, vigorous). Terms like farewell and goodbye are used at the conclusion of the letters: e.g. P. Princ. 72; P. Princ. 163; P. Oxy. 2786.

8   The present active imperative of εὐτυχέω: e.g. P. Tebt. 41, P. Tebt. 53. This form was expanded to διευτυχέω· e.g., P. Oxy. 2342, P. Oxy. 2713.

9   Roller identifies the distinction in the two forms of the final wish: ἔρρωσο is used in letters to peers or inferiors, while εὐτύχει occurs in letters to superiors and seems to be less likely because, Gamble suggests, the distinction is not so obvious. Gamble agrees with Ziemann in this view. See O. Roller, *Das Formular der Paulinischen Briefe; Ein Beitrag zur Lehre vom Antiken Briefe, BWANT* 4/6 (58) (Stuttgart: Kohlhammer, 1933), 481–82; F. Ziemann, *De Epistularum Graecarum,* 350–56; Gamble, *Textual History*, 58.

10   Weima, *Neglected Endings*, 31.

11   The farewell wish is brief and has a fixed form but it has three types of elaboration which begin to appear in the second century BCE: (1) the recipient is referred to in a term of relationship or endearment such as ἀδελφέ ('brother'), πάτερ ('father'), κύριε ('lord'), etc. The vocative case also denotes a relationship beyond the family boundary: e.g. P. Ryl. 233, P. Oxy. 1296; (2) the prepositional phrase such as μετὰ τῶν σῶν πάντων ('with all of yours'), σὺν τοῖς σοῖς πᾶσι ('with you all'), or ἐν πανοικησίᾳ ('in all [your] household'): e.g. P. Giss. 24, P. Hamb. 54, P. Amh. 135; (3) an adverbial phrase such as διὰ ὅλου βίου ('throughout [your] whole life'), εἰς τὸν ἀεὶ χρόνον ('for all time'), εἰς μακροὺς αἰῶνας ('for many years'), πολλοῖς χρόνοις ('for many years'). Weima, *Neglected Endings*, 32.

12   See for detailed description, Ziemann, *De Epistularum Graecarum,* 302–25; Exler, *Ancient Greek Letter,* 107–11; Koskenneimi, *Studien zur Idee und Phraseologie des griechichen Briefes,* 130–39; cf. Roller, *Das Formular,* 62–65; Gamble, *Textual History,* 60–61; White, 'Epistolary Formulas and Clichés', 295–99; Weima, *Neglected Endings,* 34–39.

13   Weima, *Neglected Endings,* 35. Exler suggests that the health wish comes in the body of the Hellenistic letter, which is less likely because the health wish has a role of maintaining relationships between the persons involved and the frequent occurrence of the health wish in the letter closings indicates the improbability of its position in the body of the letter. See Exler, *Ancient Greek Letter,* 101–13; *contra* Weima, *Neglected Endings,* 34–35.

structure: εἰ ἔρρωσθαι, εὖ ἄν ἔχοι· ἐρρώμεθα (ὑγιαίνομεν) καὶ ἡμεῖς (αὐτοί) ('If you are well, it would be good. We too are well').[14] The health wish (in the closing section of the letter) comes before the farewell wish and takes the basic form: ἐπιμέλου σεαυτοῦ ἵν' ὑγιαίνῃς ('Take care of yourself in order that you may be healthy'), which has no reference to the writer's own well-being.[15]

The other parts of letter closings contain greeting (which is the focus of this chapter and will be dealt with separately below), the concluding autograph, date, illiteracy formula,[16] and postscript. When a secretary was employed to assist in the writing of letters, a concluding autograph from the sender in his or her own hand carried brief closing remarks. The dating formula occurs in most official or business letters, and (if it occurs) it comes after the farewell wish in the final position of the closing section. A postscript was sometimes added to the end of the letter to include any final information not mentioned earlier.

It is rare that any one letter has all the above elements in the closing section because the context and style of the letter differ in each instance.

2.2.1. Greetings

Greeting is the third epistolary convention commonly found in ancient Hellenistic letters. Although concluding greetings are not frequently present in the letters before the first century CE, greetings attained a fixed position at the close of a letter from then onwards. The greeting of the writer to the addressee was located at the beginning of the letter (χαίρειν) and the closing greeting can be considered as a 'secondary' greeting. Both opening and closing greetings were employed to maintain good relations with the recipients. As Weima suggests, the greetings were one of 'the key means of expressing "philophronesis" – that is, the friendly relationship that existed between the sender of the letter and its recipient'.[17] The concluding greetings are directed to the friends or family members of the addressee.

---

14   The basic form varies: the common changes are καλῶς –εὖ, ἐρρώμεθα –ὑγιαίνομεν, αὐτοί– ἡμεῖς and the additions are πρὸ μὲν πάντων or πρὸ τῶν ὅλων, τὰ λοιπά or τἆλλα, βούλομαι or θέλω, κατὰ λόγον, κατὰ νοῦν or κατὰ γνώμην. The opening health wish was a separate formula and comes after the opening greeting from the third century BCE to the middle of the second century BCE, e.g. PSI 331; PSI 364; UPZ 64; from the mid second century BCE to the early second century CE the health wish began to be combined with the opening greeting, e.g. P. Tebt. 12; P. Oxy. 2979; BGU 1204; in the latter part of the second century CE and the third century CE the health wish appears as a separate formula. See Weima, *Neglected Endings*, 35, 36; Exler, *Ancient Greek Letter,* 103–105.

15   There are variations although not in an extensive manner as in the opening health wish, e.g. P. Mert. 62; P. Petr. 2; P. Oslo. 47. The health wish in the closing of the letter disappears by the first century CE and the beginning of the second, probably due to the combined form of the health wish and the farewell wish: ἐρρῶσθαί σε εὔχομαι ('I pray that you may be well'). See Weima, *Neglected Endings*, 38.

16   The illiteracy formula is a brief note at the end of the letter showing that a secretary has written the document since the person who is actually sending the letter is illiterate. See Weima, *Neglected Endings*, 50; Exler, *Form of the Ancient Greek Letter*, 124–27.

17   Weima, *Neglected Endings*, 39.

The basic form of the concluding greetings consisted of the verb of greeting and its object. Moreover, both verb and object could be subjected to various modifications. The verb commonly used for expressing greetings in letter closings is ἀσπάζεσθαι[18] ('to greet, welcome, salute'). Προσαγορεύειν[19] (to address, call by name) and ἐπισκοπεῖσθαι ('to look after, watch over')[20] are also used infrequently. In addition, the writer wants the addressee to convey the greetings to others when the verb is presented imperatively (ἀσπάζου, ἀσπάσαι).[21]

2.2.1.1. Types of greeting

There are three types of greeting corresponding to the three persons of the verb: the first-person form, the second-person form, and the third-person form.[22] The first and third-person greeting types can be put together under the banner of informational greeting (which is an informative greeting from the sender to the addressee), whereas the second-person type of greeting can be called an instructional greeting (specifically instructing the recipient to greet other parties).

1. The first-person form ἀσπάζομαι is very rarely used in the final greetings of the first century CE, and only began to be employed in the final greetings during the second century CE.[23] In the first-person form of greeting the writer of the letter greets his or her recipients directly: this is considered the most direct and personal form of greeting formulae; e.g. P. Wash. 30: ἀσπάζομαί σε ἄδελφε Νεικῆτα ('I greet you, brother Neicetes').[24] The first-person type of greeting usually occurs in the opening (χαίρειν) and it emphasises the friendly relationship between the person who does the greeting and the persons being greeted. If the first-person greeting is directed at someone other than the person mentioned in the opening, it shows that the writer wants

---

18   ἀσπάζεσθαι means 'to effect ἀσπασμός, mostly to proffer the greeting which is customary on entering a house or meeting someone on the street or parting'. An 'ἀσπασμός in a letter is a greeting from a distance, which is a substitute for a greeting and embrace in personal encounter. It expresses sincere attachment in separation and thus serves to strengthen personal fellowship'. K. H. Windisch, 'ἀσπάζομαι', *TDNT* 1, 496–502, at 496.

19   E.g. P. Geiss. 12; P. Mert. 63; P. Tebt. 58, 768; P. Oslo. 153; P. Oxy. 293, 294, 743.

20   The plain meaning of the verb is not related to greeting. However, it is used as a technical term for greeting which means 'send regards to'; e.g. P. Mert. 63; P. Oslo. 153. John White argues that the indicative form of the verb has this meaning while the imperative does not have the same meaning; Weima disagrees by suggesting that the indicative as well as the imperative of the verb have the same meaning. White, 'Epistolary Formulas and Clichés', 298–99; White, *Light from Ancient Letters*, 202, fn. 63. Weima, *Neglected Endings*, 40.

21   Gamble, *Textual History*, 59.

22   Mullins, 'Greeting as a New Testament Form', 418; Weima, *Neglected Endings*, 40; Koskenniemi, *Des griechischen Briefes*, 148–51. Koskenniemi describes the types in a different way: (1) the writer greets the addressee; (2) the writer greets others through the addressee; and (3) the writer conveys greetings from another party to the recipient.

23   Gamble, *Textual History*, 59.

24   Weima, *Neglected Endings*, 40.

to communicate with more persons than in the previous list.[25] As Mullins suggests, one of the important aspects of the first-person type of greeting is 'its potential for spelling out the intended readership of the letter'.[26]

2.   In the second-person form of greeting, the writer requires the addressee to convey the greetings to someone on his behalf: e.g. P. Tebt. 412: ἀσπάζου τὴν μετέρα σου καὶ τὸν πατέρα σου ('Greet your mother and your father'). Thus the addressee becomes the agent of communication between the sender and the third party. (The greeting can be rendered in either the present imperative ἀσπάζου or the aorist imperative ἀσπάσαι.) Second-person greetings occur in the final section of the letter and stand in contrast to the first-person greeting, which is usually located in the letter's opening. The second-person greeting is also less personal than the first-person greeting.[27]

On the one hand, this type of greeting implies a closer relationship between the writer of the letter and the addressee than between the writer and the person greeted, and on the other, it suggests a closer relationship between the addressee and the person greeted than between the writer and the person greeted. Thus the appearance of a second-person type of greeting indicates a series of close and friendly bonds. Mullins suggests that relationships between the persons in the letter can also be determined by the epistolary situation (in addition to the greeting formula); the second-person type of greeting is significant since it informs the reader of the relationships that exist beyond the scope of the letter – not just the relationships overtly indicated within the text.[28]

3.   In the third-person form of greeting, the letter writer becomes an agent through whom a third party greets either the addressee or some other fourth party: e.g. P. Mich. 464: ἀσπάζονταί σέ σου τὰ παιδία ('Your children greet you').[29] Like second-person greetings, the third-person greeting is located in the letter's closing section.[30] The third-person greeting is also the least personal form of greeting. However, it gives readers information about relationships existing beyond that of the letter writer and the addressee.

2.2.1.2. Elements of greeting

The three basic elements in the secondary (closing) greetings are: (1) the greeting verb; (2) the sender of the greeting; (3) the recipient of the greeting. The elaborating phrase is an optional fourth element in secondary greetings. The first three elements are essential but can vary in different types of greeting. In the first and second-person types of greeting, the verb alone functions as the first and second elements. An example of each type is as follows:[31]

---

25   See, e.g., BGU 276; P. Fay. 116; P. Mert. 81, 82, 85; P. Oxy. 123, 1067, 1494; P. Princ. 70; P. Tebt. 415.

26   Mullins, 'Greeting as a Letter Form', 420.

27   See e.g., BGU 632; P. Fay. 112, 123; P. Mert. 22, 81, 82; P. Oslo. 47, 48, 49, 150, 161; P. Oxy. 114, 295, 300, 1061, 1489; P. Princ. 68, 70; P. Ryl. 230, 231; P. Tebt. 412.

28   Mullins, 'Greeting as a New Testament Form', 420, 421.

29   Weima, *Neglected Endings*, 42. The third-person indicative singular or plural is used.

30   For example, P. Mert. 22, 81, 82, 83; P. Oxy. 2981, 2982, 3312; P. Princ. 70.

31   The examples are given by Mullins, 'Greeting as a New Testament Form', 419.

P. Herm. 14: ἀσπαζόμεθα Διόσκορον καὶ Εὐσδαίμονα καὶ τοὺς παρὰ σοὶ παῖδας

P. Oxy. 1016: ἀσπάζου τοὺς σοὺς πάντας

The person doing the greeting is expressed in the third-person type. For example,

P. Iand. 9: ἀσπάζεται ὑμᾶς πάντας κατ' ὄνομα Λοπεινᾶς

2.2.1.3. Elaborating/descriptive phrases
In the Hellenistic letters, the elaborating phrases used in the closing greetings indicate some details about the writer–reader relationship. The elaborating phrases emphasise some aspect of greeting that usually serves to modify or call particular attention to one of the basic elements of greeting (the greeting verb, the person doing the greeting, or the person being greeted).[32] The elaborating phrases used are different according to their function.

(a)   One type of phrase, the *modifier*, is used to strengthen the relationships indicated by the basic elements. The verb of greeting is sometimes elaborated by the modifier πολλά, and can be used with either the first, second, or third-person type of greeting (ἀσπάζεσθαι πολλά, 'to greet warmly'). 'Here the writer seeks to convey to the reader the thought that his greeting is something special, and that it is not just a conventional gesture.'[33] The use of πολλά, is the most general method of modifying the effect of the verb, and it is intended to intensify the warmth of the greeting. At other times, the entire clause is introduced with πρὸ πάντων or πρὸ τῶν ὅλων ('above all', 'by all means').

(b)   An *interjection* is another elaborating phrase. It is a 'fairly irrelevant comment thrown in as part of the greeting'; 'a simple pious wish for good luck of one sort or another for the person greeted', or a curse against a mutual enemy.[34] It can also take the form of telling something about the greeter, which, as Mullins suggests, is a type of 'personality signature'.[35]

(c)   The third kind of elaborating phrase is the *personal description*: a phrase used to describe the person being greeted. The phrase shows the special relationship between the writer and person greeted, and it might include a word of endearment. The objects of greetings are usually designated by proper names, but sometimes they are done so by a personal description that states the form of the relationship, e.g. P. Oxy. 533, ἀσπάσασθε Στατίαν τὴν θυγατέρα μου καὶ Ἡραχλείδην καὶ Ἀπίονα τοὺς υἱούς μου.

In some cases, the objects of the greetings are not named but appear in a general collective designation: e.g. πάντας τοὺς ἐν οἴκῳ (ἐνοίκους), 'all among your household', 'your whole family'. But considering that this was

32   Mullins, 'Greeting as a New Testament Form', 419.
33   Mullins, 'Greeting as a New Testament Form', 422.
34   Mullins, 'Greeting as a New Testament Form', 422.
35   Mullins, 'Greeting as a New Testament Form', 422.

too impersonal a way of greeting friends, some writers added a *personalizing phrase*, κατ' ὄνομα which means 'by name': e.g. P. Mich. 206, ἀσπάζου τοὺς σοὺς πάντας κατ' ὄνομα. ἀσπάζονταί σε καὶ τοὺς σοὺς πάντας οἱ ἐμοὶ πάντες κατ' ὄνομα.

(d)　　The fourth kind is the *identifying phrase*. The role of the identifying phrase is to characterise the person who does the greeting. It can occur in a first or third-person type of greeting. An example of this rare type of elaborating phrase is P. Oxy. 1067, κἀγὼ Ἀλέξανδρος ὁ πατὴρ ὑμῶν ἀσπάζομαι ὑμᾶς πολλά.

It should be noted that although Paul adapted the Hellenistic epistolary models for Christian purposes, he expressed a sense of freedom in literary matters. He was not tied to any fixed models and he often combined non-Jewish Hellenistic customs with Hellenistic Jewish ones.[36] 'That Paul envisioned a worship setting as he composed his letters is evident in the manner in which he altered customary conventions and/or by the way in which he used Christian formularies as a substitute for set epistolary phrases.'[37]

2.3. Letter closing in the Semitic letters

It is also important to have a look at the closing conventions of ancient Semitic letters because Paul claims to have had a Jewish Pharisaic background (Rom. 11.1; 2 Cor. 11.22; Phil. 3.5-6; Gal. 1.13-14; 1 Cor. 15.9). The Semitic letters fall under two categories: primary and secondary. The primary letters have two basic epistolary conventions: first, a farewell wish of *shalom* ('peace', 'health', and 'well-being'), which has the double function of saying farewell and proclaiming a good health wish. Second, a personal signature from the writer (full postscripts were rare occurrences). Weima suggests that the Semitic letters differ from the Hellenistic ones because it is less common for Hellenistic letters to carry a signature.[38] He also notes that Paul might have been influenced by Semitic signature practice in his writing: 'I, Paul, write this in my own hand' (Philemon 19; 1 Cor. 16.21; Gal. 6.11; 2 Thess. 3.17; Col. 4.18). The secondary (literary) letters have epistolary conventions such as a farewell wish (Ep. *Arist.* 33; 2 Apoc. Bar. 86.1; Josephus, *Life* 365), a date (2 Macc. 11.33), a health wish (opening health wish: e.g. Ep. *Arist.* 35; 2 Macc. 1.10; 2 Macc. 11.28; closing health wish: e.g. Josephus *Ant.* 17.135).[39]

36　　P. T. O'Brien, 'Letters, Letter Forms', *DPL*, 550–53, at 551; see also R. W. Funk, *Language, Hermeneutic, and Word of God: The Problem of Language in the New Testament and Contemporary Theology* (New York: Harper & Row, 1966), 270. For more discussion see Weima, *Neglected Endings*, 57–76.

37　　J. L. White, 'Saint Paul and the Apostolic Letter Tradition', *CBQ* 45 (1983), 433–44, at 437.

38　　Weima, *Neglected Endings*, 67. For more discussion see pp. 57–76.

39　　Weima, *Neglected Endings*, 74–75.

Compared to the Hellenistic letter closing, the Semitic letter closings are shorter and less elaborate with fewer letters found containing links between the body of the letter and its closing sections. Weima notes, 'As we found with respect to ancient Hellenistic letters, there does not appear among the Semitic letters to be any deliberate and careful adaptation of closings so that they summarise and echo key issues previously taken up in their respective bodies.' However, he also notes a few exceptions with links between Semitic letter closings and the main body of the letter indicating the writer's intention of writing appropriate endings.[40]

2.4. Letter closing in the Pauline letters

We have discussed the epistolary forms of both the ancient Hellenistic letters and the Semitic letters to comprehend how far these forms influenced Paul's epistolary writings. Although echoes of Hellenistic influence can be seen to a greater extent, and Semitic influence to a lesser extent, Weima suggests from Paul's 'creation of the forms unparalleled in ancient letters'[41] that Pauline letter closings relate to the specific epistolary situations. As we deal with the closing conventions of the Pauline letters, we will look at the different forms used in Paul's letters in general, and Romans in particular. The conclusion of Paul's letters consists of a grace benediction, a wish of peace, greetings, an exhortation to greet with a holy kiss, an autographic conclusion, and other elements.

The grace benediction functions as a final wish (1 Cor. 16.23 is an exception, where Paul conveys his love to be with the church by a wish) and is constructed from three components: the wish, the divine source, and the recipient. The wish includes grace (χάρις) in both the disputed and the undisputed letters; 2 Cor. 13.13 has additional words such as love and fellowship. The divine source τοῦ κυρίου Ἰησοῦ Χριστοῦ ('of [our] Lord Jesus [Christ]') is present in all the undisputed letters of Paul, but is absent in the disputed letters. The genitive phrase 'of Christ Jesus' depicts that Christ Jesus is the source of grace. The variation can be found in 2 Cor. 13.13 where θεός and πνεῦμα are used. The recipient is introduced with μετά (with) and followed by ὑμῶν (e.g. Rom. 16.20b; 1 Cor. 16.23; 2 Cor. 13.13; Gal. 6.18; Phil. 4.23; 1 Thess. 5.28; 2 Thess. 3.18; Philemon 25); the divine source is absent in the disputed letters, e.g. Eph. 6.24; Col. 4.18b; 1 Tim. 6.21b; 2 Tim. 4.22b; Tit. 3.15b.[42] Variations include: τοῦ πνεύματος ὑμῶν and πάντων ὑμῶν (which has an emphatic

---

40 Weima, *Neglected Endings*, 76. Doty suggests that there are no 'direct lines of borrowing by Paul from Jewish epistolary materials in terms of form and structure'. W. G. Doty, *Letters in Primitive Christianity* (Philadelphia: Fortress, 1973), 22. Fitzmyer finds some parallels between New Testament epistolography and Aramaic letters. See J. A. Fitzmyer, 'Some Notes on Aramaic Epistolography', *JBL* 93 (1974), 201–25, at 220.

41 Weima, *Neglected Endings*, 77.

42 See Weima, *Neglected Endings*, 78–87.

function). The grace benediction's link to the early Christian liturgy can be seen in 1 Cor. 16.20-23, where Paul deviates from the simple farewell wish to the grace benediction. According to Weima, the reasons for the variations in Paul are: (1) he may be concerned about the spiritual welfare of the readers; (2) his desire to give a Christological focus; (3) to build 'inclusion' with the opening salutation (which has a grace benediction); (4) due to his theological, liturgical, and pastoral interests.[43]

The wish of peace appears early in the epistolary conclusions, and occurs in all undisputed letters except 1 Corinthians and Philemon. The wish of peace is composed from an introductory element (δέ, καί) and the divine source (Θεός). In the grace benediction Christ is the divine source, and in the wish of peace God bestows it on the recipients. The peace wish has variations in 1 Cor. 13.11 (where peace and love are used); 2 Thess. 3.16 ('may the God of peace himself give you peace at all times and all ways'); and 1 Thess. 5.23-24 ('may the God of peace himself sanctify you wholly ... till the coming of Christ'). The wish of peace and the recipient's receiving of it (μετὰ + ὑμῶν) form the basic foundation of the wish.[44] Romans has two peace benedictions (15.33; 16.20a) that include particular special features (these will be discussed below). The Semitic peace benediction originated from the Aaronic blessing in Num. 6.24-26, and conveys a blessing of complete well-being and wholeness. In the Pauline letters, the peace benediction comes at the beginning of the letter closing and serves to express concern for the spiritual welfare of the readers. The greetings are always placed between the peace wish and the grace benediction if both are present in the letter. The instruction to 'greet with a kiss' is included with Paul's other greetings and will be discussed in the next section.

The next element, the autograph statement τῇ ἐμῇ χειρὶ (Παύλου), in/with my [Paul's] own hand, appears in five (three undisputed and two disputed) of Paul's letters (1 Cor. 16.21; Gal. 6.11; 2 Thess. 3.17; Philemon 19; cf. Col. 4.18a).[45] The autograph formula indicates that Paul used a secretary to write the letter, and his personal handwriting is used as a signature for the letter.

Doxology is another important element in letter closing, and differs from benediction: 'whereas the benediction is an invocation to God to bestow a blessing on some person(s), the doxology is an expression of praise to God'.[46] The doxology is made up of the following elements: the object of praise (God in the undisputed letters), the element of praise (glory), the signal of time, and the affirmative response. The origin of the doxology is drawn from Jewish worship, which has the same four elements as New Testament doxologies.

---

43   Weima, *Neglected Endings*, 87.

44   There are other benedictions in Pauline letters: Rom. 15.5-6; 15.13; 1 Thess. 3.12-13; 2 Thess. 2.16-17; 2 Thess. 3.5.

45   Only Galatians and Philemon's autographic statement use the verb ἔγραψα, while others lack a main verb. The autograph statement is found with the greeting formula (three occurrences: 1 Cor 16.21; 2 Thess. 3.17; Col. 4.18a).

46   Weima, *Neglected Endings*, 135, 136.

Generally, the doxology functions as a conclusion of the arguments and exhortations of the letter.

Concluding hortatory remarks look back to the main issues of the respective letters and can be found in the closings of the undisputed Pauline letters. The other elements found in Pauline letters are the joy expression, the letter of recommendation, and the postscript.

The Pauline letters' conclusions generally follow a pattern of: hortatory remarks, a wish of peace, greetings, exhortation to greet with a kiss, and a grace benediction. According to Gamble, whether these elements are present or absent, or with the addition of other items, the sequence is never violated.[47] In the structure of the individual components, Pauline epistolary conclusions have a regular pattern. However, no two conclusions are the same in all their features.

2.4.1. Form of greetings in the Pauline letters

The Pauline epistolary conclusion is marked by the greetings to the addressees. These can be found in all the undisputed Pauline letters except Galatians.[48] Although there are similarities between the Pauline greeting formula and the Hellenistic greeting formula, there is a considerable diversity of form and scope within the Pauline greetings. In both the Pauline and the Hellenistic letters, ἀσπάζεσθαι with the object is the basic formula of greeting; all three types of greeting (first, second, and third-person types) are used, but the second-person instructional type is more common.

2.4.1.1. Informational greetings

Both the first-person and third-person types contain information about the greetings and will be elaborated on below.

1. *First-person type greetings*: The first-person type of greeting ἀσπάζομαι ('I greet') is found only in Rom. 16.22. Tertius, the apostle's secretary, greets the readers of the letter: ἀσπάζομαι ὑμᾶς ἐγὼ Τέρτιος ὁ γράψας τὴν ἐπιστολὴν ἐν κυρίῳ. In the Hellenistic letters the use of the first-person greeting formula is also restricted. The personal greeting usually appears in the opening salutation (χάρις ὑμῖν καὶ εἰρήνη) alone.

    The distinctive formula: ὁ ἀσπασμὸς τῇ ἐμῇ χειρὶ Παύλου ('The greeting [is written] with my own hand': 1 Cor. 16.21; 2 Thess. 3.17; Col. 4.18) belongs to this greeting type. This type of greeting seems to have no parallels

---

47   Gamble, *Textual History*, 83.

48   The absence of any greetings in the epistle to the Galatians could be put down to the rebuking nature of the letter, or perhaps because the greetings would be inappropriate to a circular letter such as Galatians. Weima suggests that the omission may be due to 'the strained relations that existed between Paul and his Galatian converts'. Among the disputed letters of Paul, the greeting is only missing in Ephesians and 1 Timothy. In the other New Testament letters, the greeting occurs in Heb. 13.24 (twice), 1 Pet. 5.13-14; 2 John 13; and 3. John 15 (twice). Weima, *Neglected Endings*, 115.

in other first-century CE letters.[49] Although ἀσπασμός can be understood as a grace benediction, the grace benediction is actually a wish of grace and not simply a word of greeting. Therefore, Weima suggests that ὁ ἀσπασμὸς τῇ ἐμῇ χειρὶ Παύλου is a 'genuine greeting' from Paul, and is a 'Pauline type of first person greeting'.[50]

2.   *Third-person type greetings*: In the third-person type of greeting, Paul conveys the greetings of others to the recipients of the letter. The writer, Paul, serves as an agent in sending greetings on behalf of people who are with him. The present indicative singular ἀσπάζεται or plural ἀσπάζονται is used in the third-person type of greeting. The greetings are sent 'on behalf of specific individuals (Rom. 16:21, 23:1 Cor. 16:19b; Phlm. 23), of well-defined groups (1 Cor. 16:19a; Phil. 4:22), or of very general groups (1 Cor. 16:20; 2 Cor. 13:12b; Phil. 4:21)'.[51] Paul also sends greetings on behalf of 'the church in Asia' (1 Cor. 16.19a), for 'all the saints' (2 Cor. 13.12b), or for 'all the churches of Christ' (Rom 16.16b); this suggests Paul is concerned about the unity and fellowship of the church, and his own apostolic status, while he communicates greetings on behalf of the other churches.

2.4.1.2. Instructional greetings

Second-person type greetings: In the second-person type of greeting, Paul instructs the readers of the letter to greet other parties. Although it seems as if the recipients are acting as an agent of the letter sender by extending greetings, the implication is that the readers should greet the other parties as if the greeting was entirely of their own initiative.

It can be inferred from this type of greeting that the parties who are to be greeted are not a part of the congregation to whom the letter was addressed. Therefore, it may be assumed that one of the house churches at Rome was the actual recipient of Paul's letter, and 'Paul authorizes them to pass on his personal greetings to specific persons who belonged to other house churches in the capital city'.[52] However, Gamble suggests that even though the recipients of the letter can be seen as agents of greeting, the recipients of the greetings are among the circle of readers.[53]

The sender's greetings being conveyed by the addressees to the third party is equal to the sender himself greeting them: 'The second person imperative form of the greeting verb functions as a surrogate for the first person indicative form, and so represents a direct personal greeting of the writer himself to the addressees.'[54] It seems that 'the involvement of the congregation in passing on

---

49   Weima, *Neglected Endings*, 105.

50   Weima, *Neglected Endings*, 108.

51   Weima, *Neglected Endings*, 109.

52   Weima, *Neglected Endings*, 108. Weima refers to C.-H. Kim, *The Form and Structure of the Familiar Greek Letter of Recommendation* (SBLDS 4; Missoula, MT: Scholars, 1972), 139–40.

53   Gamble, *Textual History*, 92, 93.

54   Gamble, *Textual History*, 93; Mullins, 'Greeting', 418. Mullins suggests that the second-person imperative form shows that the recipients of the greetings stand outside the immediate readership of the letter. Gamble argues that this may be true for Hellenistic private

his greetings to others expressed a stronger sense of public commendation for those individuals being specifically greeted by the apostle'.[55]

However, the second-person greeting indicates Paul's instruction ('you greet'), which is an important factor in this study of mutuality. In Romans: Paul (A) instructs his readers (B) to greet others (C). Paul is not merely intending to pass on his own greetings, but is instructing group B to greet group C on their own initiative: ἀσπάσασθε - you (plural) greet.

The plural aorist imperative ἀσπάσασθε[56] occurs twenty times in the undisputed letters and is the most frequent of the greeting types. By way of comparison, the third-person greeting form only occurs ten times. It is also interesting to note that the second-person greeting type only occurs four times outside of Romans, and of these four occurrences, three belong to the exhortation to greet with a holy kiss (1 Cor. 16.20; 2 Cor. 13.12; and 1 Thess. 5.26). Therefore, only one second-person type of greeting is found outside of Romans: Phil. 4.21.

2.4.1.3. The elements of Pauline greetings

The closing greetings of the Pauline letters contain the same three elements as Greco-Roman letters. They are as follows: (1) the greeting verb ἀσπάσασθε; (2) the giver of the greeting; (3) the recipient of the greeting. Paul's use of these elements is consistent in all his greetings.

2.4.1.4. Elaborating/descriptive phrases

Elaborating phrases contain various personal descriptions and are abundant in the Pauline letters. (In contrast, elaborating phrases are used much less frequently in the papyri.[57]) Paul adds a number of appendages and elaborating phrases to his closing greetings in order to modify or stress the above three elements.

1. The first element of the greeting formula, the greeting verb ἀσπάσασθε, is given more weight by the addition of the adverb πολλά (see 1 Cor. 16.19b). In Hellenistic letters, πολλα is used to give a more personal tone to the greeting.[58] Another type of elaboration to the first element of the greeting formula is found in phrases such as ἐν κυρίῳ ('in the Lord') and ἐν Χριστῷ ('in Christ'). For example, ἀσπάζεται ὑμᾶς ἐν κυρίῳ (1 Cor. 16.19b) and ἀσπάσασθε ... ἐν Χριστῷ Ἰησοῦ (Phil. 4.21), which serve to modify the verb, with 'the verb being "Christianized" by the additions'.[59]

---

letters, but does not seem to be indicative of the Pauline letters. Therefore, the recipients of the second-person greetings in Romans 16 are members of the community.

55   Weima, *Neglected Endings*, 108.

56   The verb ἀσπάσασθε is used in the disputed Pauline letters. E.g. Col. 4.15; 2 Tim. 4.19; Tit. 3.15b. In the other New Testament letters, the second-person type occurs in 1 Pet. 5.14 and 3 John 15b, Heb. 13.24a.

57   Mullins, 'Greeting as a New Testament Form', 424. The interjection, which can be seen in the Hellenistic letters, does not appear at all in Pauline letters.

58   Weima, *Neglected Endings*, 110.

59   Gamble, *Textual History*, 74.

2.   The second element of the greeting formula, the one giving the greeting, is elaborated by using identification phrases. Identification phrases used can be found in Rom. 16.21, 22; 23a, 23b; Philemon 23–24; Phil. 4.22, Col. 4.10-12 (cf. 1 Pet. 5.13). Only one of the identification phrases is used with a first-person type of greeting, 'I, Tertius, who wrote the letter, greet you' (Rom. 16.22); the rest are third-person greetings. Romans 16.23a is a typical example of this type: 'Gaius, who is the host to me and to the whole church, greets you.' In these cases, the descriptive phrases are used with the pattern of a nominative in apposition to the person's name, and are followed by the first-person personal pronoun in the genitive. For example, ὁ συνεργός μου ('my fellow worker'), οἱ συγγενεῖς μου ('my kinsmen') points to the nature of the relationship that exists between the sender of the greeting and Paul.

3.   The descriptive phrases are also used with the third element of greeting: the recipient. The phrases are used to identify those who are being greeted by name and/or personal description, e.g. Rom. 16.5b, 11b, 12a, 12b. Apart from in Romans, this only occurs once: in Col. 4.15 (Ἀσπάσαθε τοὺς ἐν Λαοδικείᾳ ἀδελφοὺς καὶ Νύμφαν ...). In Col. 4.15, Nympha is the object of the greeting. It is also notable that the person being greeted is signified by means of an appositive noun or adjective followed by a genitive first-person personal pronoun.[60]

The phrases used to describe the recipient have different purposes. First, the recipient's descriptive phrase expresses strong commendation, e.g. τὸν ἀγαπητόν μου ('my beloved': Rom. 16.5b, 8, 9, 12b); τὸν δόκιμον ἐν Χριστῷ ('esteemed in Christ': Rom. 16.10a); τὸν ἐκλεκτὸν ἐν κυρίῳ ('chosen in the Lord': Rom. 16.13).

Second, the addition of phrases directed to the recipient, such as ἐν κυρίῳ or ἐν Χριστῷ (Ἰησοῦ),[61] modifies the verb (e.g. 1 Cor. 16.19b and Phil. 4.21) and emphasises the commendation of the recipient as Paul is mentioning them in relation to the Lord.[62]

Third, relative clauses are used with phrases such as: οἵτινες ὑπὲρ τῆς ψυχῆς μου τὸν ἑαυτῶν τράχηλον ὑπέθηκαν ('who risked their necks for my life': Rom. 16.4a); οἷς οὐκ ἐγὼ μόνος εὐχαριστῶ ἀλλὰ καὶ πᾶσαι αἱ ἐκκλησίαι τῶν ἐθνῶν ('to whom not only I but also all churches of the Gentiles give thanks': Rom. 16.4b); ὅς ἐστιν ἀπαρχὴ τῆς Ἀσίας εἰς Χριστόν ('who is the first convert of Asia for Christ': Rom. 16.5b). These phrases may serve to recognise the individual's achievement instead of introducing them to the recipients. It is probable that this is because the individual was already well known in the Christian community.

60   Weima, *Neglected Endings*, 111.
61   The prepositional phrase occurs eleven times in relation to the recipient of the greeting: Rom. 16.3, 5b, 7, 8, 9, 10a, 11b, 12a, 12b, 13; Phil. 4.21a.
62   Weima, *Neglected Endings*, 111.

2.5. The Romans letter closing

Compared to the other Pauline letter closings, Romans' closing words (Rom. 15.33–16.27) have unique aspects. For instance, it is the longest letter closing of the Pauline letters and includes two peace benedictions (15.33; 16.20a), a letter of recommendation (16.1-2), two greeting lists (16.3-16, 21-23), a hortatory section (16.17-20), and a doxology (16.25-27).

The first greeting list is unique due to its length and the number of people being greeted with additional descriptive phrases; it is concluded with the exhortation to greet with a holy kiss (v. 16a) and greetings to the Romans from all the churches of Christ (v. 16b). This is followed by a hortatory section including a paraenesis (vv. 17-18; 19b), a joy expression (v. 19a), and a peace benediction (v. 20a). The hortatory section is followed by a grace benediction (16.20b), which normally forms the final section in Paul's other letters. However, Romans' initial greeting list is followed by an additional list of greetings, where Paul passes on his greetings from his co-workers including his amanuensis (Rom. 16.21-23). Romans' letter closing ends with a long doxology (16.25-27). The closing can be outlined as follows:

15.33	Peace benediction	
16.1-2	Letter of recommendation	
16.3-16	First greeting list	
	vv. 3-15	Second-person greetings
	v. 16a	Greeting with a holy kiss
	v. 16b	Third-person greeting
16.17-20a	Hortatory section (autograph)	
	vv. 17-18	παρακαλέω unit
	v. 19a	Joy expression
	v. 19b	General paraenetic command
	v. 20a	Peace benediction
16.20b	Grace benediction	
16.21-23	Second greeting list	
16.25-27	Doxology	

The closing conventions in the ending of Romans are briefly discussed in the following section.

The two peace benedictions are a distinctive feature of Romans' letter closing and mark it out from the standard pattern followed in Paul's other letters. The range of the peace benediction (15.33) is expressed by the adjective πάντων (all) and reflects the practice of papyrus letters of the day. It seems that Paul is intending to bring about peace for 'all' in the collective sense through his dealing with the problems and divisions in the previous chapters. Weima notes, 'The addition of πάντων would thus be a subtle attempt by Paul to tailor the peace benediction so that it reinforces his previous calls for peace and unity among *all* the members of the church.'[63] The peace benediction in 16.20a is the second peace benediction in Romans' letter closing and is placed before the grace benediction;[64] it calls for God to act for someone ('The God of peace will crush Satan under your feet speedily'), and it forms part of the hortatory section in which Paul himself addresses the readers and strongly urges them to work towards unity.

The letter of recommendation for Phoebe is the second epistolary form in Romans' letter closing, and it has a similar structure and content to that of ἐπιστολὴ συστατική or *littera commendaticia* in Greco-Roman letters.[65] The Hellenistic letters have a fixed form (to some extent) and consist of the following elements: a verb of recommendation, the name of the person recommended, a describing phrase, a request clause, a circumstantial clause, and a purpose clause. Phoebe's letter of recommendation has all the above-mentioned forms except for the circumstantial clause, and therefore implies that Paul is following the example of contemporary letters of introduction.[66]

---

63   Weima, *Neglected Endings*, 96.

64   Some manuscripts place the grace benediction in 16.24, and others place it in 16.27; however, the widely held view supports16.20b as its original location.

65   The ancient letters of recommendation have been studied by C. W. Keyes and Chan-Hie Kim. C. W. Keyes, 'The Greek Letter of Introduction', *AJP* 56 (1935), 28–44; Kim, *Familiar Letter of Recommendation*. Phoebe's letter of introduction has the following contents: (1) Συνίστημι δὲ ὑμῖν (I commend to you); (2) Φοίβην (Phoebe); (3) τὴν ἀδελφὴν ἡμῶν, οὖσαν [καὶ] διάκονον τῆς ἐκκλησίας τῆς ἐν Κεγχρεαῖς (our sister, a deacon of the church at Cenchreae); (4) ἵνα αὐτὴν προσδέξησθε ἐν κυρίῳ ἀξίως τῶν ἁγίων καὶ παραστῆτε αὐτῇ ἐν ᾧ ἂν ὑμων χρήζῃ πράγματι· (so that you may welcome her in the Lord as is fitting for the saints, and help her in whatever she may require from you); (5) καὶ γὰρ αὐτὴ προστάτις πολλῶν ἐγενήθη καὶ ἐμοῦ αὐτοῦ (for she has been a benefactor of many and of myself as well). The letter of recommendation although not in the standard form can be found in 1 Cor. 16.15-18, cf. Eph. 6.21-22 and Col. 4.7-8. Those who argue 1 Cor. 16.15-18 is a formal letter of introduction include Gamble, *Textual History*, 97; L. L. Belleville, 'Continuity or Discontinuity: A Fresh Look at 1 Corinthians in the Light of First Century Epistolary Forms and Conventions', *EvQ* 59 (1987), 15–37, 34; G. D. Fee, *The First Epistle to the Corinthians* (Grand Rapids: Eerdmans, 1987), 832.

66   The notion that ancient letters of recommendation are independent letters that are not found in the letter closings made some scholars argue that Phoebe's letter was originally an independent letter of recommendation. However, Gamble cites several examples that have the letter of introduction in the closing of the letters; this probably places Phoebe's letter as one of Romans' letter closing conventions because she is the bearer of the letter. See Gamble, *Textual History*, 84–87. Those who hold the view that Rom. 16.1, 2 is a separate letter are A. Deissmann, *Light from the Ancient East*, trans. L. R. M. Strachen (London: Hodder and Stoughton, 1910), 171, 235; J. Moffatt, *Introduction to the Literature of the New Testament* (New York: Charles

Nevertheless, this does not reduce Paul's purpose of recommending Phoebe to the Romans, as she is the bearer of the letter.

The commonly held view is that the hortatory section in Rom. 16.17-20 was written by Paul's own hand (although this is not explicitly mentioned) and serves as an autograph. It echoes the concerns of the apostle by strongly cautioning those who cause dissensions and divisions in the community. Karl Donfried observes that Rom. 16.17-20 is a conclusion of the issues raised in the previous chapters, and that Rom. 16.17-20 appears as a 'final warning'. Paul Achtemeier suggests that Rom. 16.17-20 not only summarises Paul's exhortations in chs. 12–16, but also reflects the 'whole of his theology, namely the unity of Jews and Gentiles'.[67]

The doxology in Romans (16.25-27) is one of two doxologies in the undisputed Pauline corpus that appear in the letter's closing (cf. Phil. 4.20).[68] Many scholars have noticed the verbal and thematic links between the doxology in Romans and the earlier parts of the letter (e.g. 16.25a–1.11, 16; 9.17; 15.13, 19; 16.25b-26a–3.21).[69]

Paul reflects the practice of first-century letter closings by summarising and reinforcing the main arguments of the letter in his letter closing.

2.6. Greetings in the Romans letter closing

The form of the greetings in the Romans letter closing is significantly different when compared to other Pauline letters: it contains a total of twenty-one greetings (more than the other undisputed Pauline letters contain), and it has two distinct greeting lists (16.3-16 and 16.21-23), and there are a total of twenty-one greetings (seventeen greetings are in the first list and four are in the second).[70] The first list has more of the instructional, second-person type greetings.

Scribner's Sons, 3rd edn, 1918), 135; E. J. Goodspeed, 'The Ancient Letter of Introduction', 55–57; Fitzmyer, *Romans*, 292; McDonald, 'Was Romans XVI a Separate Letter?', 369–72.

67   K. Donfried (ed.), *Romans Debate*, 44–52; P. J. Achtemeier, *Romans* (Atlanta: John Knox, 1985), 238.

68   The authenticity of the doxology in Romans has been questioned on textual and literary grounds since different manuscripts place the doxology in various places (14.23; 15.33; 16.23). See above p. 3, section 1.3. But there are still scholars who support its authenticity. See L. W. Hurtado, 'The Doxology at the End of Romans', in E. P. Epp and G. D. Fee (eds.), *New Testament Textual Criticism: Its Significance for Exegesis. Essays in Honour of Bruce M. Metzger* (Oxford: Clarendon, 1981), 185–99. Weima, *Neglected Endings*, 142.

69   See Gamble, *Textual History*, 123; Dunn, *Romans 9–16*, 913; Dunn observes that the 'doxology has summarized well some of the basic concerns of the letter' (917).

70   The second list of greetings (Rom. 16.21-23) consists of individual and group greetings. Paul uses the third-person greeting formula and fewer descriptive phrases to communicate to the Romans greetings from the following people: (1) Timothy, ὁ συνεργός μου; (2) Lucius, Jason, Sosipater οἱ συγγενεῖς μου; (3) Tertius, the writer of the letter; (4) Gaius, whose hospitality Paul and the whole church enjoyed; (5) Erastus, city οἰκονόμος; (6) Quartus, our brother.

2.6.1. The first greeting list (16.3-16)

The first greeting contains both group and individual greetings. Altogether, twenty-four persons are mentioned by name, and two further individuals are simply mentioned in relational terms. Out of the twenty-six people in the first list, nine are women.[71] The individuals greeted are: Mary, Persis, Epaenetus, Amplias, Urbanus, Herodion, Apelles, Rufus, Rufus' mother; and the couples or groups who are greeted are: Prisca and Aquila; Andronicus and Junia; the household of Aristobulus; the household of Narcissus; Tryphaena and Tryphosa; Asyncritus, Philegon, Hermas, Patrobas, Hermes and the brethren; Philologus and Julia, Nereus and his sister, Olympas and all the saints. The final two general greetings mentioned in Romans 16 are: 'greet one another with a holy kiss'[72] and 'all the churches of Christ greet you'.

I will now briefly examine the descriptive phrases used to detail the men in the greeting list.[73] Epaenetus is described as 'the first fruits in Asia into Christ' (ἀπαρχὴ τῆς Ἀσίας εἰς Χριστόν; 16.5) like Stephanas, who is 'the first convert in Achaia' (1 Cor. 16.15; cf. 2 Thess. 2.13). It is possible that the first converts are devoted to ministry and later emerged to be leading figures in the church.[74]

Paul often indicates his affection for particular Christians by referring to them as 'my beloved [name]' (Rom. 16.5, 8-9b; Epaenetus, Amplias, Stachys); cf. 'the beloved Persis' (Rom. 16.12). ἀγαπητός denotes a warm personal relationship (16.5, 8, 9, 12); Amplias is described as Paul's 'beloved in the Lord' (ἀγαπητόν μου ἐν κυρίῳ), which shows Paul's relationship with him as well as Amplias' position in relation to the Lord and the Roman church (v. 8). The description of some individuals as ἀγαπητός is important since Paul emphasises the theme of ἀγάπη in Romans 12–15.

δόκιμος may refer to Apelles' maturity (16.10), indicating that he is respected and esteemed (cf. Rom. 14.18), but it is more likely that Paul was intending to convey that Apelles had been proven to be a Christian through testing.[75] Moreover, δόκιμος involves the testing or proof of one's character elsewhere in Paul's letters (2 Cor. 2.9; 8.2; 9.13; 13.3; Phil. 2.22). Conclusively, it seems that Paul is recognising these men's positive efforts for the expansion of the church as well as one another in the Lord.

ἐκλεκτός is used to describe individuals chosen for a particular task; Rufus was such an individual, and he was specially chosen for some particular role

---

71   It is possible to add Phoebe to the list of greeted women too, since she was to be welcomed (in the letter of recommendation) which implies a connotation of greeting.

72   The holy kiss is discussed as a separate section. See below 2.6.2.

73   For the phrases used of women, see chapter 4 below.

74   See Moo, *Romans*, 920; L. Morris, The *Epistle to the Romans* (Grand Rapids: Eerdmans, 1988), 533.

75   Godet (F. L. Godet, *Commentary on the Epistle to the Romans*, vol. 2 [Edinburgh: T&T Clark, 1880], 492); Murray (J. Murray, *The Epistle to the Romans* [vol. 2; Grand Rapids: Eerdmans, 1965]); Moo, *Romans*, 924; Dunn, *Romans 9–16*, 896 accept it as a character that is tested and proved.

or position of significance (16.13). It is less plausible to identify Rufus as the son of Simon of Cyrene, since Paul evidently knows of no other Christian named Rufus in Rome. Interestingly, Mk. 15.21 gives evidence of a Christian named Rufus who was well known to the Christian community.[76]

The final greeting in the first list ('all the churches of Christ greet you') is significant because Paul speaks in wider terms than he has previously to express greetings to the Romans. As Weima puts it, 'so here it seems, Paul presents himself to the Romans as one who has the official backing of all the churches in Achaia, Macedonia, Asia, Galatia, Syria and elsewhere in the eastern part of the empire'.[77] Out of seventeen greetings, this is the only third-person greeting in the first list, and it has a universal implication for the exhortations in the letter; this greeting shows that Paul was not alone in his missionary endeavour but was joined by a large number of churches who were keen to pass on their greetings. It is also significant to note the important bearing that the greeting has on the instructions given in earlier chapters. The greeting highlights the mutual interdependence of being one body in Christ and the necessity that relationships within the church should be constructive and uplifting in order to conform to this.

The first greeting list in Romans has many peculiarities. For instance, the recipients of the letter are not merely readers of the letter, but are asked by Paul actively to participate in carrying out the greetings, i.e. they are not silently accepting the exhortations in the letter but have an active role in contextualising the exhortations. This is observed through the second-person-plural greeting formula ἀσπάσασθε (you pl.) that reveals the recipients are being addressed as a group.

What are the social dynamics of the greeting being conveyed by the verb ἀσπάσασθε? Does ἀσπάσασθε intend to communicate Paul greeting the third party, or the second group greeting the third party? Gamble suggests that the imperative form of the greeting verb 'represents a direct personal greeting of the writer' and has the effect of 'Paul's own greetings' to those addressed in the letter.[78] However, the plural instruction 'you greet' also deepens and strengthens relationships between B (the recipients of the letter) and C (the recipients of the greeting), thus establishing a mutual bond between all three parties. It also modifies the relationships between B and C by strengthening friendships and increasing respect for the persons being greeted. If the greeting were considered as having the same effect as a normal Pauline greeting, then the mutuality between all three parties would be diminished because the recipients of the letter would simply be acting as Paul's agents instead of extending greetings to the third parties themselves. It is important

---

76   See Cranfield, *Romans,* 2: 794; Moo, *Romans,* 926; Dunn, *Romans 9–16,* 897; *contra* Käsemann, *Romans,* 414; H. Schlier, *Der Römerbrief* (HThKNT 6. Freiburg: Herder, 1977), 445.

77   Weima, *Neglected Endings,* 227.

78   Gamble, *Textual History,* 93. The closing greetings function as a 'more direct and personal way of expressing and developing an intimate bond between Paul and his readers, as well as promoting unity and fellowship among the various churches'. Weima, *Neglected Endings,* 115.

to note that greetings rendered in the second-person imperative induce a web of relationships irrespective of whether the different parties belong to the same congregation or not. When one person is being greeted, the whole Roman community joins in the greeting and vice versa. This act of mutual greeting implies a call to strengthen ἀγάπη between the Roman Christians. It is significant that the greetings function in representing or repositioning one another or relating to one another.

The commendatory element in the first list is also unique in Romans because no other Pauline letters have such elaborative phrases that praise the persons greeted. According to Gamble the use of descriptive phrases denotes a significant relationship between the persons greeted and Paul himself (16.3-4, 5, 7-9, 13): 'He ties them to himself and himself to them.'[79] Paul is not using these descriptive phrases to 'help the Roman Christians identify the persons being greeted', since such persons would have already been known to the Roman community. Rather, Paul uses the descriptive phrases to emphasise his commendation.[80] Weima points out that the greetings contain 'laudatory phrases' that emphasise positive relations between the person greeted and Paul and support the apostle's credibility among the Roman Christians who do not know him personally.[81] However, the relationship between the persons who are greeted and Paul himself is only one of the social dimensions that Paul wants to express through greetings.

Paul acknowledges certain women's toil and hard work in the same way as he describes his ministry. The women greeted in the list with the descriptive phrases indicate their active part in the Christian church. The names of ten women appear in Rom. 16.1-16: Phoebe, Prisca, Mary, Junia, Tryphaena, Tryphosa, Persis, Rufus' mother, Julia, Nereus' sister. Phoebe, Prisca (with Aquila), and Junia (with Andronicus) are introduced with more descriptive phrases. All of the women except Julia and Nereus' sister are given descriptive phrases detailing their active roles in the church. For example, Phoebe is referred to as διάκονος (deacon); Prisca as a συνέργος (co-worker); Junia as being 'prominent among the apostles'; Mary, Persis, Tryphoena, and Tryphosa are described as hard working members; Rufus' mother is like a mother to Paul; and Julia and Nereus' sister are mentioned in connection with the group greeting (these are analysed in the fourth chapter below).

Romans 16 has an extensive number of descriptive phrases among the Pauline letters, and apart from Romans (and except one instance in Col. 4.15) 'there is no individualization of the recipients of greetings through naming names or adding descriptive phrases'.[82] The greetings in Romans 16 are

---

79   Gamble, *Textual History*, 92.

80   Weima, *Neglected Endings*, 226.

81   Weima, *Neglected Endings*, 226.

82   Gamble, *Textual History*, 75. Although Nympha's name is mentioned in Col. 4.15, no descriptive phrase is used. Therefore the descriptive phrases used in the second-person type of greetings in Romans 16 are significant and a number of phrases are used qualifying the persons mentioned.

addressed to specific individuals and groups, while in other letters Paul uses a general and collective greeting. As Gamble suggests, 'The particularisation of the greetings is accomplished not only by the naming of names, but in many cases by supplying the names with rich descriptive characterizations.'[83]

The relational character of the greetings in Romans can be seen in the way the individuals are greeted in relation to Paul, Christ, and the church. The descriptive phrases in the greeting list emphasise the strong relations that existed between the persons greeted and/or praised by Paul.[84] By acknowledging Paul's relations with certain people in the Roman community, Paul is strengthening his relationship with them by including himself in the commendations he gives them. As Gamble suggests, 'Paul's commendatory greetings to specific individuals serve to place those individuals in a position of respect vis-à-vis the community, but also, by linking the Apostle so closely with them, place Paul in the same position.'[85] Greetings given 'in the Lord' reveal an individual's alignment with Christ, but also imply that love, solidarity, and affection exist between them and others who 'belong to the Lord'.[86] The phrase 'in the Lord' serves as a unifying factor that redefines the identity of the Christian community in relation to Christ and one another; this new identity centres the members of the community, irrespective of gender, status, and ethnicity, around one axis: Christ. Phoebe, Prisca, and Aquila are all mentioned in relation to the church: Phoebe is the διάκονος of the church, and Paul identifies Prisca and Aquila's house-church with the acknowledgement that 'all the churches of the Gentiles' are grateful to them. This acknowledgement seems to be an approval of their role and support for many groups of Gentile Christians.

The type of relationship Paul wants to cultivate in the Roman Christians, through the greetings, is of the utmost importance to this study. It is very clear from Paul's praise of the women in the greetings of Romans, that he does not want to exclude their participation in the church. The women named and greeted in Rom. 16.1-16 were involved in greeting others – not

---

83   Gamble, *Textual History*, 91.

84   Käsemann, *Romans*, 412; Gamble, *Textual History*, 92; Weima, *Neglected Endings*, 226.

85   Gamble, *Textual History*, 92.

86   Schreiner, *Romans*, 790. They are not merely secular 'hellos' but are rooted in the new life of Christ. Thus the phrases with κύριος that occur in the greetings show the impact of one's relationship with Christ in the practical and ethical context of the whole church. It denotes the 'present sovereign dominion in the life of a Christian', and it implies the solidarity, affection, and mutuality between the people of the community through being in Christ. See J. A. Fitzmyer, *Paul and his Theology* (New Jersey: Prentice Hall, 1989), 90.

Apart from the two group greetings in Rom. 16.14, 15, and the household of Aristobulus, all of them are mentioned in relation to the Lord. They are greeted 'in Christ Jesus' (ἐν Χριστῷ Ἰησου v.3), in Christ (ἐν Χριστῷ v. 9), beloved 'in the Lord' (v. 8), tested in Christ (ἐν Χριστῷ v.10), those in the Lord (v. 11), those who labour 'in the Lord' (v. 12), or who are elect in the Lord (v. 13). Epaenetus is the first fruits of Asia 'in Christ' (v. 5), and Andronicus and Junia are notable because they were 'in Christ' (v. 7) before Paul.

simply as passive recipients – but as individuals commissioned to pass on the welcome and greetings to others. All the members of the community are active participants in it, and giving greetings is a way of acknowledging and welcoming others into the life of the community. Moreover, the Christological significance in the relationship of the church is emphasised as Paul describes people who are 'in the Lord' and 'in Christ'; this gives impetus for the church to maintain a mutual dynamic in their relationships with one another. The church has no existence without Christ, and Paul maintained that relationships should be maintained in Christ's likeness.

2.6.2. Greeting with a holy kiss

The imperative mood is used in the greetings of Rom. 16.16a to convey the exchange of the holy kiss. This is significant because it is the summation of the whole greeting list.[87] What does this signify? Is the exchange of the holy kiss given among the members of a closed community of friends or relatives? Where does it originate? What was the meaning of the 'holy' kiss?

The practice of the 'holy kiss' is regarded as originating in the community of believers,[88] since the role of the kiss has its specific importance among the believers rather than being found in the Greco-Roman world[89] or ancient Judaism.[90] Others find the custom has its origin in 'the life and ministry of

---

87   The Greek noun for kiss is φίλημα, which comes from the verb φιλέω, whose primary meaning is 'to love', and the expression of love can be in the outward act of a kiss. For more discussion see Stählin, 'φιλέω κτλ.', *TDNT* 9, 113–71, at 128–46.

88   In the New Testament, the noun φίλημα (kiss) is used seven times (Lk. 7.45; Lk. 22.48; Rom. 16.16; 1 Cor. 16.20; 2 Cor. 13.12; 1 Thess. 5.26; 1 Pet. 5.14). The verb καταφιλέω appears six times (Mt. 26.49; Mk. 14.45, Lk. 7.38, 45; 15.20; Acts 20.37). The erotic sense of a kiss is not found in the New Testament and there is only one reference to a woman kissing a man (Lk. 7.38, 45).

89   In Greco-Roman society, the nature of the kiss differs with the levels of society and region. A public kiss (both heterosexual and homosexual) is not encouraged in Greco-Roman society. W. Klassen, 'Kiss', *ABD* 4, 89–92, at 91.

'There is no basis in ancient texts, Jewish and Greco-Roman, outside the New Testament for the transformation of the kiss into a sign of religious community'. W. Klassen, 'The Sacred Kiss in the New Testament: An Example of Social Boundary Lines', *NTS* 39 (1993), 122–35, at 128; see also K. Thraede, 'Ursprünge und Formen des "heiligen Kusses" im frühen Christentum', *JAC* 11/12 (1967–68), 124–80, at 145.

90   It is difficult to trace the origin of this custom in Judaism or Christianity. See Klassen, 'Kiss', 90. Some similarities can also be seen in the practices of Judaism. Josephus referred to a kiss four times (*J.W.* 7.321; *Ant.* 7.284; *Ant.* 8.387; *Ant.* 11.59).

In the Old Testament, it is recorded that Jacob kissed Rachel at their first meeting (Gen. 29.11). See Klassen, 'Kiss', 90; cf. *Ant.*1.288–91. Other examples of kisses in the Old Testament are Gen. 29.11, 13; 33.4; 45.15; 48.10; Exod. 4.27; 18.7; Gen. 31.28.

In Judaism, the kiss has three different functions as a 'kiss of reverence, kiss of reunion or reconciliation (Gen 45:15), and kiss of farewell' and there is no general advice given to kiss each other in Jewish sources. Klassen, 'Sacred Kiss', 124. The story of Joseph and Aseneth, which is pre-Christian, has references to a number of kisses. C. Burchard, 'Joseph and Aseneth', in J. H. Charlesworth (ed.), *The Old Testament Pseudepigrapha* 2 (London: Darton, Longman and Todd, 1985), 177–248, at 206f. See also Klassen, 'Sacred Kiss', 124, 125.

Jesus': primarily in the post-resurrection experiences of Jn. 20.21-23 or Judas' betrayal of Jesus in the garden.[91]

Paul's exhortation to greet with the 'holy kiss' (φιλήμα ἅγιον) is found four times in his epistolary conclusions (1 Thess. 5.26; 1 Cor. 16.20b; 2 Cor. 13.12; Rom. 16.16, cf. 1 Pet. 5.14 and the 'kiss of love' [φιλήμα ἀγάπης]). ἀσπάσασθε is the verb and the object of the action is expressed with ἀλλήλους ἐν φιλήματι ἁγίῳ ('greet one another with a holy kiss').

Variations include the reversed order of ἁγίῳ φιλήματι in 2 Cor. 13.12a and τοὺς ἀδέλφους πάντας in 1 Thess. 5.26 ('greet all the believers with a holy kiss'),[92] which are preceded by Paul's request to his readers to pray for him. Klassen suggests that 'since the admonition [in 1 Thess. 5.26] is in the midst of the discussion of greetings, to and from others, it seems evident that the imperative is meant to assume that mutual greeting should not be neglected'.[93]

It is likely that the practice of the 'holy' kiss emerged from early Christian practice. As Klassen argues, 'Paul was the first popular ethical teacher known to instruct members of social groups to continue to greet each other with a kiss whenever or wherever they meet.'[94] The imperative does not draw boundaries regarding gender; however, the greeting kiss was not an erotic act, but rather an act meant to express ἀγάπη (1 Pet. 5.14).

It is worth noting that the admonition to practise the holy kiss, in the context of a letter's concluding greetings, has an impact on the focus of the entire letter. In Romans 16, the instruction to kiss comes at the end of the instruction to greet a number of individuals and groups made up of both men and women. The opposing genders are expected to be 'kissed as equals', although they 'represented separate branches of the believing community in Rome'.[95] The consensus is that the holy kiss should be practised only when the

---

The kiss was not seen as a formal act by Jews in the first century. Jews had set limitations, 'as Egyptian men and women would not kiss Greek lips defiled by animal sacrifice (Herodotus 2.41) and later Christians would not kiss pagans'. Klassen, 'Sacred Kiss', 125. There is less evidence for the practice of the public kiss among Jews in the Second Temple Period.

In one of the rabbinic commentaries on Genesis (*Gen. Rab.* 70[45b]) it is written: 'in general, kissing leads to immorality: there are however three exceptions, namely kissing someone to honour that person (Samuel kissing Saul, 1 Sam 10:1), or kissing upon seeing someone after a long absence (Aaron kissed Moses, Exod 4:27), and the farewell kiss (as when Orpah kissed Naomi (Ruth 1:14)'. Klassen, 'Sacred Kiss', 126.

91   See Klassen, 'Sacred Kiss', 128; S. Benko, *Pagan Rome and the Early Christians* (Bloomington: Indiana University Press, 1969), 82. Benko finds the beginnings in the post-resurrection appearances (Jn. 20.21-23).

92   NRSV translates τοὺς ἀδέλφους as 'the brothers and sisters'.

93   Klassen, 'Sacred Kiss', 130.

94   Klassen, 'Sacred Kiss', 130. The practice was not restricted to worship but was assumed to be something the Christians should practise wherever they meet.

95   Jewett, *Romans*, 974. Jewett suggests the holy kiss is not limited to the familial boundary but is practised among all members of the body of Christ irrespective of their custom or culture.

church is gathered or in a context of worship.[96] It is a sign of love and affection displayed wherever Christians meet.

The 'holy' kiss can be an expression of the oneness of people who represent different social classes, and it expresses the warmth of love transcending gender, religious, national, and ethnic divisions. It signifies that they see themselves as being 'in Christ' and that 'the new reality is affirmed in the freedom of quite innocently greeting each other with a holy kiss'.[97] Thus this practice strengthens the relationship between one another.

It is possible that Paul's request to greet with a 'holy' kiss emphasises the word 'holy' to imply the kissing should be done with a holy motive. This may have been to prevent it from being associated with an erotic kiss.[98] Therefore, in such a background, Paul's admonition may be a warning against such unholy practices. However, the reference to a 'holy' (ἅγιον) kiss indicates the way Paul wants to distinguish believers' greeting kiss (ἅγιοι) from others who practised it. Among Christians, the kiss symbolised unity and togetherness, but for others it could be simply be an expression of friendship and goodwill.[99]

Therefore, the practice of the holy kiss serves to hold a community together without divisions and disparities. On the other hand, the possibility of the kiss merely becoming a ritual cannot be overlooked. It is 'a sign of fellowship within the community, of the community with the Apostle, and indeed of one community with others'.[100] As Klassen rightly suggests, 'The admonitions to kiss one another serve to stress the liberty to express without inhibition to all people of whatever background, rank or gender, the ardour of agape in any context.'[101]

Paul's admonition to greet one another with a holy kiss in the context of Romans' greetings is significant because it includes all members of the Roman church, even those he has not mentioned in the greeting list. It has a function of creating love, affection, and mutual care among the believers and signifies Paul's strategy to bring about mutuality in the community (as in Romans 12–15). The Pauline second-person imperative greeting reaches its peak in Rom. 16.16a: ἀσπάσασθε ἀλλήλους. This phrase shows how the people are important to Paul's own ministry, the wider church, and one another (ἀλλήλους).

---

96   Benko suggests that the holy kiss draws its significance in relation to the Holy Spirit, which was transmitted and received through the kiss. He claims that the kiss becomes 'the life giving breath of God'; see Benko, *Pagan Rome*, 81, 82, 92.

97   Klassen, 'Sacred Kiss', 133.

98   Weima, *Neglected Endings*, 113. The erotic element found in Song of Songs is taken as an allegory. But the Old Testament warns of the dangers of the 'woman kiss' (Prov. 7.13). In addition, the woman kissing Jesus' feet can be viewed as an act of reverence or gratitude or an expression of agape, see Klassen, 'Kiss', 129.

99   Benko, *Pagan Rome*, 98.

100   Gamble, *Textual History*, 76.

101   Klassen, 'Sacred Kiss', 135.

2.7. Conclusion

The greetings in Paul's letters clearly reflect the epistolary practice of his day. Paul uses elaborations and additions in his greetings to make them relevant to the particular situations his letters are concerned to address. The form of greeting in the closing of Romans is significant since among other Pauline letter closings, Romans contains more instructional greetings. In the instructional form, the writer instructs the addressee to greet a third party. The extensive use of instructional greetings in Romans, which are very specific as well as loaded with descriptive phrases, implies that Paul wishes to preserve a close rapport with the congregations as he instructs them to act for him.

Although Paul instructs the readers to greet a third party, this is intended to increase the bond between his recipients and the other party, and not just to promote Paul himself before the third party. The instruction to greet one another is the climax of the greetings and throws light on the intended mutuality that should exist between people. Paul's instruction to greet others reveals his desire to bring unity among the Romans and the wider Christian community.

The mutuality of relationships in Romans shows that Paul accepts men and women as his associates. This fact is significant to my study. The women are greeted with descriptive phrases that imply that they held leadership roles in the church. I will now examine what potential leadership roles are implied by the descriptive phrases. In the following chapters I will analyse the implications of the greetings for women's leadership in the early church by viewing it against the backdrop of contemporary Greco-Roman society. In the next chapter, I will focus on leadership roles of women in Greco-Roman society.

CHAPTER 3

WOMEN IN THE ROMAN EMPIRE

3.1. Introduction

In *Roman Wives, Roman Widows*, Winter has successfully shown that women were evidently engaged in *politeia* (πολιτεία). This is contrary to the common perception that wives in the first century were a 'monochrome group' who were 'confined to domestic dwellings in order to fulfil the role of dutiful wife engaged primarily in childbearing and managing the household'. This attitude was assumed of women in the early Christian communities.[1] In his reconstruction of the social settings of women's lives in the first century, Winter is aiming to deconstruct the common perception that women were kept away from the public and played the role of the stereotypical housewife. Winter gathers evidence that women were involved in the public sphere, claiming that 'it is very unlikely that one could epitomize all first-century marriages by a single stereotype of restriction to the home and reproductive activity in the vast Roman Empire, any more than it would be possible to do so today in our multicultural world'.[2]

This chapter focuses on the roles of women in the public areas of religious and non-religious life in the Roman Empire, and will help us to understand their possible influence on women in Pauline communities. While basically agreeing that Winter's presentation of 'new women' in the Roman Empire does help readers to understand women in Pauline communities, I will carry his point further to show that the epigraphic evidence can provide a solid backdrop against which the leadership roles of women (Rom. 16.1-16) can be properly situated. In doing so, I will draw from other scholars of first-century social and religious life as I discuss women in courts, politics, magistracy, patronage, priesthood, and Jewish synagogues.[3]

---

1   Winter, *Roman Wives*, 6. Winter defines *politeia* in terms of 'all activities outside the home' and not in terms of women's involvement in the political sphere. Winter, *Roman Wives*, 173.

2   Winter, *Roman Wives*, 6.

3   Half of this chapter focuses on Jewish synagogues because Paul might be more influenced by Jewish culture and practice. He often went to the synagogues after his conversion experience (Acts 13.42; 17.1, 2, 10, 17; 18.4, 7, 8, 17, 19, 26; 19.8; 22.19; 26.11).

3.2. Women in courts

It is interesting to note that a women's ability was used in an effective manner in the political sphere in the early centuries in the Greco-Roman world. As Bauman writes:

> there were from about the turn of the third century (BCE), women lawyers, some of whom not only had a theoretical knowledge of the law, but also gave opinions to consultants. ... And women did put their knowledge to good use in the political sphere, though unlike men they could not use it to attract votes in the chase for public office.[4]

There were women who argued for themselves or on behalf of others in the courts. Valerius Maximus refers to women's defence in courts as they were compelled against their will to testify before a large gathering of men around the time of Cicero (106–43 BCE).[5] Fannia is recorded as the first woman who conducted her own defence against her husband regarding the return of her dowry (100 BCE). Her husband married her with the aim of divorcing her on the grounds of unchastity (which was known to him before marriage) since he wanted to acquire her property.[6]

Another example is of women who became legal advisors after their training in first-century (BCE or CE) law before actively prosecuting cases against their fellow people.[7] Maesia of Sentinum, in the early first century, was highly proficient in the law and demonstrated her skill in male-dominated courts to the extent that she was called an 'Androgyne' (man-woman).[8]

Carfania, a senator's wife (died c. 48 BCE), was 'ever ready for lawsuit and always spoke on her behalf before the Praetor, not because she could not find advocates but because she had impudence to spare'.[9] Carfania's act resulted in the change of the law that prohibited women from making claims for others before magistrates.

---

4   R. A. Bauman, *Women and Politics in Ancient Rome* (London: Routledge, 1992), 45–46. Bauman comments that the opinions of women lawyers 'did not have the same capacity to make law as the *responsa* of male practitioners'. His comparison of the skills of the women lawyers with that of male counterparts is not appealing.

5   Valerius Maximus, *Memorable Doings and Sayings*, VIII. 3.

6   Valerius Maximus, *Memorable Doings and Sayings*, VIII. 3

7   Valerius Maximus, *Memorable Doings and Sayings*, VIII. 3. 2. See also Bauman, *Women and Politics*, 50.

8   Bauman, *Women and Politics*, 50.

9   Valerius Maximus, *Memorable Doings and Sayings*, 8.3.2; see also Winter, *Roman Wives*, 177; Bauman, *Women and Politics*, 50. The Velleian decree of the Senate was put into practice in the time of Claudius or Nero and resulted in discouraging women from bringing requests for another person. The reason for the edict was Carfania who brought requests without shame and dishonour before magistrates. See J. E. Grubbs, *Women and the Law in the Roman Empire: A Sourcebook on Marriage, Divorce and Widowhood* (London: Routledge, 2002), 60–61.

The Justinian code supports women in litigation concerning 'civic status, obligations of freed condition, marriage, divorce, support, dowry, minority status and child custody – essentially private matters, though also among those most often of concern to men, too'.[10] Juvenal (c. CE 60–100) gives evidence of women conducting cases, learning civil laws, and making judgments. It is interesting to note the questions raised by women as he states, 'Do we as women ever conduct cases? Are we learned in civic law? Do we disturb your courts with our shouting?', questions all answered by 'yes'.[11]

The above evidence shows that some women were learned in law and were active in prosecution as well as defence. The prohibitions concerning their involvement lead us to wonder whether those were caused by a few women trespassing on male-dominated spheres. However, the participation of women in these areas could not be entirely forbidden.

3.3. Women in politics

Women's names are seen in election posters in Pompeii asking electors to vote for their candidate; interestingly, the majority of supporters were women. Husbands and wives also supported candidates together and encouraged others to vote.[12] MacMullen notices that when the wife's name precedes her husband's in writing it shows 'an inversion of the status explained by neither of the parties having any sense of status between them at all, or by the woman being free or freed, the man freed or slave'.[13] This signifies the importance of the wife's higher rank or higher social status than her husband. Women also supported the candidates for civic office along with their husbands. At least one married woman was allowed to speak in the forum before the Triumvirs. Valerius Maximus refers to Hortensia, who argued against the heavy tax imposed on women and won the case. This resulted in lesser financial obligations for women.[14]

Therefore, there are good reasons to doubt Cotter's generalisation that 'in the matter of public presence, Roman culture did not allow women to call attention to themselves. In legislative and juridical assemblies women were excluded from any leadership role and any role that would bring attention to themselves'.[15]

10   See R. MacMullen, 'Women in Public in the Roman Empire', *Historia* 29 (1980) 208–18, at 210.

11   Juvenal, *Satires*, 2. 51–52, see also Winter, *Roman Wives*, 179.

12   MacMullen, 'Women in Public in the Roman Empire', 209; see also Winter, *Roman Wives*, 180.

13   MacMullen, 'Women in Public in the Roman Empire', 209; see also Winter, *Roman Wives*, 180.

14   Valerius Maximus, *Memorable Doings and Sayings*, VIII. 3. 3. He writes, 'Hortensia, daughter of Q. Hortensius, pleaded the cause of women before the Triumvirs resolutely and successfully when the order of matrons had been burdened by then with a heavy tax and none of the other sex ventured to lend them his advocacy.'

15   Cotter, 'Women's Authority Roles', 367.

3.4. Women magistrates and patronage

Apart from the evidence of literary and legal sources (which limits women's roles to the private sphere), some inscriptions throw light on the significance of women in the public life of the ancient world. As Rives comments, 'the importance of women in civic life is another aspect of the ancient world that is known almost entirely from inscriptions, since legal and literary sources usually depict women as largely relegated to private life'.[16] Some examples follow.

Phile, the daughter of Apollonius and wife of Thessalus, was honoured as 'the first woman in Priene to hold the office of magistrate' (first century BCE).[17] Her position in the public sphere and her benefactions certainly highlight the fact that wealth had an important role in public life and could alter the position of women in society.[18]

Another woman worth noting is Plancia Magna from Perge. She was the magistrate of her city and influenced the priesthood of Artemis and the imperial cult. She was honoured with two statues which record her as 'the daughter of the city' and 'the benefactor'.[19] Claudia Metrodora from Chios was an influential woman who was powerful in the public sphere and a contemporary of Junia Theodora.[20] She financed festivals and buildings associated with her native city and acted as a civic patron.[21]

Another example of a woman combining public office with her role in the household is Aurelia Leite of Paros, who was honoured by the erection of 'a marble statue of the wisdom-loving, husband-loving, children-loving woman'.[22] After the first century, women also formed a magistracy of the city,

---

16   J. Rives, 'Civic and Religious Life', in J. Bodel (ed.), *Epigraphic Evidence: Ancient History from Inscriptions* (London: Routledge, 2001), 118–36, at 135, 136.

17   *Die Inschriften von Priene*, no. 208. Winter, *Roman Wives*, 181. Women holding the position of magistrates in the ancient world are in contradiction to Grubbs' view that women did not serve as magistrates or senators at all in Roman history. See Grubbs, *Women and the Law in the Roman Empire*, 71.

18   Rives, 'Civic and Religious Life', 136.

19   *L'Année épigraphique* (1958), 78; (1965), 209. See Winter, *Roman Wives*, 182; Rives, 'Civic and Religious Life', 136; M. T. Boatwright, 'Plancia Magna of Perge: Women's Roles and Status in Roman Asia Minor', in S. B. Pomeroy (ed.), *Women's History and Ancient History* (London: The University of North Carolina Press, 1991), 249–72.

20   The inscriptions of Claudia Metrodora are found in L. Robert, 'Inscriptions de Chios du Ier siècle de notre ère', *Études épigraphiques et philologiques* (Paris: Champion, 1938), 133–34; J. and L. Robert, 'Bulletin épigraphique', *Revue der études grecques* 69 (1956), 152–53, no. 213; J. Keil, 'Inschriften', in *Forschungen in Ephesos* III (Vienna, 1923), 94–95, no. 3; *Die Inschriften von Ephesus,* VII.1 no. 3003. See pp. 26, 85.

21   R. A. Kearsley, 'Women in the Public East: Iunia Theodora, Claudia Metrodora and Phoebe, Benefactress of Paul', *TynBul* 50 (1999), 189–211, at 199. Claudia Metrodora was the magistrate of the city on two occasions and was gymnasiarch four times. See also J. M. Arlandson, *Women, Class, and Society in Early Christianity: Models from Luke-Acts* (Peabody: Hendrickson, 1997), 36.

22   *IG* xii.5.292 (c. CE 300).

as there were seventeen women, compared to 214 men, found on coins in the East from CE 180 to 275.[23]

A contemporary inscription from Corinth (c. CE 43) testifies that the Roman colony honours a benefactress, named Junia Theodora, described by the cognate noun προστασία of the noun προστάτις.[24] She had involvement with commercial patronage and lived in Corinth during Paul's mission there. Moreover, 'The public honouring of Junia occurs in five separate decrees or official letters that were recorded on a composite inscription erected in Corinth.'[25] The inscriptions testify that 'Junia was a Roman citizen with considerable wealth which she used to offer hospitality to ambassadors and to care for Lycian exiles in Corinth.' She is described in a decree by the people of Patara (in Lycia) as:

> a woman held in highest honour ... who copiously supplied from her own means many of our citizens with generosity, and received them in her home and in particular never ceased acting on behalf of citizens in regard to any favour asked – the majority of citizens have gathered in assembly to offer testimony on her behalf.[26]

As noted in the examples given above, public patronage, by which a 'wealthy benefactor endowed a city' and received approval by means of 'statues, inscriptions and public office' (and also of clubs, associations, trade guilds, etc.), was common in the Greco-Roman world.[27] The patrons of clubs presided at meetings, where leadership titles and the right to perform special ceremonial duties were given to them. Female benefactors described by the term προστάτις are present in epigraphic sources.[28] As MacMullen also

---

23   MacMullen, 'Women in Public', 213.

24   D. I. Pallas, S. Charitonidis, and J. Venencie, 'Inscriptions lyciennes trouvées à Solômos près de Corinthe', *Bulletin de Correspondance héllenique* 83 (1959), 496–508; Kearsley, 'Women in the Public East', 194–95. 'The value of this epigraphic material to our understanding of Phoebe's activity lies in its contemporaneity, its location, and its detailing. Theodora is recognized by the federal assembly of the Lycians for her hospitality to Lycians travelling to Corinth, and her meeting of their needs, possibly commercial. The text alludes to the elevated civic circles in which she had influence, and among which she was able to act on behalf of the Lycians.' See Clarke, 'Jew and Greek', 116. See also Winter, *Roman Wives*, 186. She acted as a patron of thirty-six cities of the Lycian Federation. See pp. 26, 84.

25   Winter, *Roman Wives*, 183. The official letters include: a decree of the federal assembly of the Lycian cities; a letter from the Lycian city of Myra to the magistrates of Corinth; a decree of the Lycian city of Patara; a letter and decree of the federal assembly of Lycia; a decree of the Lycian city of Telmessos.

26   M. R. Lefkowitz and M. B. Kant, *Women's Life in Greece and Rome: A Source Book in Translation* (London: Duckworth, 1992), 160.

27   C. Osiek and D. L. Balch, *Families in the New Testament World: Households and House Churches* (Louisville: John Knox, 1997), 50; C. Osiek and M. Y. MacDonald, *A Woman's Place: House Churches in Earliest Christianity* (Minneapolis: Fortress, 2006), 199–209. For 'Benefactors and the Institution of Patronage', see L. Y. Cohick, *Women in the World of the Earliest Christians: Illuminating Ancient Ways of Life* (Grand Rapids: Baker Academic, 2009), 285–301.

28   See G. H. R. Horsley, *NewDocs*, 4.239–44. Examples include *PGM* 36, 338; *1 Eph.*

observes, 'perhaps a tenth of the protectors and donors that the *collegia* sought out were women'.[29]

As Kloppenborg suggests, inscriptions from the fourth century BCE to the later Roman Empire demonstrate that 'voluntary associations represented a cultural institution integral to Hellenistic and Roman society where they played a significant role in mediating various kinds of social exchange'.[30] Members exerted the freedom to speak their opinions and were bound together by fellowship and friendliness. Moreover, they were granted the opportunity to become an officer or magistrate and 'to participate in a *cursus honorum* to which he or she could never aspire outside of the association'.[31] Due to their greater independence in possessing money and power in the imperial period,[32] women often take the role of benefactor for clubs and associations.[33] It is also striking to see the occurrence of *mater collegii* in inscriptions connected with

IV.1063. The term προστάτις (*patronus* in Latin) denoted an official of the *collegium*. J. S. Kloppenborg, 'Collegia and Thiasoi: Issues in Function, Taxonomy and Membership', in J. S. Kloppenborg and S. G. Wilson (eds.), *Voluntary Associations in the Graeco-Roman World* (London: Routledge, 1996), 16–30, at 26.

29   MacMullen, 'Women in Public', 211. See also G. Clemente, 'Il Patrnato Nei Collegis Dell'Impero Romano', *Studi classici e orientali* 21 (1972), 142–229, at 160–213.

30   Kloppenborg, 'Collegia', 17.

31   Kloppenborg, 'Collegia', 18. Franz Poland assumes that 'every association is in some sense a cult association', while Kloppenborg argues that a more helpful categorisation is based on membership (rather than purposes) identified by shared occupation, household connections, and common cult. F. Poland, *Geschichte des griechischen Vereinswesens* (Leipzig: Teubner, 1909), 5; Kloppenborg, 'Collegia', 23, 24; see also P. A. Harland, *Associations, Synagogues and Congregations: Claiming a Place in Ancient Mediterranean Society* (Minneapolis: Fortress, 2003), 29.

32   Women enjoyed more freedom and privileges under the Roman law. There are a number of examples of this: (1) free marriage (*sine manu*) enabled them to escape the fetters of *manus mariti*. There was an expectation that men married in their early thirties, and it is likely that a wife would outlive her husband and become *sui iuris* along with her grown daughters. In *sine manu*, 'women were on equal par with their husbands in terms of ownership and disposal of property by the system of separation of goods'; (2) the *ius trium liberorum*, the law of three or four children, allowed women to act without a guardian and transact business without a tutor; (3) the *tutor optivus* gave women the right to choose their own guardian; (4) the *tutor fidiuciarius* gave women the right to make a will. Whelan, 'Amica Pauli', 73, 74; Cotter, 'Women's Authoritative Roles in Paul's Churches', 363–66; M. S. Collins, 'Money, Sex and Power: An Examination of the Role of Women as Patrons of the Ancient Synagogues', in P. J. Hass (ed.), *Recovering the Role of Women: Power and Authority in Rabbinic Jewish Society* (Atlanta: Scholars Press, 1992), 7–22, at 15.

33   Evidence can be seen from the inscriptions of clubs and associations praising women who built houses to meet in, financed dinners, and received public honour in the cities where their generosity was carried out. Clemente, 'Il Patroneiato Nei Collegis Dell'Impero Romano', 142–229. Clemente suggests that of 147 inscriptions, from professional *collegia* in Italy, twelve have names of women as patrons as *patrona* (nine) and *mater* (three), and there are women identified as wives (four) and a daughter (one) of certain men. In most cases the women were identified independently from their husbands. Only one inscription identifies a woman (*mater*) as the wife of a certain man. See also *prostates* in Franz Poland, *Geschichte des Griechischen*, 363–66; Cotter, 'Women's Authority', 364.

professional guilds.[34] Additionally, Harland identifies mothers and daughters of civic and official organisations.[35]

Therefore, women were probably leading members of professional guilds as well as standard members. Some of the titles used in associations carry important overtones for our study of Romans 16, which might help us to identify the roles women held in Pauline communities. However, I will not assume complete equivalence between the Pauline community and the model observed in various societal associations without extensive investigation.[36] I will focus on this in the next chapter.

3.5. Priesthood (Greco-Roman)

In classical Greek tradition, the existence of priestesses in service to Greek goddesses is well attested in inscriptions and ancient writings.[37] There was an assumption that the gender of the deity was associated with that of the priest, but evidence shows that gender difference was not a hindrance to the service of the male and female deities.[38] Their roles included service for a

34   Examples are *CIL* IX 2687 (*mater collegii centonariorum*); III 7505; XIV 69 (*c. dendrophorum*); XIV 256 (*corporis fabrum navalium*); (*CIL* VI 10234.10–12). The similar view that *mater synagogoi* was purely honorific was challenged by Brooten's study followed by van der Horst (1991) and Cohen (1980). See B. J. Brooten, *Women Leaders in the Ancient Synagogue: Inscriptional Evidence and Background Issues* (Brown Judaic Series, 36; Atlanta: Scholars Press, 1982), 55–65; P. W. van der Horst, 'The Jews of Ancient Crete', *Journal of Jewish Studies* 39 (1988), 183–200; S. J. D. Cohen, 'Women in the Synagogues of Antiquity', *Conservative Judaism* 34 (1980), 23–29.

35   Daughter: *SEG* 37 (1987) 1099bis (Amorion; II–III CE); *IGR* III 90 (Ankrya; II CE), 191 (Ankrya; mid II CE); *MAMA* VIII 455, 514–17 a-b (Aphrodiasias; II–III CE), 191; *I Ephesos* 234, 235, 239, 424, 424a, 1601e (late I–early II CE); Mother: *IGR* III 191 (Ankyra; mid II CE); *MAMA* VIII 492b (Aphrodisias; ICE); *IG* V. 1 499, 587, 589, 597, 608 (Sparta; early III CE); *IKilikia*BM 1 27 (early III CE); P. A. Harland, 'Familial Dimensions of Group Identity (II): Mothers and Fathers in Associations and Synagogues of the Greek world', *JSJ* 38 (2007), 57–79. I accessed this article from: www. philipharland.com, 1–16, at 4, 5, in June 2008.

36   See C. Osiek, '*Diakonos* and *Prostatis*: Women's Patronage in Early Christianity', *HTS* 61 (2005), 347–70. R. S. Ascough raises problems for using the model of associations to understand Christian, especially Pauline, communities. R. S. Ascough, 'Voluntary Associations and the Formation of Pauline Christian Communities: Overcoming the Objections', in Andreas Gutsfeld und Dietrich-Alex Koch (eds.), *Vereine, Synagogen und Gemeinden im kaiserzeitlichen Kleinasien* (Studies and Texts in Antiquity and Christianity 25; Tübingen: Mohr Siebeck, 2006), 149–83, at 182.

37   R. S. Kraemer, *Her Share of the Blessings: Women's Religions among Pagans, Jews, and Christians in the Greco-Roman World* (Oxford: Oxford University Press, 1992), 81. Priestesses are found in service of Demeter, Hera, Athena, Artemis, Eileithyia, Isis, Bona Dea, Cybele. For discussion on 'Greek standards for women in public' see J. G. Sigountos and M. Shank, 'Public Roles for Women in the Pauline Church: A Reappraisal of the Evidence', *JETS* 26 (1983), 283–95, at 288–92.

38   Athena Polias was attended by a priest, and Dionysos, Helios, and Apollo were served by a priestess. See R. Garland, 'Priests and Power in Classical Athens', in M. Beard and J. North (eds.), *Pagan Priests: Religion and Power in the Ancient World* (London: Duckworth, 1990), 73–91, at 77.

particular deity in their sanctuary, and comprised of the 'care and upkeep of the sanctuary and the statue of the deity, the performance of rites of purification, and safeguarding the sanctuary treasures and gifts'. A small amount of money and a portion of the sacrifices were given for undertaking these services.[39] Kraemer writes, 'although the majority of priests for official Roman cults were male and organized into colleges, particularly during the republican period, one of the most famous of all official Roman priesthoods was held by women, that of the Vestal Virgins'.[40] According to Beard, the Vestals functioned like virgins, matrons, and aristocratic males, while playing 'an important part in their symbolic position'.[41]

From the Hellenistic period onwards, women's cultic offices began to flourish in Greek and Roman worship alongside the new mystery religions and the worship of the emperor. Examples include the Priestess of Athena, who is recorded in an inscription from Delphi (Chrysis, *IG* II, 1136) in the second century CE and is described as receiving honours for taking part in a procession to Apollo. Tata of Aphrodisias, in western Asia Minor, was a priestess of Hera and of the imperial cult who also held the office of *stephanophorus* 'crownbearer'.[42] Her responsibilities included providing funds for religious festivals and public entertainments, supplying oil free of charge to the athletes who competed in public games, offering sacrifices throughout the year for the health of the imperial family, and sponsoring banquets open to the public.[43]

Women had numerous official positions in the worship of Isis. Aba of Histiria in Thrace was high priestess of Cybele in the second century CE, and there are other priestesses mentioned in the inscriptions too.[44] Aba of Histiria not only looked after the great festival of Cybele but also funded a public banquet excelling all previous generosity. In Hellenistic Greek cities and towns, women and men who held cultic offices paid very large sums of money for public religious festivals and entertainment.

39   Kraemer, *Her Share of the Blessings*, 81. See also Garland, 'Priests', 77.

40   Kraemer, *Her Share of the Blessings*, 81. Plutarch has shown that the Vestals' period of service lasted about thirty years, after which they were permitted to marry. Plutarch, *Life of Numa Pompilius*, 10. 'The privileges accruing to Vestal virgins were considerable, including freedom from any male guardianship and the right to make a will and bequeath property during the lifetime of their fathers ... Vestals who broke their vows of chastity during their term of office were walled up in a small chamber furnished with a couch, a lamp, minimal food, and left to die.' See Kraemer, *Her Share of the Blessings*, 81, 82.

41   M. Beard, 'The Sexual Status of Vestal Virgins', *JRS* 70 (1980), 12–27, at 21.

42   Family position also played an important part in attaining priesthoods. Tata of Aphrodisias in the second century CE (Tation, *CIJ*, 738) was a member of an illustrious family of the first rank and she held the title of the mother of the city. Her husband's status is secondary compared to her father's. Similarly, Aba of Histiria and Menodora came from prominent families. Marital status is secondary to that of the actual position held, and the example of Tata, whose husband held the office of *stephanophorus*, does not indicate that she received her position by virtue of his.

43   Kraemer, *Her Share of the Blessings*, 84.

44   Kraemer, *Her Share of the Blessings*, 84, 223. The inscriptions are *CIL* 6.502; *CIL* 6.508; *CIL* 6.2257; *CIL* 6.2260; *CIL* 6.2259; *CIL* 14.371; *CIL* 14.408; *CIL* 10.6075; *CIL* 10.6074.

Menodora is mentioned in inscriptions from Sillyon (in Pamphylia) for her benefactions in the early third century CE (*IGRR* III, 800–802). Moreover, she had a variety of careers in religious affairs and civic office. Examples include: 'high priestess of at least two emperors (probably Septimius Severus and Caracalla), priestess of Demeter, and of "all the gods," hierophant for life of the city's gods, *dekaprotos, demiourgos and gymnasiarch*'. She also 'distributed money and corn to the entire populace, 300,000 denarii to orphans and children, financed the building of a temple, and provided numerous other benefactions'.[45]

Women were able to take public roles in special cases, and they were notably wealthy. If they had their name placed before their husband's, their status was probably higher than their husband's. Thus, the discussion on the position and status of women in Greco-Roman paganism helps one to understand their roles in religious leadership in the private and public spheres.

3.6. Jewish synagogues

As far as the position and function of women in Jewish religious life is concerned, there are very diverse and conflicting portrayals depending on whether they come from rabbinic sources or archaeological discoveries. Rabbinic writings caricature Jewish women as those who 'led restricted, secluded lives and were excluded from much of the ritual life of Jewish men especially from the study of Torah'. However, evidence from the Greco-Roman diaspora suggests that at least some Jewish women played active religious, social, economic, and even political roles in the public lives of Jewish communities.[46]

Brooten's work, *Women Leaders in the Ancient Synagogue*, focused on women who played significant leadership roles in synagogues in the ancient world. These included heads of synagogues, leaders, elders, priestesses, and 'mothers of synagogues'. These roles are observed in inscriptions dating from the second century BCE to the sixth century CE, and they come from different locations and communities. In addition, women were involved as donors to the synagogue buildings.[47] Trebilco records that four out of fifty-three inscriptions regarding donations mention that they were provided by women alone, and another fifteen were from women and their husbands.[48] I will deliberately limit my exploration to the leadership roles of women in the synagogues, which seem to be at odds with the commonplace portrayal of Jewish society as ostentatiously male centred.

---

45   Kraemer, *Her Share of the Blessings*, 85.
46   Kraemer, *Her Share of the Blessings*, 93.
47   For example, Tation from Phoecaea funded a whole synagogue building and held the position of προεδρία, which was a prominent position in the synagogue. She was possibly a wealthy and independent woman (*CIJ* 738; *IGR* 4.1327). See P. R. Trebilco, *Jewish Communities in Asia Minor* (Cambridge: Cambridge University Press, 1991), 110.
48   Trebilco, *Jewish Communities*, 112.

3.6.1. ἀρχισυνάγωγος *(head of the synagogue)*

ἀρχισυνάγωγος was the title of a leading official in the synagogue and has the primary position in the list of officials. This particular official seems to be 'the spiritual and intellectual leader of the synagogue and responsible for its spiritual direction and regulation, including at times teaching the community and on other occasions inviting someone else to preach'.[49]

3.6.1.1. Inscriptional evidence

Three Greek inscriptions have been found with women bearing the title of 'head of the synagogue'. Although there is an interpretation that understands the title as purely honorific, the different aspects of the title's use for men and women are dealt with in Brooten's *Women Leaders in the Ancient Synagogue*; he concludes that there were presumably women leaders in the synagogue. The three inscriptions cite the names of the women such as Rufina from Smyrna, Ionia (*CII* 741; *IGR* IV 1452), Sophia from Crete (*CII* 731c), and Theopempte from Caria (*CII* 756).

The inscription (*CII* 741; *IGR* IV 1452) with Rufina titled ἀρχισυνάγωγος is probably dated around the second or third century CE.

> Rufina, a Jewess, a head of the synagogue (ἀρχισυνάγωγος), built this tomb for her freed slaves and the slaves raised in her house. No one else has the right to bury anyone (here). If someone should dare to do, he or she will pay 1,500 denars to the sacred treasury and 1,000 denars to the Jewish people. A copy of this inscription has been placed in the (public) archives.

From the inscription, it is clear that Rufina was a woman of affluence who had the means to build a tomb for her freed slaves and the slaves who were raised in her house. 'This tomb may be that of her slaves, to whom Rufina would have been a patron.'[50] It is not clear from the inscription whether she was married or not since there is no mention of her marital status. This type of inscription is quite usual in both Jewish and non-Jewish communities of Asia Minor, and there are two other Jewish inscriptions from Smyrna that refer to office holders.[51] Rufina

---

49   Trebilco, *Jewish Communities,* 104, 105. *CII* 1404 mentions that the role of the heads of the synagogue includes the reading of the law and teaching of the commandments. The exhortation and spiritual direction of the congregation is attested in Lk. 13.10-17; cf. Acts 18.12-17; Justin Martyr, *Dialogue with Trypho,* 137, Epiphanius, *Panarion,* 30.18.2. They invited members of the congregation to preach (Acts 13.15). The synagogue heads together with the elders collected money to be sent to the patriarch (*Cod. Theod.* 16.8.14, 17) and were likely the leaders of the congregation. See Brooten, *Women Leaders,* 28–29.

50   Brooten, *Women Leaders,* 10.

51   The inscriptions are found in *CII* 739, which describes Irenopoios as 'an elder and father of the tribe and the son of the elder'; *CII* 740 is an additional inscription from the same synagogue. Another inscription included the name of the scribe of a Jewish community in Smyrna. Titles such as elder, scribe, and father of the tribe were used in the inscriptions; the first two are common titles whereas the 'father of the tribe' is possibly equivalent to the father of the synagogue. See Brooten, *Women Leaders,* 11.

was a wealthy and independent Jewess who was able to handle the business matters of her time. She was possibly a member of a leading family of Smyrna. Moreover, Trebilco suggests that she was an active head of the synagogue, in the whole sense of the title, due to her administrative and managerial skill, her educational qualifications, and her economic background.[52]

The second inscription (*CII* 731, c. fourth or fifth century CE) mentions Sophia of Gortyn as elder and head of the synagogue of Kisamos:

> Sophia of Gortyn, elder and head of the synagogue (ἀρχισυναγώγισσα) of Kisamos (lies) here, the memory of the righteous one for ever. Amen.

It is interesting to note that the two roles 'elder and the head of the synagogue' take feminine forms (πρεσβυτέρα, ἀρχισυναγώγισσα) of the title. As we shall see below, some opinions suggest that the title was honourably bestowed upon her due to her husband's role as πρεσβύτερος and ἀρχισυνάγωγος. Another view makes the comparison with other Jewish titles possessed by women such as ἀρχηγισσα, ἱέρισα, ἀρχισυνάγωγος, and πρεσβυτέρα. Sophia's marital status is not mentioned in the inscription and therefore it is unlikely that she received the title from her husband. It is obvious from the inscription that she was an important figure in the Jewish community of Kisamos, acting as both elder and head of the synagogue.

The third inscription (*CII* 756, fourth or fifth century CE) reads: '[From Th]eopempte, head of the synagogue, and her son Eusebios.' It is uncertain whether the inscription is funerary or donative, since it is carved into the top of a white marble quadrangular post. The inscription shows that Theopempte, the head of the synagogue, and her son are donors of the post. Her husband's name is not mentioned but the son's name being mentioned points to the fact that she was married. Her son did not possess a title. If his father had a title, it would have been carried on to the son. The picture that emerges from this inscription suggests that she was both the donor and the head of the synagogue.

3.6.1.2. Role identification
There are different lines of interpretation regarding women as heads of synagogues. For example, was the title purely honorific?[53] And did women play an equal role to that of male officials?[54]

---

52   Trebilco, *Jewish Communities*, 106.

53   See E. Schürer, *History of the Jewish People in the Age of Jesus Christ*, Geza Vermes, Fergus Millar, Mathew Black, and Pamela Vermes (rev. and ed.; 2 vols.; Edinburgh: T&T Clark, 1973–79), 2.435.

54   The New Testament gives evidence about the head of synagogues (Mk. 5.22, 35, 36, 38; cf. Lk. 8.49). Cf. Lk. 8.41, ἄρχων τῆς συναγωγῆς, whereas in Mt. 9.18, 23 ἄρχων is used. However, the question of whether these titles denote the same functions arises. The Jairus passage raises another question, since Jairus is mentioned as one of the heads of the synagogue (Mk. 5.22), was there more than one head of the synagogue? Luke 13.10-17 suggests that the role of the head of the synagogue was to prevent people moving away from Torah. The Acts of the Apostles also mentions the head of the synagogue inviting apostles to give sermons, which possibly shows a

The general consensus is that the title was entirely honorific and carried no responsibility. It is assumed that the title had been handed down from the husband, who was an ἀρχισυνάγωγος. However, there are weaknesses in this presupposition because out of the three inscriptions, two did not give any evidence that the women mentioned were married. The inscriptions detailing Rufina and Theopempte give the impression that they are fairly independent in controlling funds, household, and business affairs; in the inscriptions, 'where wives of synagogue heads are named (*CII* 265, 553, 744), they do not in fact bear the title of their husbands'.[55] Therefore, the assumption that the title is purely honorary and non-functional for women is unlikely. Brooten's suggestion is more plausible: on the basis of the evidence, the role of a female synagogue head is the same as her male counterpart, i.e. they 'were active in administration and exhortation'.[56] They possibly had administrative roles as well, as was the case with Rufina, who administered her entire household.

How did these women acquire official status? It is understood, from the inscription, that Rufina was possibly wealthy and a member of a leading Roman family. Theopempte also had funds. Sophia fulfilled two roles as elder and ἀρχισυνάγωγος, which might indicate her involvement in the matters of the synagogue. Therefore, their active involvement in the synagogue (which was on a par with the male officials) and wealthy family connections may have been the factors that helped them to assume leadership roles.

3.6.2. ἀρχήγισσα (leader)

3.6.2.1. Inscriptional evidence
The Peristeria inscription gives evidence for female leadership. It was first published in 1937 from Thebes in Phthiotis in Thessaly (*CII* 696b): Μνῆμα Περιστερίας ἀρχηγίσις (Tomb of Peristeria, leader).

Another inscription, *CII* 731g, reads῾ Ὑπὲρ εὐχῆς῾ Ἰακωβ ἀρχιγοῦ πιννωνᾶ᾽ ('in accordance with a vow of Jacob, president, the setter of pearls'). These inscriptions date from around the fourth or fifth century CE. The title ἀρχηγός occurs only once in Jewish inscriptions and *principalis* is its Latin parallel.

---

leadership role (Acts 13.15). Acts 18.1-17 refers to two synagogue officials: Crispus (v. 8), who had become a believer in Christ, and Sosthenes, who had not (v. 17).

The early rabbinic sources such as m. *Yoma* 7.1 refer to the head of the synagogue when they mention reading from the Torah on *Yom Kippur.* Other evidence includes *t. Meg.* 4. 21 (Zuck. 227); *b. Pesah* 49b; *y. Ber.* 6a.28–29.

Several fourth-century laws indicate that the head of the synagogue was one of the important official positions in the synagogue. Examples include, *Cod. Theod.* 16.8.4; *Cod. Theod.* 16.8.13; *Cod. Theod.* 16.8.14. Further evidence can be obtained from the Patristic Fathers such as Justin Martyr, *Dialogue with Trypho,* 137, Epiphanius of Salamis (c. 315–403) and Palladius, *Dialogue on the Life of John Chrysostom.* Pagan sources also used this title. In Flavius Vopiscus' *Life of Saturninus* 8, *Scripores Historiae Augustae* 3.398–99, the emperor Alexander Severus was called the Syrian ἀρχισυνάγωγος by his opponents. Thus the title was well known in the ancient world.

55   Brooten, *Women Leaders,* 30.
56   Brooten, *Women Leaders,* 30.

Example, *CII* 681 – *Ioses arcisna et principalis filius Maximini Pannoni sibi et Qyriae Coniugi sui vivo suo memoria dedicavit* ('Ioses, head of the synagogue and leader, son of Maximinus Pannonus, dedicated this monument, while still alive, for his wife and himself'). Due to the lack of context, in order to understand the meaning of ἀρχήγισσα a study of its use in different literature is required.

3.6.2.2. Literary evidence

ἀρχηγός in ancient literature functions as an adjective and a noun. As an adjective it means 'beginning', 'originating', 'primary', 'leading', 'chief'; and as a noun it translates as 'founder', 'ancestral hero', 'prince', 'chief', 'first cause', 'originator', and 'originating power'.[57] The word conveys the 'human ancestor of a tribe or family' or a 'leader'.[58]

The LXX uses the term to translate a number of Hebrew words, such as *rosh* in the sense of military, political, or clan leader (e.g. Exod. 6.14; Num. 13.3; 14.4; 25.4; Deut. 33.21); *qasin* in the sense of chief, ruler (Judg. 11.6, 11; Isa. 3.6,7), and *sar* in the sense of prince, official, governor (Judg. 5.15; 1 Chron. 26.26; Neh. 2.9; Isa. 30.4).

Josephus uses ἀρχηγός five times: three in the sense of 'originator' or 'author', and twice in the sense of 'ancestor' or 'founder of the race'.[59] Philo uses it with the meaning of leader, chief.[60] The New Testament speaks of Christ as the ἀρχηγός, originator of life (Acts 3.15), of salvation (Heb. 2.10), of faith (Heb. 12.2), and as leader and saviour (Acts 5.31).

Therefore, the three basic meanings of the term centre on the ideas of 'ancestral hero' or 'heroine', 'founder/originator', and 'leader/chief'.

In Jewish inscriptions (*CII* 696b, 731g) the meaning is probably 'leader' or 'chief' rather than 'originator'. However, Jewish titles differed with respect to locality, and it is quite difficult to decide on the definite original meaning. Moreover, there is the question whether ἀρχηγός and ἀρχισυνάγωγος refers to the same position or not, as in *CII* 681. It is not explicitly mentioned in the inscriptions whether ἀρχηγός denotes the leadership role in the Jewish community.[61]

---

57   G. Delling, 'ἀρχηγός' *TDNT* 1, 487–88; see also *MM*, 81.

58   The ancestor of a tribe or family is used as in Aristotle, *The Nicomachean Ethics* 8.12.4, whereas 'leader' is the sense in Eusebius, *De ecclesiastica theologia* 2.9; Brooten, *Women Leaders*, 37.

59   Josephus used ἀρχηγός in the sense of the originator and author of crimes (*Ant.* 7.207), of trouble (*Ant.* 20.136), of legal violations (*Ag.Ap.* 1.270), and in the sense of an ancestor or founder (*Ag.Ap.* 1.71, 130).

60   Philo uses ἀρχηγός in *Leg. Alleg.* 3.175; *De somn.* 1.89.

61   Brooten asks whether 'founder' might be the best translation as it is paralleled with fatherly figures in early Christian texts. However, she thinks this is speculative and supports 'leader' as the more likely translation. See Brooten, *Women Leaders*, 38, 39.

3.6.3. πρεσβυτέρα *(elder)*

3.6.3.1. Inscriptional evidence

The title of elder being used for women (πρεσβυτέρα/ πρεσβυτέρησα) has been found in some Greek inscriptions, and there is another inscription in which a woman is called πρεσβῦτις. The examples are:

1.   *CII* 731c (fourth/fifth century CE), Sophia of Gortyn was both the head of the synagogue as well as an elder (see above).
2.   'Tomb of Rebeka, the elder who has fallen asleep.' *CII* 692 (fourth/fifth CE).
3.   Three Greek inscriptions found in Apulia mention women elders that date from the third to the sixth centuries CE. *CII* 581; *CIL* IX 6226 'Tomb of Beronikene, elder and daughter of Ioses'. Here Beronikene's father bears no title. She is described as the daughter of her father rather than the wife of a man. Other inscriptions include *CII* 590; *CIL* IX 6230 and *CII* 597; *CIL* 6209.

3.6.3.2. Literary evidence

The term πρεσβυτέρα can bear several different meanings. It denotes a political function such as the 'elders of Israel' (Num. 11.16-30; 2 Sam. 3.17; 5.3; 17.4; etc.) and/or judicial functions such as the 'elders of the city' (Deut. 19.12; 21.2-9, 19-20; 2.15-21; 25.7-9). Philo and Josephus mention the *gerousia* of Alexandria, and the members of the *gerousia* are called πρεσβυτέροι.[62] The New Testament cites members of the Sanhedrin as 'elders' (Mt. 16.21; Mk. 8.31; 11.27; Lk. 9.22).

The meaning of an elder is varied, and it is hard to define. The Talmud refers to an elder as a scholar (*b.Qidd.* 32b). The *Theodosian code* (16.8.13) and *Justinian Code* (*Cod. Iust.* 1.9.15) refer to elders as synagogue officials. Another meaning corresponds with *seniores* and *maiores*. It occurs in the plural in inscriptions (*CII* 663, 731f, 803, 1404), and its parallel with the New Testament references is striking. In Lk. 7.3-5, the centurion considers the elders as the official representatives of the Jewish community. The 'elders' in the New Testament refer to the decision-making body of the church, e.g. Acts 11.30; 15.2, 4, 6, 22-23; 16.4; 21.18; Jas. 5.14.

3.6.3.3. Role identification

The evidence in the inscriptions and literature suggests that women could be regarded as elders. However, an elder's function might have differed between periods and regions. The title is sometimes used in the plural where it refers to a council of elders, and it appears most often in a religious context to describe functionaries.[63] The assumption that the title was merely honorary for women

---

62   Philo (*In Flacc.* 74, 76, 80; *Leg. ad Gaium* 229) and Josephus (*J.W.* 7.412).

63   There are four inscriptions, which refer to 'elders' in the plural (e.g. *CII* 663, 731f, 803, 1404) and also the New Testament references to Jewish and Jewish Christian elders (Lk. 7.3-5; Acts 11.30; 15.2, 4, 6, 22-23; 16.4; 21.18; Jas. 5.14). The functions in the religious context can be seen in *Cod. Theod.* 16.8.13: related to the worship service in *Corpus Iuris Civilis*, Nov. 146.1; collecting money in the synagogue in *Cod. Theod.* 16.8.14; the special seating arrangements during the worship service denote their religious function (*t. Meg.* 4.21).

(being inherited from their husbands), and the issues this raises, is discussed in the section on ἀρχισυνάγωγος. Nevertheless, the fact that the husband's name is not mentioned with the female elder in the inscriptions reduces this possibility. Six, possibly seven, inscriptions with women bearing the title 'elder' show the possibility of them fulfilling leadership roles.[64] Therefore, it is most likely that women were the members of the council of elders; they would have been involved in financial matters and were possibly seated facing the congregation like the male elders.[65]

3.6.4. μήτηρ συναγωγῆς *(mother of the synagogue)*

3.6.4.1. Inscriptional evidence
The evidence includes two Greek inscriptions with μήτηρ συναγωγῆς *CII* 496, *CII* 166 (c. first century BCE to third century CE); two Latin inscriptions with the equivalent of μήτηρ συναγωγῆς *CII* 523, *CII* 639, *CILV* 4411; one Latin inscription with *pateressa CII* 606 (*CIL* IX 623); one inscription with μήτηρ *CII* 619d (c. third to sixth century CE).[66] It is interesting to note in *CII* 523 that Verturia Paulla, of Rome, was the mother of the two synagogues belonging to Campus and Volumnius; this is paralleled with *CII* 508, where a father of synagogues is mentioned. Mother (or father) of the synagogue is a key term relating to leadership, and it most likely denotes their active involvement in the synagogues. In addition, it is difficult to conclude that Verturia obtained this title from her husband since, again, no husband's name is mentioned in the inscription. However, the Menorah inscription (*CII* 166) does give the name of a husband. It seems that she was an office holder just like a πατήρ συναγωγῆς. The title *pateressa* is the feminine of *pater*, and there is the question as to whether *pateressa* and μήτηρ συναγωγῆς referred to one and the same function, or whether *pateressa* refers to a less official position or implies a synagogue function.

πάτηρ/μήτηρ is also used outside the context of the synagogue, which leads one to ask what would the implied role be when it is used as such? Did it refer to a civic function? It is a common title among the Jewish Venosan inscriptions, and Brooten records that 'πατήρ occurs nine times outside of our inscription while μήτηρ and *pateressa* occur one time each'.[67] The number of occurrences of the title in the inscriptions stresses its significance in the Venosan Jewish community.

---

64   Brooten, *Women Leaders*, 55.
65   The question can be raised as to whether women could be full members of the judicial council, whether they could have been scholars, or whether they could read the Bible in the synagogue. See Brooten, *Women Leaders*, 55.
66   They are all from Italy, Rome (*CII* 523, *CII* 496, *CII* 166); Venosa (*CII* 606: *CIL* IX 6231, *CII* 619d, *CII* 619c); Venetia (*CII* 639; *CIL* V 4411). Brooten, *Women Leaders*, 57.
67   Seven out of the ten inscriptions with πάτηρ are named Faustinus and μήτηρ in *CII* 619d is named Faustina, which probably suggests both are from the same family. See Brooten, *Women Leaders*, 63. Some of the examples are *CII* 590, *CII* 599, *CII* 611, 612, etc.

3.6.4.2. Literary evidence

There is one literary reference to Jewish mothers of the synagogue in the Christian anti-Jewish polemic 'De altercatione ecclesiae et synagogae'. The polemic takes the form of a dialogue between two matrons: *synagoga* and *ecclesia*.[68] The mothers of the synagogue, mentioned as outstanding women in the Jewish community, attest to the fact that the title was well known even outside the Jewish community, and, by doing so, reveal their leadership position. *Theodosian code* 16.8.4 refers to the three synagogue officials – 'priests', 'heads of the synagogues', and 'fathers of the synagogues' – along with 'all others who serve the synagogue'. This fourth-century law gives evidence on the functions of the synagogue officials, although it is hard to define their actual function and distinction in the community.[69] The literary evidence is too limited clearly to define the functions of mother/father when used independently.

3.6.4.3. Role identification

One interpretation that has been made about the role of the mother of the synagogue is gender-biased, again proposing that the title was merely an honorary bestowal.[70] Another suggestion is that πάτηρ συναγωγῆς and μήτηρ συναγωγῆς were responsible for caring for the sick and dying; that the former also made arrangements for funerals, while the latter had responsibility for providing money for poor brides. Some understand the title as an 'active role in administration', while others find roles parallel with patronage.[71]

The evidence clearly shows that women bore the title of 'mother of the synagogue' or simply 'mother', and although this function is not clearly defined, it seems that women held some administrative position in the synagogue.

3.6.5. ἱερεία / ἱέρισα (priestess)

3.6.5.1. Inscriptional evidence

Three ancient Jewish inscriptions have the title ἱερεία/ἱέρισα referring to women between the first century BCE and the fourth century CE. These

---

68   The work, dated fifth century CE, is discussing a controversial point on the bestowal of the eternal life only for the circumcised, which excludes women in general and even the mothers of the synagogue, who are outstanding women of the Jewish community. Brooten, *Women Leaders*, 63.

69   Jesus refers to the title 'fathers' in Mt. 23.9: 'And call no one your father on earth, for you have one father, the heavenly one', which seems to be an honorific title. There is also the prohibition to call any one '*rabbi*' (vv. 7-8). The title '*abba*' occurs as an honorific title in the rabbinic sources.

70   See S. Krauss, *Synagogale Altertümer* (Berlin: Benjamin Harz, 1922), 166.

71   Brooten, *Women Leaders*, 64, 65.

inscriptions were found in Tell el-Yahudiyyeh in Lower Egypt, in Beth She'arim in Galilee, and in Rome.[72] They are:

1. *CII* 1514 (SEG 1 (1923) no. 574) Μαριν ἱέρισα χρηστὴ πασίφιλε καὶ ἄλυπε καὶ φιλογίτων ... ('O Marin, priest, good and friend to all, causing pain to no one and friendly to your neighbours, farewell!'). She died at approximately fifty years old, in the third year of Caesar (Augustus), on the thirteenth day of Payni (7 June 28 BCE). Brooten writes that 'C. C. Edgar, who first published the inscription in 1922, thought that ἱέρισα was "the name of Marion's father; whether it is an indeclinable noun or whether this is a genitive in -α I do not know".'[73] But Hans Lietzmann assumed it to be ἱέρισα, 'priestess'.[74] Women bearing the title ἱέρισα were interpreted as not really performing the actual function of a priestess in the Jewish community, but rather belonging to the family of priests. (Aaron's family).[75]

2. *CII* 315 (c. third to fourth century CE) from the Monteverde catacomb in the Via Portuensis. Ενθάδε χιτε Γαυδεντια ἱέρισα ... ('Here lies Gaudentia, Priest, (aged) 24 years. In Peace be her sleep!'). The name Guadentia appears in another inscription from the same place (*CII* 314); she is the daughter of a man named Oklatios. Galudentis (the male form of the name) occurs in *CII* 316. Inscriptions with men (possibly five) bearing the title ἱερεύς have also been found in the Monteverde catacomb.

3. *CII* 1007 Σαρα θυγάτηρ Ναιμιας μήτηρ ἱερείας κύρα Μαρ[ει]ης [ἐν]θα κ[εῖται?] ('Sara, daughter of Naimia, mother of the priest, Lady Maria, lies here'). This inscription is dated to the fourth century CE. Miriam has been interpreted as a *kohenet*, wife of a *kohen*.

3.6.5.2. Role identification

Scholars interpret ἱέρισα as probably designating the wife or daughter of a ἱερεύς and as a member of the priestly family, since presumably there is no priestess in the Jewish system.[76] The three possible interpretations regarding this are: first, ἱερεία/ ἱέρισα is simply the Greek equivalent of *kohenet* (wife of a priest); second, ἱερεία/ ἱέρισα in the inscriptions means the priest in the cultic sense; third, it denotes a function of the synagogue as *kohenet* is

---

72   Brooten, *Women Leaders*, 73.

73   Brooten, *Women Leaders*, 73. Brooten cites from C. C. Edgar, *Annales du Service des Antiquités de l'Egypte* 22 (1922) 13, no. 25.

74   Hans Lietzmann, *Kleine Schriften* (ed. Kurt Aland; 3 vols.; *Untersuchungen zur Geschichte der Altchristlichen Literatur* 67, 68, 74; Berlin: Akademie-Verlag, 1958–62), 1.442; Brooten, *Women Leaders*,73. The name Marion occurs in Greek inscriptions such as *SEG* 17 (1960), 818 (Cyrenaica), *SEG* 17 (1960), 819.

75   Brooten, *Women Leaders*, 74. In Tell el-Yahuddiyyeh, there was a Jewish temple founded by Onias IV during the time of Ptolemy VI Philometor and Cleopatra (181–146 BCE), who, because of the Maccabean revolt, was unable to continue the Jerusalem High priesthood.

76   See E. Goodenough, *Jewish Symbols in the Greco-Roman Period* (13 vols.; Bollingen Series 37; Princeton, Princeton University Press, 1953–68), 1.253–57; see also Brooten, *Women Leaders*, 78, 79.

an exclusivley rabbinic term.[77] The passages referring to *kohenet* show the rights and privileges of a *kohenet*; they also show how she loses *kohenet*, and its general inferiority when compared to the priestly privileges of a man. The *kohenet* passages do not speak about leadership in a congregation or in terms of cultic functions, but rather in terms of the rights of becoming a member of a priestly class.

The possibility of women performing religious functions in ancient Israel[78] poses a question about the masculine nature of the Israelite priesthood. Brooten suggests that 'there are scraps of scattered evidence which could indicate a more varied historical reality than we are accustomed to imagine'.[79] She also suggests that the cultic or priestly functions may include 'singing psalms, providing musical accompaniment, performing priestly blessings, examining the priestly offerings and animals and performing sacrifices'.[80]

The function of a priest as bestowing blessings and reading the Torah in the synagogue can be seen in M. Git 5.8 (cf. Philo of Alexandria, *Hypothetica* 7.13; Philo suggests that the priest has preference to the elder). The *Theodosian code* (16.8.4) gives preference to the priests as the synagogue functionaries. Is it possible for the women to perform the same functions as their male counterparts? It is unlikely that the women carrying the title in the inscriptions were forbidden the functions of the priests; it seems that they received the title by virtue of their rights of priestly descent, and perhaps due to their donations to the synagogue.

There are also inscriptions and papyri referring to ἱερεύς dating from the first century BCE to the third century CE (*CII* 346; *CII* 347; *CII* 355; *CII* 375). Women were possibly involved in cultic functions. They might have performed priestly duties and performed leadership roles in the congregation in Jewish synagogues.

---

77 A man becomes a *kohen* by birth but a woman becomes a *kohen* by birth and by marriage. The Old Testament refers to the priest's daughter having rights to eat priestly offerings (Lev. 22.12-13). The Holiness Code speaks of the priest's daughters and wives (Lev. 21.7, 9). It is said in Lev. 22.13 that the daughter of a priest could lose her privileges in a priestly family by marrying a non-priest. The Mishnah lists a number of occasions and reasons when a *bat kohen* loses her right to eat of the priestly heave-offering (m. *Yebam* 7.4–6; m. *Sota* 3.7 (priestliness of a *kohenet* implies less than the priestliness of a *kohen*); m. *Sota* 3.7 (the priestly role of a woman was much more fragile and open to profanation than a man's role was). See Brooten, *Women Leaders*, 78.

78 The two texts that allude to priestesses in ancient Israel are Exod. 38.8 and 1 Sam. 2.22 (*hassobot* – ministering women). There are differing opinions about 'the women who ministered at the tent of meeting' as housekeepers or doing menial duties, which is quite unlikely and Brooten regards this as over-interpretation. See Brooten, *Women Leaders*, 85. The other possible suggestions for priestesses in the Bible are Zipporah, who performed the ritual of circumcision on her son (Exod. 2.16, 21; 4.24-26); Jael the wife of Heber the Kenite (Judg. 5.24); and Miriam, who is called a prophet and led the Israelite women in dancing and worship (Exod. 15.20-21; Mic. 6.4).

79 Brooten, *Women Leaders*, 88.

80 Brooten, *Women Leaders*, 88.

3.7. Conclusion

It is clear that some women enjoyed considerable freedom and independence in the socio-political, religious, and cultural context of the Greco-Roman world. Although wealth and status were assumed as the rationale for taking on leadership, the evidence shows women had the skill and potential to become lawyers, politicians, magistrates, patrons of associations, priestesses of cultic worship, and leaders of synagogues. Women bore the same titles as men in the synagogues, being identified as heads of synagogues, elders, priestesses, leaders, and mothers of synagogues. Most of the references I examined were not from the first century, but originated a short while later. However, by cautiously using this evidence, it could be postulated that Jewish culture was not opposed to women's leadership.

On the one hand, it is argued that the above titles are simple honorary designations for women with husbands of stature, but on the other hand there are convincing claims to the contrary, predominantly the examples of women who were not mentioned alongside their husbands. Although their function is not clearly defined in the inscriptions, these titles possibly denote leadership roles, administrative capacity, and organisational character. Additionally, some of the titles used for women in the Pauline churches are similar to those of the Greco-Roman world. Although the exact nature of these leadership roles remains obscure, it implies a functional similarity from a different context. This provides a clear vantage point in our analysis of the roles of the women in Romans 16 and their contribution to the Pauline communities. This will be the task of the next chapter.

CHAPTER 4

WOMEN IN ROMANS 16.1-16

4.1. Introduction

Among the Pauline letter closings, Romans 16 contains more greetings and personal names than any other. Moreover, the individuals are greeted regarding their activities in relation both to the church and to Paul. The greeting formula and the rhetoric of the passage support the construction of mutual relations between the different parties.

The passage (16.1-16) seems to be Paul's acknowledgement of some people's hard work and their roles in relation to the Roman believers and himself. Women appreciated for their roles denote Paul's attitude to the general role of women in the church and ministry. The tone of his speech to restrict their involvement in the church elsewhere in his letters (1 Cor. 11.1-16; cf. 1 Cor. 14.34, 35) strikes a notable dissonance with what we find in Romans 16, where he appreciates their work. This chapter consists of a detailed analysis of the women named and portrayed with descriptive phrases. In turn, this helps us understand the roles they played in the Pauline mission as well as in the Roman church.

The major focus of this chapter is to deduce the leadership roles of the women and the implication of Paul's rhetoric of mutuality. The roles of the women are discussed as follows: first, the role of Phoebe; second, Prisca; third, Junia; fourth, the hardworking members: Mary, Persis, Tryphoena, and Tryphosa; finally, other members: Rufus' mother, Nereus' sister, and Julia.

4.2. The role of Phoebe (Rom. 16.1, 2)

Rom. 16.1, 2:

> v. 1. Συνίστημι δὲ ὑμῖν Φοίβην τὴν ἀδελφὴν ἡμῶν, οὖσαν [καὶ] διάκονον τῆς ἐκκλησίας τῆς ἐν Κεγχρεαῖς,
> v. 2. ἵνα αὐτὴν προσδέξησθε ἐν κυρίῳ ἀξίως τῶν ἁγίων καὶ παραστῆτε αὐτῇ ἐν ᾧ ἂν ὑμῶν χρῄζῃ πράγματι· καὶ γὰρ αὐτὴ προστάτις πολλῶν ἐγενήθη καὶ ἐμοῦ αὐτοῦ.

I commend to you our sister Phoebe, a deacon of the church at Cenchreae, so that you may welcome her in the Lord as is fitting for the saints, and help her in whatever she may require from you, for she has been a benefactor of many and of myself as well (NRSV).

It has been widely accepted that Rom. 16.1, 2 is a letter of introduction for Phoebe to the Romans. Although Phoebe's relation to the Romans is not particularly explicit, the social and theological role of Phoebe in Cenchreae can be clearly deduced from the passage. It is probable that Phoebe was a Gentile Christian since her name has connections with pagan mythology.[1] Her home town is Cenchreae and she is the διάκονος of the church of Cenchreae.[2] She is also the προστάτις of many others including Paul. *Prima facie*, Rom. 16.1, 2 appears as a letter of recommendation for Phoebe, but one may be able to pick up some hidden motives such as recommendation for Paul himself, an intention for the Spanish mission, or to prepare for Paul's visit. What is the importance of the relationship between Phoebe and Paul? What is the significance of the descriptive phrases used for her? Why is she recommended to the Romans? What is her expected mission portrayed in the epistle to the Romans?

In order to analyse the role of Phoebe and her significance in the Pauline mission, the titles used for Phoebe, her contribution to the Spanish mission (as proposed by R. Jewett), and the relation of reciprocity as evident in the structure and content of the passage are dealt with in the following sections.

4.2.1. διάκονος

The role of Phoebe as διάκονος has long been a subject of debate. διάκονος generally expresses the concept of serving.[3] 'διακονέω has the special quality of indicating very personally the service rendered to another.'[4] Although it generally denotes the concept of serving, Paul uses the term with a special relation to the church (ἐκκλησία) throughout his letters.[5] Of all the uses, only

---

1   The mythical Phoebe was the daughter of Heaven and Earth, the wife of Coeus, mother of Leto, and the grandmother of Apollo and Artemis. Fitzmyer, *Romans*, 729.

2   Cenchreae was the eastern port of Corinth. Six possible towns are known with the names of Cenchreae. Fitzmyer lists the towns: (1) a place in Argeia in the eastern Peloponnesus; (2) a town in Troas in Asia Minor; (3) a town near Lindos on the island of Rhodes; (4) a place near the town of Mitylene on the island of Lesbos; (5) a place near Lampsakos in the Troas; and (6) one of the two ports of Corinth. Cenchreae is the port of Corinth (situated 7 kilometres southeast of Corinth, on the Saronic Gulf, serving trade with Asia), and is associated with Paul's mission. See Fitzmyer, *Romans*, 730.

3   Other Greek words which have the notion of serving are δουλεύω, θεραπεύω, λατρεύω, ὑπηρετέω. δουλεύω means 'to serve as a slave with a stress on subjection', θεραπεύω 'expresses the willingness for service', λατρεύω means 'to serve for wages', which also connotes performing religious and cultic duties. H. W. Beyer, 'διακονέω, διακονία, διάκονος', *TDNT* 2, 81. ὑπηρετέω denotes 'to act under instruction', in a sense of an assistant, servant, or an inferior officer. *LSJ*, 179, 315, 407, 736.

4   Beyer, 'διακονέω', 81.

5   Paul (and the New Testament writers) preferred to use the διακονία word group to

Rom. 16.1 designates a woman as διάκονος of a church, which is unique as well as noteworthy. It is unique because Phoebe is the only woman named with this title by Paul. Different renderings will help us to figure out the original meaning of the title used by Paul to describe Phoebe. The use of διάκονος in relation to the church could denote the function of a minister. I will now attempt to analyse the noun διάκονος in order to find out in what sense Paul intended to use it in Rom. 16.1, and to identify the role of Phoebe in regard to the church of Cenchreae. To do this, I will analyse the terminology and different notions of its use in the Pauline epistles; its wider use in the New Testament, Greek literature, and Judaism; and finally in the function of Phoebe as διάκονος of the church of Cenchreae.

4.2.1.1. διάκονος in Pauline epistles

Paul uses the concrete noun διάκονος, the abstract noun διακονία, and the verb διακονέω to address different contexts and designated individuals. In this section, the discussion is limited to the undisputed letters of Paul, to Colossians and Ephesians.[6]

The verb διακονέω is used in relation to Paul himself (Rom. 15.25; 2 Cor. 3.3; 8.19-20) and Onesimus (Philemon 13). In Rom. 15.25, Paul expresses that he is going to minister to the saints (διακονῶν τοῖς ἁγίοις), which is important to our discussion because Phoebe's ministry is also in relation to the saints in Cenchreae.

He uses the abstract noun διακονία in a range of contexts and in relation to a variety of individuals. It includes himself (Rom. 11.13; 15.31; 2 Cor. 4.1; 5.18; 6.3; 2 Cor. 11.8); Stephanas and his household (1 Cor. 16.15); Archippus (Col. 4.17); Roman Christians (Rom. 12.7); Corinthian Christians (1 Cor. 12.5); Christians in general (Eph. 4.12); the ministry of death and condemnation (2 Cor. 3.7, 9); the ministry of the Spirit (2 Cor. 3.8); and the relief aid in the form of the collection (2 Cor. 8.4; 9.1, 12-13).

It is interesting that 1 Cor. 16.15 talks about the service of the household of Stephanas 'to the saints'.[7] Service to the saints implies service to a group of people gathered together as a church and is probably related to a leadership role. Early Christianity regarded the all-important activity of the edification of the community as διακονία (Eph. 4.11f.).[8] Paul describes διαιρέσεις

---

speak of service or ministry rather than the terms 'office'/'rule' (ἀρχή), 'honour' (τιμή), or 'power' (τέλος), which denote positions of ecclesiastical office.

6   Although the authenticity of Colossians and Ephesians is widely disputed, I assume those to be Pauline, or very closely connected to Paul, since they have similar themes and structures to the undisputed letters.

7   Other instances where διακονία is related to the saints are Rom. 15.31 (my *service* in Jerusalem may be acceptable to the saints); 2 Cor. 8.4 (the fellowship of *ministering* to the saints); 1 Cor. 9.1 (concerning the *ministering* to the saints); Eph. 4.12 (for equipping of the saints for the work of the ministry).

8   Beyer, 'διακονία', 87.

διακονιῶν, and διαιρέσεις χαρισμάτων (1 Cor. 12.4, 5).[9] The different services in the early church were performed by different members of the community, and were rendered to the same Lord. διακονία is placed between προφητεία and διδασκαλία (Rom. 12.7). It also denotes obligations and responsibilities in the community.

Moreover, the concrete noun διάκονος occurs frequently in the Pauline letters to denote different functions in the context of ἐκκλησία. It is used to denote Paul himself (1 Cor. 3.5, 6; Eph. 3.7; Col. 1.23, 25); Apollos (1 Cor. 3.5); Tychicus (Eph. 6.21; Col. 4.7); Epaphras (Col. 1.7); Phoebe (Rom. 16.1); the Philippian deacons (Phil. 1.1); the false apostles (2 Cor. 11.15, 23); the Roman authorities (Rom. 13.4); and Christ (Rom. 15.8; Gal. 2.17). They are described in relation to God (2 Cor. 6.4); Christ (2 Cor. 11.23; Col. 1.7); the church (Col. 1.25); the new covenant (2 Cor. 3.6); righteousness (2 Cor. 11.5); and the gospel (Eph. 3.7; Col. 1.23).

The opinion that the word group denotes 'humble service of other people' is criticised by Collins, who argues that the term denotes the task of carrying messages that emphasise the notion of an agent or messenger in non-Christian sources. The same idea can be seen in the New Testament use of the term too. He argues that the words διάκονος, διακονία, and διακονέω 'do not speak directly of "attitude" like "lowliness" but express concepts about undertakings for another, be that God or (hu)man, master or friend'.[10] In the New Testament, διακονία is a task entrusted by divine authority.

The beneficiaries of διακονέω are the members of the community. It affects the life of a community in its entirety. Paul specially mentions the beneficiaries as the saints in general or a church in particular. The verb denotes that the benefactor specified in each context plays an important role in that particular community or congregation.

First Corinthians 16.15, Phil. 1.1, Col 4.7, 17, and Rom. 16.1 are significant to the discussion.[11] They are chosen because: (1) the individuals or the group mentioned are Paul's associates in ministry; (2) their contribution is to the

9   Different charisms are for the common good and for building up the body of Christ. Paul's account of ministries shows no evidence for only one group exercising or controlling all ministries in the early church; rather, different groups within the community shared the responsibility for ministry or service.

10   J. N. Collins, *Diakonia: Re-interpreting the Ancient Sources* (Oxford: Oxford University Press, 1990), 194. See also Robert Hannaford, 'The Representative and Relational Nature of Ministry and the Renewal of the Diaconate', in *The Ministry of Deacon: Ecclesiological Explorations* (Uppsala: NEC, 2000), 245. Georgi also shares the same opinion that διακονία refers to the service performed by those whom God has chosen to be messengers; see D. Georgi, *The Opponents of Paul in Second Corinthians* (SNTW; Edinburgh: T&T Clark, 1987), 27–32; A. D. Clarke, *Serve the Community of the Church: Christians as Leaders and Ministers* (Grand Rapids: Eerdmans, 2000), 239.

11   For more discussion on the ministry in the New Testament, see A. Hentschel, *Diakonia im Neuen Testament:Studien zur Semantik unter besonderer Berücksichtigung der Rolle von Frauen* (Tübingen: Mohr Siebeck, 2007), 90–137. Romans 16.1 is discussed as a separate section, see 4.2.1.7.

community of saints; (3) they are mentioned as διάκονος or otherwise identified by their service.

Stephanas and his household devoted themselves to the service (διακονία) of the saints (1 Cor. 16.15). According to Banks, Stephanas appears as a 'co-worker ... in the founding of the church'.[12] Being 'devoted for work' should be understood as an individual setting themself aside to focus on a specific task.

Archippus' service (διακονία, Col. 4.17) denotes a special act of 'service' of a διάκονος, though it could not be equated with the later technical sense of deaconate.[13] The use of διάκονος to denote a title for a specific function in the developing church is found first in Phil. 1.1 (σὺν ἐπισκόποις καὶ διακόνοις), where Paul sends greetings to all the saints in Philippi. It is notable that deacons are greeted with the overseers (ἐπίσκοποι)[14] and named after them. This raises the question of how these offices were integrated or coordinated. Although it is difficult to determine the specific duties of deacons and overseers, it is implausible that both denote the different duties of one person. Some scholars suggest these titles are 'functional' rather than 'titular', thus describing 'someone who serves others' rather than a title denoting leadership.[15] Elsewhere Paul refers to church workers without mentioning an office (Rom. 12.8; Gal. 6.6; 1 Thess. 5.12). However, as O'Brien suggests, with Beyer and others, 'he [Paul] has in view particular members of the congregation who are specifically described and known by these two titles; otherwise the addition seems to be meaningless' and they 'have special, self-evident authority'.[16] Best rightly argues that the two groups mentioned particularly (with the saints) suggest a distinction between ordinary believers and ministers as they are particularly mentioned.[17]

Ephaphras (Col. 1.7) and Tychicus (Col. 4.7; Eph. 6.21) are specially called διάκονος. Epaphras is σύνδουλος of the apostle and διάκονος τοῦ Χριστοῦ (Col. 1.7). Tychicus is διάκονος ἐν Κυρίῳ (Eph. 6.21; Col. 4.7). Dunn suggests that the term may describe 'an individual's sustained commitment like Paul's co-worker and not the title of a defined office'.[18] But as Paul's fellow worker, the person probably shared the responsibilities of Paul and had an effective participation in ministry.

12   Banks, *Paul's Idea of Community*, 164; I. H. Marshall and D. A. Hagner, *1 Corinthians* (Grand Rapids: Eerdmans, 2000), 1339. See also S. Schreiber, 'Arbeit mit der Gemeinde (Rom. 16:6, 12). Zur versunkenen Möglichkeit der Gemeindeleitung durch Frauen', *NTS* 46 (2000), 204–26, at 214–17.

13   J. D. G. Dunn, *The Epistle to the Colossians and to Philemon: A Commentary on the Greek Text* (Grand Rapids: Eerdmans, 1996), 288.

14   Lightfoot, *Epistle to the Philippians*, 82.

15   G. D. Fee, *Paul's Letter to the Philippians* (Grand Rapids: Eerdmans, 1995), 69.

16   P. T. O'Brien, *The Epistle to the Philippians: A Commentary on the Greek Text* (Grand Rapids: Eerdmans, 1991), 48, [Paul] is an addition; Beyer, 'διακονία', 616; M. Silva, *Philippians* (Grand Rapids: Baker Academic, 2005), 40, 41.

17   E. Best, 'Bishops and Deacons: Phil. 1.1', *SE* 4 (1968), 371–76, at 372–74; O' Brien, *Philippians*, 49.

18   Dunn, *Colossians and Philemon*, 65, 272.

4.2.1.2. διάκονος in the New Testament (outside the Pauline literature[19])
Service in the New Testament has a special significance as far as Jesus' life
and ministry are concerned. He bases his teaching on the commandment of
loving one's neighbour, and an attitude of serving was an essential prerequisite
of being a disciple and in alignment with the virtues of the kingdom of God.

διακονέω is used with the meaning 'to wait at table' (Lk. 17.8; Jn. 12.2;
Lk. 12.37; Lk. 22.26).[20] It is used in a sense 'to supervise a meal' (Acts 6.2).
In a broader sense, it means 'to be serviceable', which includes many different
activities such as provision for bodily sustenance. The Son of Man came not
to be served, but to serve others (Mk. 10.45). Moreover, διακονεῖν denotes
the service to the community (cf. Heb. 6.10). The charismata are divided into
ministry of the word and deed (1 Pet. 4.10, 11; cf. 1 Pet. 1.10-11). διάκονος
specifies 'the waiter at a meal' (Jn. 2.5, 9) and the servant of a master (Mt.
22.13).

4.2.1.3. διάκονος in the Pastoral Letters
The deaconate related to the episcopate is also found in 1 Tim. 3.1f.; a list of
requirements for an overseer (vv. 1-7), followed by those for a deacon (vv.
8-13). A specific group is later assigned to be deacons and possibly used in a
technical sense, which integrated the 'function' with the 'office'.[21] The lack
of reference to teaching or authority in the list of qualifications of deacons
does not imply that their responsibilities are limited to fulfilling practical
needs; rather, to become effective leaders in their household suggests their
responsibility to the church (v. 9).[22]

4.2.1.4. διάκονος in extra-biblical Greek literature
διακονέω is first found in contemporary Greek in Herodotus with the meaning
'to wait at table' (cf. Aristophanes *Acharnenses* 1015ff.; Diodorus Siculus V.
28, 4; Athenaeus of Naucratis IX, 21). In particular, it means to taste or to
direct a marriage feast, and more generally 'to provide or care for', which is
often used to describe the work of a woman (Athenaeus of Naucratis IX 20,
Dion of Chrysostomus *Orationes* 7, 65; Sophocles *Philoctetes* 285f., Plato

---

19   The Pastoral Letters are discussed below, since they have a special reference to the role
and function of the deaconate, although it is debated whether they represent a later development
and are deutero-Pauline in origin.

20   διακονεῖν is also used to describe Martha's care (Lk. 10.40); Peter's mother-in-
law's service (Mk. 1.31) and angels ministering to Jesus (Mk. 1.13; Mt. 4.11). See G. Lohfink,
'Weibliche Diakone im Neuen Testament', in J. Blank et al. (eds.), *Die Frau Im Urchristentum*
(QD 95; Freiburg: Herder, 1983), 320–38; Philsy, Sr., 'Diakonia of Women in the New Testament',
IJT 32 (1983), 110–18.

21   I. H. Marshall and P. H. Towner, *A Critical and Exegetical Commentary on the
Pastoral Epistles* (Edinburgh: T&T Clark, 1999), 489.

22   I disagree with Beyer's suggestion that the primary functions of deacons are those
pertaining to practical needs and inferior to that of overseers. Beyer, 'διακονέω', 90. Acts 6 hints
that deacons are selected to carry out practical service rather than minister the word. However, the
origin of the deaconate is primarily in relation to the episcopate, and not as described in Acts 6.

Leges VII 805e).[23] Based on the above meanings, the comprehensive meaning is 'to serve' (Herodotus IV, 154, P. Oxy. II, 275, 10). Greeks, on the other hand, considered serving as undignified, lowly, and inferior in status.

4.2.1.5. διάκονος in Judaism

In the Jewish tradition, the master–servant relationship is used to describe the relationship between God and humanity. διακονεῖν is used by Philo to convey the meaning 'to serve' or 'to wait at a table' (Vit. Cont. 70; cf. Vit. Cont. 75). Josephus uses it with three meanings such as 'to wait at table' (*Ant.* 11.163), 'to serve' with the notion of obedience (*Ant.* 17.140), and 'to render priestly services' (*Ant.* 7. 365).[24]

4.2.1.6. διάκονος in inscriptional evidence

There are extant inscriptions citing female διακόνοι of cultic organisations in non-literary sources from Ephesus.[25] It is also interesting to note that an inscription from the fourth century recognises a lady called Sophia, who is described in four ways: a 'second Phoibe', δούλη, νύμφη of Christ, and also διάκονος (Guarducci *EG* 1V 445).[26] The title 'second Phoibe' seems to be an allusion to Phoebe in Rom. 16.1. There are other women mentioned by the title διάκονος,[27] which is further evidence of women holding this title.

4.2.1.7. Phoebe as διάκονος (Rom. 16.1)

In Rom. 16.1 Phoebe is designated the διάκονος of the church of Cenchreae. The discussion is mainly centred on whether Paul is referring to her leadership in the church or to a general service she provided. It is probable that her title denotes a significant role since she is singled out as the διάκονος of the church of Cenchreae. As Thomas suggests, 'the term deacon was used to designate a believer who had been set apart for work in the church with the added authority which came with an act of setting apart'.[28] The term is referring to a special office, but the nature of the special office is not clearly depicted in the New Testament.[29]

The title is translated as 'servant' (NIV), 'deaconess' (RSV, NAB, NJB, JB, Philips), 'who serves' (GNB), 'who holds office in the congregation' (NEB), 'active in the service of the congregation' (William Barclay), and 'a deacon in the church of Cenchreae' (NRSV). Some of the translations may be based on

---

23   Beyer, 'διακονέω', 82.

24   See for more discussion Beyer, 'διακονέω', 82.

25   *IG* 111, 2.x.3527; *SEG* 425; Guarducci, *EG* 1V 345–47; Guarducci *EG* 1V 368–70.

26   See G. H. R. Horsley, *New Docs*, 4.239–41.

27   See Horsley, *New Docs*, 4.239–40. Examples are *IG* III, 2.x.3527, *SEG* 425, Guarducci *EG* IV 345–47, Guarducci *EG* IV 368–70.

28   W. D. Thomas, 'Phoebe: A Helper of Many', *ExpTim* 95 (1984), 336–37, at 337.

29   C. S. Keener, *Paul, Women and Wives: Marriage and Women's Ministry in the Letters of Paul* (Peabody: Hendrickson, 1992), 238. Although the office of the deacon is interpreted in the light of Acts 6 as one who is called to serve, the particular title is not used in Acts 6. That is, there is no reason to suggest that Acts 6 is the origin of the office.

the general sense of the term denoting 'one who serves at the table'. Whelan suggests that translating διάκονος in Rom. 16.1 as a synonym for the later office of deaconess (in the third or fourth century CE) would limit the function and responsibility of the role when compared to the male deaconate.[30] Since there is no separate Greek word for deaconess in the first three centuries CE, the English translation of διάκονος as deaconess is incorrect and misleading. It might have been during the fourth century when the Greek word διακόνισσα was developed, and the role and responsibility is vastly different from that of the first-century διάκονος,[31] which can designate both a man and a woman.

Some commentators interpret διάκονος in terms of informal service or a limited ministry to helping women or the sick. For example, Cranfield suggests that Phoebe's activities are to 'the practical service of the needy'; Käsemann considers her ministry was the 'charitable care of the poor, sick, widows and orphans'.[32]

On the other hand, some consider Phoebe as the leader of a particular congregation. Dunn indicates that 'διάκονος together with οὖσαν points more to a recognized ministry or position of responsibility within the congregation'.[33] Fitzmyer regards Phoebe as the minister and leader of the congregation.[34] Although a developed form of the deaconate is hard to distinguish from when Romans was written, the role and function should be determined by the context of each letter and each particular congregation.[35]

The term διάκονος can be used in a general sense for exercising some role of service. But in certain respects it seems to go hand in hand with a designated office, e.g. when related to 'the saints' or 'the church'. This is clear when it is placed with other titles (Phil. 1.1 and the Pastorals) and is probably the case in Rom. 16.1 with Phoebe.

It is noteworthy that Rom. 16 is the only occasion in which Paul describes Phoebe. Paul's description of Phoebe includes her title as the διάκονος, and also her roles as ἀδελφὴν ἡμῶν and προστάτις. Although it seems difficult to locate the specific role of Phoebe in the church of Cenchreae, it is possible

---

30   Whelan, 'Amica Pauli', 67.

31   See Whelan, 'Amica Pauli', 68. *Contra* Romaniuk suggests, 'Paul knowingly magnifies the role of Phoebe when he likens her role in the community to that of an officed deacon', and is a 'pleasant exaggeration', which can be accepted only if there is any evidence of Paul speaking that is not totally true and for his own personal benefit. K. Romaniuk, 'Was Phoebe in Romans 16, 1 a Deaconess?' *ZNW* 81(1990), 132–34, at 133, 134. See also D. C. Arichea, 'Who was Phoebe?', 407. I disagree with the term 'pleasant exaggeration' and his view that Phoebe was 'an ordinary lay-woman'; if Paul exaggerates women's roles, it should be true for Paul's statements for others elsewhere.

32   Cranfield, *Romans*, 2.781; Käsemann, *Romans*, 410; Clarke, 'Jew and Greek', 117.

33   Dunn, *Romans 9–16*, 886, 887.

34   Fitzmyer, *Romans*, 729–30. See also B. Holmberg, *Paul and Power: The Structure of Authority in the Primitive Church as Reflected in the Pauline Epistles* (Philadelphia: Fortress Press, 1980), 99–102; Ellis, 'Paul and his Co-workers', 185.

35   Dunn, *Romans 9–16*, 886, 887.

to make some deductions from the form of recommendation and the titles used by Paul. The way he recommends Phoebe to the Romans, and the requests he gives to the Romans to receive her and 'assist her in whatever she needs of you' certainly give some evidence of her role in the church of Cenchreae. Ellis equated διάκονος with that of 'a special class of co-workers, those who are active in preaching and teaching'.[36] As noted above, when Paul uses διακονέω or διάκονος in relation to a congregation, it implies the notion of some role in leading the congregation.

The early Christian movement was spread by travelling missionaries, but Phoebe could not be understood as an itinerant missionary[37] because her responsibilities as διάκονος are centred on the local church of Cenchreae. As Klauck rightly asserts, her 'ministry' or 'office' could not be regarded as equal to the later deaconesses, whose ministry is limited to women; rather she was the διάκονος of the whole church in Cenchreae.[38]

It is also striking that Fiorenza tries to equate Phoebe's title with that of the charismatic preachers in Corinth (suggesting they were co-workers); the major difference is that Phoebe is not Paul's opponent, but has friendly relations with him.[39] I presume that the hermeneutical tool to interpret Phoebe's role as διάκονος of the church of Cenchreae should be Paul's use of διάκονος in relation to the community or the church. The responsibilities of a διάκονος involve some form of leadership, which probably includes teaching and preaching.[40]

I suggest that Phoebe's relation to the community at Cenchreae is the same as the house of Stephanas, who committed themselves 'to the διακονία of saints' (1 Cor. 16.15) and Timothy, co-worker of Paul[41] (1 Thess. 3.2).[42] In 1 Cor. 3.5, 9 Paul uses the expression to confirm that Apollos and himself were called by God and entrusted with a common ministry.[43] The terms Paul uses to describe the members of the community (co-workers, deacons, and patrons) carry no gender distinctions. It can be translated as 'minister', which

36   Ellis, 'Paul and his Co-workers', 442.

37   Fiorenza, *In Memory of Her*, 171; Jewett suggests Phoebe's role is that of a local leader rather than a travelling missionary; Jewett, *Romans*, 945.

38   H. J. Klauck, *Hausgemeinde und Hauskirche im frühen Christentum* (Stuttgart: Katholisches Bibelwerk, 1981), 31; Fiorenza, 'Missionaries, Apostles, Co-workers, 425.

39   Fiorenza, 'Missionaries, Apostles, Co-workers', 426. See also Georgi, *Opponents of Paul in Corinth*, 29–32. The word group διάκονος, διακονία, διακονέω is used in 2 Cor. 11.13 to characterise the false apostles, who were the charismatic preachers, visionary prophets, and spirit-filled apostles.

40   See Croft, 'Text Messages', 89. See also A. Hentschel, *Diakonia im Neuen Testament*, 167–72.

41   1 Thessalonians 3.2 poses a textual question whether συνεργόν or διάκονον should be read. Metzger suggests the best reading is συνεργὸν τοῦ θεοῦ ἐν τῷ εὐαγγελίῳ τοῦ Χριστοῦ. See Metzger, *A Textual Commentary*, 563.

42   See Cotter, 'Women's Authority Roles in Paul's Churches', 354. Tychicus is also called as 'our beloved brother' and faithful διάκονος (Col. 4.7; cf. 2 Cor. 3.6).

43   1 Corinthians 3.5 shows that the Pauline concept of leadership is task-oriented rather than person-oriented. See A. D. Clarke, *Secular and Christian Leadership in Corinth: A Socio-Historical & Exegetical Study of 1 Cor. 1–6* (New York: Brill, 1993), 119.

is a significant title to denote a specific role in the church: a person with a special function who is engaged in leading the church.[44] This title 'clearly points to a leadership role over the whole church, not just a part of it; and the way the title is introduced suggests a recognized office, though doubtless not as well defined as it later became in the church (1 Tim 3.8-13)'.[45]

Phoebe's title διάκονος shows her leadership role was exercised in the church of Cenchreae, although it cannot be placed in the hierarchy of the developed church. Paul's use of the term in Rom. 16.1 is also used to describe his fellow workers as well as himself. The correct rendering would be a minister of the church of Cenchreae. Although there is no question of a fully-fledged diaconate's office at this early stage, Phoebe could be identified as a διάκονος: a women of recognised status and significance. Having looked at the role of Phoebe as διάκονος, I will now focus on the next significant title προστάτις.

4.2.2. προστάτις

In addition to διάκονος, Paul uses the title προστάτις (Rom. 16.2) to describe Phoebe's function and role in relation to his ministry. προστάτις is a unique word in the New Testament, occurring only in Rom. 16.2. As I observed previously, epigraphic evidence suggests the existence of female 'patrons' who took an active part in voluntary associations and guilds; patronage was a well-established institution in the first century.[46]

This section attempts to make a study of the term προστάτις in order to find its meaning for Phoebe in Rom. 16.2. After analysing different translations and interpretations, I will suggest the role Phoebe had possibly played as the προστάτις of Paul and many others.

4.2.2.1. Translations and interpretations

προστάτις is the feminine form of προστάτης and is used for a sponsor of a private association. προστάτης could mean one who stands before as the leader, president, or ruler, or one who stands to protect as a guardian, champion, or patron.[47] The title occurs in six Jewish inscriptions in which it is difficult to decide whether leader or patron is the most suitable translation.[48] Trebilco comments that the inscriptions testify that 'there was often more than one προστάτης in the community and that it was a significant position in some synagogues'.[49] In the LXX, the term has the meaning of 'leader' or 'ruler' and not 'patron'. Josephus and Philo used meanings such as 'leader',

---

44   Arichea, 'Who was Phoebe?' 409.

45   Bassler, 'Phoebe', 135.

46   See chapter 3 for more discussion.

47   *LSJ*, προστάτης, 1526–27.

48   Horsley, *NewDocs*, 4.242. The inscriptions are *CPJ* 3, 1441 (Xenephyris); *CPJ* 2, 149 (Alexandria, the prostates of a loan society); *CPJ* 1, 101f. (Oxyrhynchus); *CIJ* 100 and 365 (Rome); *SEG* 29.969 (Naples).

49   Trebilco, *Jewish Communities*, 109.

'patron', and 'champion' too. Philo usually employs προστάτης and προστασία to convey the title or office of the 'president' of a community.[50] It is also important to note that the term is commonly used in the ancient world to denote 'the patron of a pagan religious society', who looked after the group's interests.[51] The role of μήτηρ συναγωγῆς is assumed to have parallel roles with that of προστάτης.[52]

προστάτις has been translated in different forms, including: 'she has been a great assistance to many' (BGD), 'a helper of many' (RSV), 'a good friend to many' (NEB), 'a great help to many people' (NIV), 'has come to the help of many' (NJB), and 'a benefactor of many' (NRSV). Whelan suggests that the problem concerning the translation of the term is in connection with the 'hidden assumptions of Bible translators regarding the position of women in primitive Christianity and more importantly a lack of understanding of the position of women in the imperial period'.[53] I will now analyse the different renderings.

i. Helper
A number of English versions translate προστάτις as helper, and include final forms such as 'succourer' (KJV), 'helper' (RSV, NAS, and NKJV), 'a great help' (NIV), and 'has come to the help of' (NJB). Some commentators also interpret προστάτις with the same meaning. For example, Käsemann suggests that:

> προστάτις ... cannot in the context have the juridical sense of the masculine form, i.e. the leader or representative of a fellowship. There is no reference, then to a 'patroness' who could not take on legal functions. ... The idea is that of personal care which Paul and others have received at the hand of the deaconess.[54]

The plausibility of this translation could be due to two factors. First, the cognate verb προΐστημι has the meaning 'to have an interest in, show concern for, care for, and give aid'.[55] Second, the term προστάτις and the request of Paul to assist (παραστῆτε) Phoebe in whatever she needs resulted in some manuscripts

---

50   Trebilco, *Jewish Communities in Asia Minor*, 109. See also J. M. Reynolds and R. Tannenbaum, *Jews and God Fearers at Aphrodisias: Greek Inscriptions with Commentary* (PCPSSV vol. 12; Cambridge Philological Society, 1987), 41. In the LXX it translates the word as ruler (1 Chron. 27.31; 29.6; 2 Chron. 8.10), overseer (2 Chron. 24: 11), and commissioner (2 Chron. 24.11). See also 1 Esd. 2.12 (cf. 6.18); Sir. 45.24; 2 Macc. 3.4. In Josephus προστάτης means patron nine times (e.g. *Ant* 14.157, 444), leader nine times (e.g. *BJ* 1.633), and champion once (*BJ* 2.135); Philo uses the term three times with the meanings of leader, patron, and champion (*Virt.* 155; *Abr.* 221).

51   Trebilco, *Jewish Communities*, 109.

52   Brooten, *Women Leaders*, 65. See 3.6.4

53   See Whelan, 'Amica Pauli', 69.

54   Käsemann, *Romans*, 411; see also Barrett, *Romans*, 282–83. Although Cranfield assumes a general sense of a 'helper' role for Phoebe, he agrees that Phoebe is possessed of 'some social position, wealth, and independence'; Cranfield, *Romans*, 2.782.

55   *BDAG*, 870.

(F, G) replacing προστάτις by παραστάτις. On the basis of Paul's request 'to receive her worthily of the saints' and 'to stand by her in whatever she requires of you', the term is rendered as 'she has been the assistant (παραστάτις) of many and Paul as well' and corresponds with the translation of προστάτις as 'helper'. However, as we have discussed in the previous section, the rendering of διάκονος as 'helper' is unlikely in the context of Rom. 16.2.[56] The lexical evidence indicates προστάτις should be translated as 'protectress' or 'patroness', and it is misleading to translate προστάτις as 'helper', since those who were in the position of προστάτις enjoyed a high position and were more than simple 'assistants' to others.

ii. Leader or president of the congregation
Another suggestion is that προστάτις could be translated as the leader or president of the congregation. The arguments[57] are as follows:

1. The related term προΐστημι in 1 Thess. 5.12; and 1 Tim. 3.4-5, 5.17 speak about someone with authority and who presides or governs over a community of believers.
2. The masculine form of the noun προστάτης is used for stewards of the king's property or for the chief officers over the people (1 Chron. 27.31; 2 Chron. 8.10; 24.11; 1 Esd. 2.12; Sir. 45.24; 2 Macc. 3.4).
3. Justin Martyr used the word προστάτης for a person presiding over the communion (*First Apology* 65).
4. The passive form ἐγενήθη in the clause describes an appointment to an office; the clause καὶ γὰρ αὐτὴ προστάτις πολλῶν ἐγενήθη καὶ ἐμοῦ αὐτοῦ should be rendered 'for she has been appointed, by my own action, as an officer presiding over many'.

These arguments each have their own shortcomings, since προστάτις is used here not in relation to the church but in relation to individuals. It is important to consider how she could be the president of Paul and many others as well. It is also dubious to take the phrase καὶ ἐμοῦ αὐτοῦ as indicating the agent of the action. The idea of presidency is unlikely in this case.[58]

iii. *Patroness, protectress, benefactress*
The appropriate translation could be patroness, protectress, or benefactor. The rendering 'benefactor' is adopted by NRSV and TNIV, and recent commentators also interpret along this line of thought.[59]

This line of interpretation is built upon the assumptions that προστάτις is equivalent to the more common προστάτης, the masculine counterpart, and

---

56   Fiorenza, 'Missionaries', 425.

57   This argument is put forward by R. R. Schulz, 'A Case for "President" Phoebe in Romans 16:2', *LTJ* 24 (1990), 124–27; see also E. Y. Ng, 'Phoebe as *Prostatis*', *TJ* 25 (2004), 3–13, at 4.

58   Murray, *Romans*, 2.227; Schreiner, *Romans*, 788.

59   Dunn, *Romans 9–16*, 887; Jewett, *Romans*, 946, 947. See also B. Reike, 'προΐστημι', *TDNT* 6, 700–703, at 703; *MM*, 551.

that the Greek words are equivalent to the Latin words *patronus* and *patrona*. The Latin equivalent, *patronus*, is used to refer to patronage of collegia or clubs.[60] It is possible to argue that Phoebe is similar to the patrons/patronesses of individuals, of voluntary associations, clubs, and professional guilds. Hence she may have offered monetary support, procured political advantages, served as a legal representative for individuals, opened her house to receive visitors or provide space for meetings, etc. Reynolds and Tannenbaum suggest that the position of the patronage, if it did refer to the community, would be similar to that of the *pater* or *mater* of synagogues and the Hellenistic cult societies.[61] Judge evaluates that the better attested meaning 'protectress' suffered from appearing to assign Phoebe a much higher social status than might have been anticipated,[62] an issue which will be discussed in the following section.

4.2.2.2. Social status

There are differing views about the social status of Phoebe. On the one hand, many scholars suggest that she is a woman of high social standing since προστάτις denotes an 'upper class benefactor'.[63] They base their argument on the fact that she is a wealthy patron, and that the references to offices, households, and help rendered to the congregation, not to mention the fact that she has funds to travel, reveal her high social status. The role of wealthy women in the early church is well documented in providing hospitality, space for gatherings, and leading roles in the congregations.[64]

On the other hand, some scholars suggest that wealth is not a guiding factor to decide independence and influence. For example, Meggitt suggests that it is not plausible to infer that the individuals mentioned by Paul in his letters are mentioned due to the fact that they were 'elite or prosperous in society'.[65] He supports this point as follows: (1) independence could not be regarded as a deciding factor to determine whether she is elite or non-elite;[66] (2) the term

---

60   Trebilco, *Jewish Communities*, 116; R. MacMullen, *Roman Social Relations: 50 BC to AD 284* (London: Yale University Press, 1974), 74–76.

61   Reynolds and Tannenbaum, *Jews and God Fearers*, 41.

62   E. A. Judge, 'Cultural Conformity and Innovation in Paul: Some Clues from Contemporary Documents', *TynBul* 35 (1984), 3–24, at 21.

63   Theissen, *Social Setting of Pauline Christianity*, 252–57. The other scholars who share a similar view about the leading role of male and female upper-class benefactors in early Christian communities are Holmberg, Funk, Murphy-O'Connor, Meeks, Kearsley, Trebilco, Garrison. Jewett portrays Phoebe as the patron for the Spanish mission; see Jewett, *Romans*, 947; Meeks, *First Urban Christians*, 57; Kearsley, 'Women in the Public East', 189–211; Trebilco, *Jewish Communities*, 109.

64   S. R. Llewelyn, 'Changing the Legal Jurisdiction', *New Docs*, 9.45–53, at 50.

65   Meggitt, *Paul, Poverty, and Survival*, 134. Meggitt proposes that the reference to the household with slaves, hospitality and material help rendered to the members of the community and travel are not secure evidence of a high social-economic status in the Pauline community. See Meggitt, *Paul, Poverty and Survival*, 128–35.

66   Meggitt agrees that Phoebe is definitely an independent woman since she is not mentioned with any male names. She is also capable of conducting business tours, but both elite and non-elite women alike enjoyed independence. See Meggitt, *Paul, Poverty and Survival*,

προστάτις cannot be taken in reference to her wealth; (3) Phoebe's ability to travel cannot be 'an indicator' of her elite status.[67] Rather, he agrees that Phoebe had some significant contribution in Pauline communities, but not on the basis of her wealth. Although Phoebe did not play the traditional role of a patron, he agrees that Paul's words indicate her significance in the church at Cenchreae.[68]

Moreover, Meggitt doubts whether Paul is using προστάτις for Phoebe in a sense of 'social superiority'.[69] His argument is based on three issues: first, she is not equal to the patrons of the Greco-Roman world; second, he infers that χρῄζῃ πράγματι is a request for material help for Phoebe, which is unusual in a patron–client relationship where patrons required political or social support in return; third, sending a recommendation on behalf of a patron was quite unusual in Paul's day since the recommendee was socially inferior to the patron and not superior.

Having described the above two viewpoints, my suggestions are: first, Phoebe is not necessarily elite or of high status, but rather relatively wealthy when compared to the members of the church of Cenchreae; second, patron in the full sense of the Greco-Roman world is unwarranted; however, she may have some informal role as a benefactress; third, I disagree with Meggitt that Paul requested material help for Phoebe, since the expression does not point to any specific help and leaves the request open-ended.

What made Paul recommend Phoebe to the church at Rome? What is the significance of their relationship? The ancient letters of recommendation testify to recommendees in two different ways: one as inferior to the letter writer (as a client to the writer) and the other as more or less social equals.[70] In the light of Romans 16, an inferior role for Phoebe can hardly be found. Rather on the basis of her social role as προστάτις and her ecclesiastical role as διάκονος, it is far more plausible to find mutuality in the relationship between Paul and Phoebe. Whelan suggests that Phoebe's description as 'the patron of many and of myself' implies that Paul accepts her as his social superior

---

145; cf. A. Cameron, 'Neither Male nor Female', *GR* 27 (1980), 60–68, at 62, 63. In her article, Cameron remarks that the women of the lower and middle classes 'lived relatively active lives' in late Republican and early Imperial Rome; Phoebe, although not belonging to the upper class, certainly has substantial means.

67   Meggitt suggests that there were lower-class patrons and travel could be undertaken by various means; wealth and status were not a limiting factor. Lydia and Phoebe are misrepresented as 'wealthy, entrepreneurial, independent women', since most women were denied access to economic resources and their jobs were basic, not skilled jobs. See Meggitt, *Paul, Poverty and Survival*, 69, 78, 144.

68   Meggitt, *Paul, Poverty and Survival*, 149.

69   Meggitt, *Paul, Poverty and Survival*, 146–48.

70   Whelan, 'Amica Pauli', 80, 81. The first type shows an unequal relationship and the writer may be superior to the recommendee, while in the second type, the writer assumes the role of a mediator introducing the person to a new group of friends. The recommendee being the superior of the writer is rarely found.

to some extent.[71] That Phoebe was merely a financial benefactor is less clear but both share their honour and prestige in acting reciprocally: Phoebe acts as Paul's patron, and Paul recommends or sponsors her. Whelan rightly suggests that patronage here implies 'mutual obligation' or reciprocity.[72]

Therefore, I suggest that there is an element of mutual obligation in the relationship between Paul and Phoebe rather than social superiority. It is not one-way patronage, but the model of patronage is taken up into a relationship of mutuality and reciprocity. Therefore, Phoebe seems to be an influential figure with relative wealth (to entertain guests at her home) and social position, who acted as a benefactor of many people, including Paul.

4.2.2.3. Function of Phoebe as προστάτις

On the basis of the preceding discussion, it appears that Phoebe played the role of a benefactor or patron. The next task is to discover in what sense she is the προστάτις to Paul and to others.

The different possible roles may include:[73]

1. Patron of the congregation of Cenchreae.
2. Legal representative of individuals.
3. A patron–client relationship.
4. Benefaction in terms of hospitality and practical help.

Phoebe should not be thought of as merely an assistant or helper since she is acknowledged by the same title as the patrons in associations and guilds. Phoebe is not described as a προστάτις of the church of Cenchreae, nor is she described explicitly in juridical or technical terms. Moreover, it is also doubtful whether a patron–client relationship was involved between Phoebe and Paul. However, what is more overtly suggested is the notion of reciprocity involved in the request for Phoebe. The benefaction system involves reciprocal relations within networks, and the characteristic of these relations involves exchange of benefits or gifts in return for appropriate honours. 'Relations were reciprocal in the sense that both the benefactor and the beneficiary had something to gain from the exchange, whether tangible or otherwise.'[74]

---

71   Whelan, 'Amica Pauli', 83. That Phoebe is the social superior of Paul to some extent is accepted by Jewett as well as Judge. See Jewett, 'Spanish Mission', 149–50; Judge, 'Cultural Conformity and Innovation in Paul', 21. Bierinder suggests Phoebe is the superior of Paul, which is not likely; R. Bieringer, 'Women and Leadership in Romans 16: The Leading Roles of Phoebe, Prisca, and Junia in Early Christianity: Part I', *East Asian Pastoral Review* 44 (2007), 221–37, at 235.

72   Whelan, 'Amica Pauli', 84. There is a sense of mutual indebtedness between Paul and Phoebe. Whelan suggests Phoebe is sent to the Ephesian church, while I consider that Phoebe is sent to the church in Rome and that Romans 16 is an integral part of the letter to the Romans.

73   Ng, 'Phoebe as *Prostatis*', 6–9.

74   Harland, *Associations, Synagogues and Congregations*, 97.

Most scholars who agree that Phoebe's role included benefaction assume this involved hospitality.[75] Her benefaction could be compared to that of Junia Theodora, who welcomed Lycian travellers and citizens in her own house and looked after their interests.[76] Unlike Junia, who operated in a civic or federal capacity within a particular ethnic group, Phoebe acted as a patron to many individuals, presumably saints, as Paul claims that she 'has been a patron of many and myself also' (προστάτις πολλῶν ἐγενήθη καὶ ἐμοῦ αὐτοῦ; Rom. 16.2). She may have been 'a host to many and her sphere of influence was the church in Cenchreae in whose service she operated, possibly as her home'.[77]

The recipients of her patronage were 'many' (πολλῶν). They could have been people who were financially supported by her, or used her contacts and influence on their behalf. If Phoebe's patronage is limited to the church of Cenchreae, Paul would have mentioned it more clearly as the προστάτις of the church. 'Many' implies that those who benefited from her patronage were uncountable. Paul himself was also the recipient of patronage which was expressed by a double pronoun καὶ ἐμοῦ αὐτοῦ, emphasising, perhaps, her patronage to his missionary work. As described above, the mutual obligation between Phoebe and Paul is significant.

The specific situations in which Phoebe extended patronage to others is unknown, but it can be assumed that hospitality is the main issue under consideration. Although Phoebe might have been noted simply for her hospitality, like other women associates in Pauline communities, I doubt whether Paul used the term προστάτις just to refer to her hospitable character. It could be assumed that Phoebe played a substantial role in the community that was significant, noteworthy, and in need of reciprocation. Phoebe could have supplied 'aid to others, especially foreigners, providing housing and financial aid and representing their interests before local authorities'.[78] Thus we find a mixture of many potential roles undertaken by a patroness, including formal, legal, and social expectations. As Fiorenza rightly affirms:

> The well-to-do converts to Christianity must have expected to exercise the influence of a patron in the early Christian community. Christians such as Phoebe acted as benefactors for individual Christians and the whole church. In dealings with the government or the courts they represented the whole community. With their network of connections, friendships with well placed persons, and public influence, such benefactions eased the social life of other Christians in Greco-Roman society.[79]

75   Schreiner, *Romans*, 788; Ng, 'Phoebe as *Prostatis*', 12.

76   See above, 3.4. See also Cohick, *Women in the World of the Earliest Christians*, 301–307.

77   Winter, *Roman Wives*, 195. Byrne suggests that through her ministry of hospitality she earned recognition among her own community and among many other believers passing through. See B. Byrne, *Romans* (Sacra Pagina Series 6; Collegeville: Liturgical, 1996), 448.

78   Moo, *Romans*, 916. Benefaction did not only include financial help, but also allowed clients to access social and economic resources. See Whelan, 'Amica Pauli', 84. *Contra* Ng, 'Phoebe as *Prostatis*', 9 (who suggests that Paul did not depend on Phoebe for monetary benefits only).

79   Fiorenza, 'Missionaries, Apostles', 426.

The preceding study showed that Phoebe's description as προστάτις is unique since she is the only woman in the New Testament holding the title. It is also significant in respect to her role as a benefactor. The term προστάτις should be understood as 'benefactor' instead of 'helper' or 'president'. The notion of reciprocity is explicit in Paul's request on her behalf, and it can be assumed that Phoebe is probably an influential and a relatively wealthy person. Because she is presented as the προστάτις 'of many and of myself (Paul) as well' (v. 2), and not specifically as προστάτις of the church, the emphasis falls on her role as a patron or benefactor, a role that reinforces her position as διάκονος. What was Paul's intention in recommending Phoebe to the Romans? Were there any hidden motives such as patronage for the Spanish mission? This will be the focus of discussion in the following section.

4.2.3. Expected role: patronage in the Spanish mission?

Although Phoebe's role in Rome cannot be clearly reconstructed from Paul's recommendation alone, Jewett correlates the role of Phoebe to her patronage for the Spanish mission on account of the background of Spain and Paul's desire to visit Spain.[80] He considers that the request in 16.2b (παραστῆτε αὐτῇ ἐν ᾧ ἂν ὑμῶν χρῄζῃ πράγματι) is important in determining Phoebe's role. 'The "matter" is her missionary patronage, which she has provided for many others and now is providing for Paul, and this help is what Paul requests from the Roman congregations.'[81]

Though Jewett aims to prove that the Spanish mission is the real purpose of the letter to the Romans, I think the letter has quite various purposes in view.[82] That the cultural, linguistic, and political contexts of Spain caused a barrier to begin the mission is unpersuasive when compared with Paul's general missionary strategy. As Barclay rightly suggests, 'As a travelling artisan, he had learned to make his way in many different cities, and, as an "apostle to the Gentiles" it is hard to imagine that he had *always* depended on local synagogue contacts (however Acts may portray matters).'[83] The letter of recommendation for Phoebe has a similar style to the recommendation letters among the papyri and literary collections.[84] The letters were carried with the individuals on their

---

80   Jewett, *Romans,* 74–91, 941–48. See also Jewett, 'Paul, Phoebe, and the Spanish Mission', 142–61. Jewett argues that Romans is an 'ambassadorial letter'; the 'theological argumentation' and the 'ethical admonitions' in the epistle are only present to seek support from the believers in Rome for the Spanish mission. See also Kümmel, *Introduction to the New Testament,* 305–307; P. Stuhlmacher, 'The Theme of Romans', in K. P. Donfried (ed.), *The Romans Debate* (Peabody: Hendrickson, 1991), 333–45.

81   Jewett, *Romans,* 90.

82   J. D. G Dunn, 'Romans', in *DPL* (Downers Grove: IVP, 1993), 838–46, at 839, 840; Käsemann also considers the Spanish mission as one of the main purposes of the letter, Käsemann, *Romans,* 398. See also Wedderburn, *Reasons for Romans,* 97–102.

83   J. M. G. Barclay, 'Is it Good News that God is Impartial? A Response to Robert Jewett, Romans: A Commentary', *JSNT* 31 (2008), 89–111, at 94, 95. (Italics as given in the article.)

84   Kim, *Greek Letter of Recommendation,* 7. See also Gamble, *Textual History,* 84. The three similar features are: the person introduced by name; a brief statement of the qualifications or

travel but the purpose of the journey is not stated.[85] The favour requested in the letters is usually general.[86] Although most of the letters share common characteristics, there are peculiar forms for each letter.

Jewett's analysis of v. 2 relates the two ἵνα and γάρ clauses to find the purpose of recommendation; this seems to be unwarranted because the two clauses have different purposes in view. Romans 16.2 (a, b) is a ἵνα clause introducing the purpose of the recommendation: 'that you may receive her in the Lord in a manner worthy of the saints, and help her in whatever matter she may need from you', whereas v. 2c begins with καὶ γάρ: 'for she has been a patron of many as well as of myself', and re-emphasises her credentials.

Jewett's translation of the expression ἐν ᾧ ἂν ὑμῶν χρῄζῃ πράγματι ('she might need in the matter') is incorrect because πρᾶγμα cannot be translated as 'the matter'. ἐν ᾧ ἂν ὑμῶν χρῄζῃ πράγματι is an indefinite clause used with the subjunctive and there is no definite article used in order to specify a particular thing.[87] The word πρᾶγμα is used eleven times in the New Testament, of which four are in the Pauline letters.[88] πρᾶγμα used without referring to a specific matter occurs only once in the Pauline letters (Rom. 16.2). πρᾶγμα is generally used in the sense of 'matter', 'thing', or 'affair'.[89] It could also have a sense of 'an open ended request for aid' in view of the

credentials of the person, followed by reference to the relationship between the parties and other background information; and a request on behalf of the person recommended. The request clause consists of ἵνα or ὅπως – purpose clause and a γάρ causal clause. See Kim, *Greek Letter of Recommendation*, 64; cf. recommendation letters in Phil. 4.2, 3; 1 Cor. 16.15-18; 1 Thess. 5.12-13a; Philemon 10–17. The request formula has a resemblance in terminology with that of the letters of recommendation. The different forms of the verbs δεχέσθαι and χρῄζειν are also used in the common letters. See Keyes, 'Greek Letter of Introduction', 41.

85   S. R. Llewelyn, 'The Christian Letters of Recommendation', *NewDocs*, 8.170.

86   Keyes, 'Greek Letter of Introduction', 40. 'To assist in whatever matter' is a general way of asking a favour (P. Cairo Zen 59101, 59192, 59284, P.S.I. 8, 969, P. Oxy. 787, P. Giss. 71; P. Giss. 88). See also; Kim, *Recommendation*, 72. The reasons why the recipient should do the favours requested is also not given in the letters, unless there were close relations with the writer or the bearer of the letter (e.g. P. Oxy. 1064, P. Flor. 2, P. Giss. 71).

87   The different translations of v. 2b do not give the meaning of πρᾶγμα precisely, but leave it with an indefinite meaning. Examples include: 'and help her in whatever she may require from you' (NRSV, RSV); cf. (REB); (NKJV); (JB); (NEB). I prefer the following translation of v. 2b: 'and help her in whatever matter she may need from you'.

88   W. F. Moulton and A. S. Geden, *A Concordance to the New Testament*, I. H. Marshall (ed.) (Edinburgh: T&T Clark, 2002), 926. Paul's references to πρᾶγμα are: Rom. 16.2 whatever matter (ἐν ᾧ ἂν χρῄζῃ πράγματι); 1 Cor. 6.1; lawsuit (τις ὑμῶν πρᾶγμα ἔχων); 2 Cor. 7.11 this very thing (τῷ πράγματι); 1 Thess. 4.6 this matter (τῷ πράγματι). Πρᾶγμα as used in 1 Corinthians refers to a lawsuit or dispute with a fellow brother as is clear from the context, whereas the other two (1 Thess. 4.6; 2 Cor. 7.11) are used with a definite article. See also Barclay, 'Is it Good News that God is Impartial?', 95, 96.

89   *BDAG*, 858, 859; *MM*, 532; G. Friedrich (ed.), 'πρᾶγμα', *TDNT* 6, 638–40. Examples in the papyri include P. Oxy. VI (ordinary meaning – an action or deed); P. Ryl. II, P. Oxy. IX (vaguer meaning – a matter or affair); P. Ryl. II, P. Strass. I (lawsuit cf. 1 Cor. 6.1); P. Oxy. IV (weaker sense of trouble); Chrest. I (business, trade).

expression ᾧ ἂν ὑμῶν χρῄζῃ.[90] Although Jewett suggests that πρᾶγμα has a vague meaning, it seems that he wants to attach a specific meaning to it; this is an unjustifiable hermeneutical choice.[91] The indefinite use of πρᾶγμα may have meant that in different matters Phoebe could stand in need of the help of the Romans and in all such matters they need to assist her.[92] Therefore, Paul's request on Phoebe's behalf could imply to the Romans that she was worthy of their assistance in carrying out a number of important tasks.

4.2.4. Relation of reciprocity

The underlying implication in the passage concerns reciprocity. An element of reciprocity is precipitated to a notable degree between Paul and Phoebe, and Paul wants to extend this to the relationship between Phoebe and the Roman church. The way Paul presents Phoebe to the Romans is significant in many respects, but especially when one is aware of the implicit reciprocity between the two. I have described some of the key ideas in the preceding sections, and my next task is to present the most significant aspect of the relationship between Paul and Phoebe: mutuality. Paul wants to present the concept of mutuality to the Romans, but it should not be misunderstood as simple equality, inferiority, or superiority. Reciprocal relationships can be seen in the structure of the passage, in the sibling relationship, and in the request for welcome and assistance.

4.2.4.1. Structure of the passage
There is a degree of mutuality evident in the structure of Rom. 16.1-2:

a. What Phoebe has done for others:
   v. 1 οὖσαν διάκονον τῆς ἐκκλησίας τῆς ἐν Κεγχρεαῖς
b. What the Romans have to do for her:
   v. 2a προσδέξησθε ἐν κυρίῳ ἀξίως τῶν ἁγίων καὶ παραστῆτε αὐτῇ ἐν
   ᾧ ἂν ὑμῶν χρῄζῃ πράγματι
a'. What Phoebe has done for others:
   v. 2b προστάτις πολλῶν ἐγενήθη καὶ ἐμοῦ αὐτοῦ

Structure a + a' shows the relationship between Paul and Phoebe, and also between Phoebe and others. Next, (a + a') + b calls for a pattern of mutuality between Phoebe and the believers in Rome. What Paul and the others have received from Phoebe is worth giving back to her. Whatever Phoebe's help looks like, the Romans are expected to reciprocate. It could be inferred that Paul's depiction of Phoebe as 'our sister' has implications for the believers in Rome. It is also possible to think that the Romans could have received Phoebe's help as a προστάτις. By expressing this in such general terms Paul includes a wide circle of beneficiaries.

90   Kim, *Greek Letter of Recommendation*, 133.
91   Jewett, *Romans*, 946.
92   Cranfield, *Romans*, 2.782; Moo, *Romans*, 915; Käsemann, *Romans*, 411.

4.2.4.2. Sibling relationship (ἀδελφὴν ἡμῶν)

Paul introduces Phoebe to the Romans as 'our sister' ἀδελφὴν ἡμῶν (v. 1). The use of the feminine ἀδελφή in contrast to masculine ἀδελφός in Phoebe's recommendation is worth noting. The designation of a female Christian as 'sister' seems to have been a distinct feature of Christianity (1 Cor. 7.15; 9.5; Philemon 2; Jas. 2.15).[93] The reference to Phoebe as 'our sister' shows her membership in the Christian community: 'It carries the nuance of her solidarity with Paul as well as with all other Christians in Rome and elsewhere.'[94] Dunn indicates that ἡμῶν denotes a universal meaning: the concept of international brotherhood and sisterhood or the role of Phoebe in relation to the churches as a whole.[95] However, Aasgaard points out that the sibling metaphor used in Phoebe's case is associated with particular status and authority; the responsibility includes both internal and external affairs: a role in the church and involvement in the proclamation of Christ to outsiders.[96]

4.2.4.3. Reciprocity in hospitality and assistance

The purpose of the recommendation is stated with a ἵνα clause to welcome Phoebe with full hospitality and to provide her with whatever she needs (v. 2). How is reciprocity attached to these requests? How is Paul emphasising Phoebe's action for others, in order to prove that she is worthy of receiving it back?

The first purpose of recommendation is stated in the expression: αὐτὴν προσδέξησθε ἐν κυρίῳ ἀξίως τῶν ἁγίων. There are differing views among scholars regarding προσδέξησθε. On the one hand, it indicates a general way of showing hospitality, but on the other hand, the welcome has some relation to her ecclesiastical position because of the use of the phrases ἐν κυρίῳ and ἀξίως τῶν ἁγίων. Käsemann thinks 'welcome' may be meant in the sense of offering her lodging and help in a 'secular way'.[97] Cranfield suggests that the expression has some significance in relation to her role in the church since the phrase 'in the Lord' was added to it.[98] In secular letters of recommendation

---

93   Dunn, *Romans 9–16*, 886. There are also examples in *Ign. Pol.* 5.1; *2 Clem.*12.5; 19.1; 20. 2; *Herm.* 2.2.3; 2.3. The Papyri letters of recommendation (PSI III 208, PSI IX 1041, P. Alex. 29, P. Oxy. XXXVI 2785, SB X 10255, SB III 7269, P. Oxy. VIII 1162, SB XVI 12304, and P. Oxy. LVI 3857) also use familial languages like 'sister', 'brother', daughter, catechumen, etc. in introducing the person who is travelling. The familial titles imply the Christian context of the letters with ecclesiastical connotations. See Llewelyn, *NewDocs*, 6.171.

94   Jewett, 'Paul, Phoebe and the Spanish Mission', 148.

95   Dunn, *Romans 9–16*, 886.

96   Aasgaard, *'My Beloved Brothers and Sisters!'*, 297–98. The person's sibling status appears to be related to their roles as missionary co-workers. Cf. 1 Cor. 1.1; 2 Cor. 1.1; Philemon 1; 1 Thess. 3.2; 2 Cor. 2.12f.; Phil. 2.25: Sosthenes, Timothy, Titus, Epaphroditus are Paul's messengers and co-workers in his missionary endeavours.

97   Käsemann, *Romans*, 411.

98   Cranfield, *Romans*, 2.781–82. Cranfield suggests the expression 'worthy of the saints' is superfluous. But ἄξιος was an important term used in the Roman government to demonstrate honour, rank, office, esteem, and worthiness. Jewett thinks the meaning is the same as in Phil.

προσδέξεσθαι is used with respect to the hospitality given to the bearer of the letter.[99] The phrase 'worthy of the saints' throws light on the fact that she should be welcomed as a fellow believer (cf. Rom. 12.13).

Earlier Paul exhorted the Romans to welcome (προσλαμβάνεσθε) one another 'just as Christ welcomed (προσελάβετο) you, to the glory of God' (Rom. 15.7). The motive for such a welcome is that, as fellow Christians, the recipients should welcome others who belong to Christ.[100] Welcoming or receiving also implies extending hospitality and fellowship. Hospitality has a significant place in the Christian community. προσδέχομαι often appears in the letters of recommendation; however, Paul adds the phrases ἐν κυρίῳ and ἀξίως τῶν ἁγίων in his requests to welcome Phoebe.

The second request on Phoebe's behalf is to 'help her in whatever matter she may need from you'. As noted above it has a sense of 'an open-ended request for aid' in view of the expression ἐν ᾧ ἂν ὑμῶν χρῄζῃ.[101] I think that Paul's requests for favours are based on her role as προστάτις for many and for Paul; in Paul's recommendation of Phoebe, her work for others is given as substantial evidence of Phoebe's entitlement to receive favours from the Romans. Therefore, the contribution for Phoebe is not futile but is intended to repay or reciprocate her contributions to a wider community and Paul.

To conclude, Phoebe plays an important leadership role in the church of Cenchreae as the διάκονος. In addition, her contribution to Paul and many others is observed in the title προστάτις. Her presumed purpose to the Roman community should not be limited to the Spanish mission since πρᾶγμα is an indefinite matter. The chiasm of the passage is woven in such a way to show the significance of reciprocity between the parties. Her action for others needs to be reciprocated, and so she should be granted hospitality and assistance in whatever matter she needs. This gives an insight into Phoebe's contribution to the Pauline mission, and Paul's presentation of her reveals his desire to reciprocate her actions.

4.3 The role of Prisca (Rom. 16.3, 4, 5)

Ἀσπάσασθε Πρίσκαν καὶ Ἀκύλαν τοὺς συνεργούς μου ἐν Χριστῷ Ἰησοῦ, οἵτινες ὑπὲρ τῆς ψυχῆς μου τὸν ἑαυτῶν τράχηλον ὑπέθηκαν, οἷς οὐκ ἐγὼ μόνος εὐχαριστῶ ἀλλὰ καὶ πᾶσαι αἱ ἐκκλησίαι τῶς ἐθνῶν, καὶ τὴν κατ' οἶκον αὐτῶν ἐκκλησίαν.

2.29, concerning welcoming back Epaphroditus; Jewett, *Romans*, 945; Jewett, 'Spanish Mission', 150. It probably has the connotation that Phoebe is to be welcomed with honour. Goodspeed suggests that since Phoebe is a person of high social status, welcoming her has the intention of providing her with good housing: Goodspeed, 'Phoebe's Letter of Introduction', 56.

99   The prepositional phrase used with προσδέχομαι reminds the recipients to offer 'proper hospitality to the recommended person' (P. Oxy. LXI 3857); see, S. R. Llewelyn, *NewDocs*, 8.171.

100   Moo, *Romans*, 915; Fitzmyer, *Romans*, 731.

101   See above 4.2.3.

> Greet Prisca and Aquila, who work with me in Christ Jesus, and who risked their necks for my life, to whom not only I give thanks, but also all the churches of the Gentiles. Greet also the church in their house. (NRSV)

Prisca and Aquila[102] were a couple who made a significant contribution to the early Christian mission. Murphy-O'Connor claims that they were 'the most prominent couple involved in the first-century expansion of Christianity'.[103] Paul's greeting in Rom. 16.3, and the fact that Prisca and Aquila come first in the long list of greetings, shows their acquaintance with him and their significant contribution to his missionary enterprise (Rom. 16.3-6). There are a number of noteworthy points regarding the greeting to Prisca[104] and Aquila: first, Prisca's name is mentioned before Aquila's; second, the greeting is combined with a cluster of appreciations (descriptive phrases) and thanks from Paul and a large group of Gentile churches; third, it is the longest greeting in the list and shows their prominence among the other people in the greetings; finally, the greetings are directed to them and the church in their house. These features signify the zealous nature of their involvement in mission. Moreover, the rhetoric Paul employs to describe this couple is also worth exploring.

The account in Acts 18 gives a picture of their background and relationship to Paul. It is possible to assume that they had been leaders in Rome and actively involved in mission prior to Paul's arrival at Corinth. Due to the edict of Claudius in 49 CE, by which Jews had been expelled from Rome, they moved to Corinth and based their business and ministry in Corinth (Acts 18.2). Paul, while on his second missionary journey, met them at Corinth and stayed with them by virtue of sharing the same vocation: tent-making (Acts 18.3). After eighteen months of their stay at Corinth, they moved to Ephesus with Paul (Acts 18.18-19). It was from Ephesus that Paul sents greetings from Prisca and Aquila's church to the church in Corinth (1 Cor. 16.8, 19). By the time Romans was written they may have returned to Rome after the lapse of the edict in 54 CE. Later, they were again mentioned in Ephesus (2 Tim. 4.19).

This section attempts to deduce Prisca's role and her contribution to the Pauline mission, and also to analyse the rhetorical method Paul uses while speaking about her and Aquila. Was her role related to her higher social

---

102   Prisca and Aquila are mentioned as a pair in the New Testament. The diminutive form Priscilla is used in Acts (Acts 18.2, 3; and 18.18, 26), whereas the proper form 'Prisca' is used in the Pauline epistles. Although Aquila was described in Acts as a certain Jew, a man of Pontus by race, we are told nothing about Prisca's origins. Both names are Latin and there is no clue about their ethnic origin. See Cranfield, *Romans*, 374; J. M. Bassler, 'Prisca/Priscilla', in C. Meyers (ed.), *Women in Scripture* (Grand Rapids: Eerdmans, 2000), 136, 137, at 136.

103   Jerome Murphy-O'Connor, 'Prisca and Aquila: Travelling Tentmakers and Church Builders', *BRev* 8 (1992), 40–51, at 40. See also F. Gillman, who suggests Prisca as 'one of the cosmopolitan and well-travelled women mentioned in the New Testament tradition'; F. M. Gillman, *Women Who Knew Paul* (Zacchaeus Studies: New Testament; Collegeville: Liturgical Press, 1992), 49.

104   Her name was not used by slaves and indicates that she was probably freeborn. See P. Lampe, 'Prisca', *ABD* 5, 467–68, at 467.

status? What type of leadership did she hold (she is mentioned as συνεργός as well as one who risked her life for Paul)? What is the reason for the Gentile churches' indebtedness to her? Why was it important for Paul to greet the church in her house? How was she engaged in ministry with her husband Aquila? These issues will be discussed in four sections: Prisca's social status; her contribution to the Pauline mission; the relational dynamic of the passage; and the rhetorical analysis of the passage.

4.3.1. Social status

In our journey to discover Prisca's (and Aquila's) social status we deal with two important issues: first, whether she belonged to an affluent group; and second, what was Paul's reason for putting Prisca's name before her husband's.

Prisca and Aquila's social status has been widely debated. Some scholars have suggested that they are of 'relatively high status because of their patronage of Paul, frequent travels, and the capacity to own property in Corinth, Ephesus, and Rome, large enough for house churches'.[105] However, other scholars do not equate Aquila's trade and travel with high social status.[106] According to Meggitt, the criteria suggesting high social status and significance (hospitality and references to travel) 'are not sustainable grounds for regarding an individual as wealthy'; he concludes that they did not differ in their economic status from the rest of the church members or society.[107] As Meggitt observes, a person's economic status is not necessarily related to their desire to be hospitable or their ability to travel. Paul's description about the couple also gives no clue regarding their social status, except that they were acquaintances and were involved in ministry. (In Acts 18.3 there is evidence suggesting their trade involved tent-making.) However, it is not plausible to

---

105   Jewett, *Romans*, 956; Theissen, *Social Setting of Pauline Christianity*, 90; Meeks, *First Urban Christians*, 59.

106   Lampe, *From Paul to Valentinus*, 195. Lampe suggests a lower status is possible because of Aquila's trade and because the cost of travel was also affordable to lower-class people. See Lampe, *Paul to Valentinus*, 192–95. However, Hock suggests that for Paul, tent-making did not mean great wealth, reputation nor prestige (1 Cor. 4.11-13; cf. 2 Cor. 11.7; cf. 1 Cor. 9.18f.) but μόχθος (1 Thess. 2.9). See R. F. Hock, 'Paul's Tent-making and the Problem of his Social Class', *JBL* 97 (1978), 555–74, at 555–64. *Contra* Hock, Jewett suggests that this argument is not convincing and fails to explain all the evidence, since he suggests: 'Prisca's house in the elegant Aventine quarter of Rome and that the names of Prisca and possibly also Aquila were associated with the noble Acilius family indicates a higher social niveau.' Jewett, *Romans*, 956, 957. *Contra* Jewett, Lampe displays high-level scepticism regarding this opinion, Lampe, 'Prisca', 468.

107   Meggitt, *Paul, Poverty and Survival*, 134, 135. He argues that hospitality is not indicative of elite status, since the desire of one to give to others is a matter of fact rather than wealth. The hospitality practised in antiquity does not signify the economic status of an individual. For example, the poor market gardener (*hortulanus*) in Apuleius' *Metamorphoses* extended hospitality to a traveller in spite of his poor condition to afford the visitor. See Ovid, *Metamorphoses* 8.631 (Philemon and Baucus). In addition, people travelled for different reasons: business, work, health, religion, sport, tourism, etc. The means of travel also vary from expensive to inexpensive, and travel per se cannot indicate status in the first-century world. See Meggitt, *Paul, Poverty and Survival*, 132–34.

assume they had high social status and belonged to an affluent group, and neither is it plausible to assign them to much lower social status. It seems that they were relatively wealthy and influential in the Christian community because of their support for Paul and their active roles in the house churches to which they had travelled.[108]

Out of the six references to the couple in the New Testament, Prisca is named first in four of them (Acts 18.18, 26; 2 Tim. 4.19; and Rom. 16.3), whereas Aquila is mentioned first in Acts 18.2 and 1 Cor. 16.19.[109] It is rare for a woman's name in a married couple to come first, and this is the only case of it occurring in the Pauline epistles. It is possible that Prisca belonged to a higher social status and was more prominent and knowledgeable than Aquila (Rom. 16.3; 2 Tim. 4.19; Acts 18.18, 26).[110]

It seems that Prisca, rather than Aquila, might have been Paul's sponsor. If so, it would exhibit her partnership in the house church leadership. Winter argues that placing a wife's name ahead of the husband's would indicate that the wife was of a higher rank or social status than him.[111] However, although it is difficult to prove the higher status of Prisca, I assume that her prominence was due to her leadership role in the early Christian missionary movement.[112] I arrive at this conclusion because although the greeting verb is directed at the couple and their church ('Greet Prisca and Aquila ... and the church in their house' [vv. 3, 4]), Prisca's name is given preference.

---

108   L. Gaston, 'Faith in Romans 12 in the Light of the Common Life of the Roman Church', in J. V. Hills (ed.), *Common Life in the Early Church: Essays Honoring Graydon F. Snyder* (Harrisburg: Trinity Press International, 1998), 258–64, at 260. See also P. Oakes, *Reading Romans in Pompeii: Paul's Letter at Ground Level* (Minneapolis: Fortress Press, 2009), 76–77.

109   Kurek-Chomycz lists the textual variants and suggests, 'It cannot be excluded that some of the textual variants in the passages mentioning Prisca and Aquila in Pauline Epistles, ... may be understood as intended to diminish the importance of Prisca.' D. A. K-Chomycz, 'Is there an "Anti-Priscan" Tendency in the Manuscripts? Some Textual Problems with Prisca and Aquila', *JBL* 125 (2006), 107–28, at 128.

110   Meeks, *The First Urban Christians*, 59; Dunn, *Romans 9–16*, 892: Prisca was the more dominant of the two or of higher social status and she may have provided the financial resources for the business. Other opinions are that Prisca may be more gifted than Aquila, the one who brought most money into the marriage, or the one who was most contributing to their 'home-based' ministry. Fiorenza finds the reason for her prominence may be her higher status, or her prominence in mission or both. Fiorenza, 'Missionaries, Apostles, Co-workers', 428.

111   'In the Roman colony of Pompeii women alongside their husbands were actively supporting candidates for civic office', Winter, *Roman Wives*, 180. MacMullen comments that 'it is also common to have a woman's name written ahead of man's ... an inversion of status explained by neither of the parties having any sense of status between them at all, or by the woman being free or freed, the man freed or slave'. See MacMullen, 'Women in Public in the Roman Empire', 209. See above chapter 3, section 3.3

112   *Contra* Jewett, who asserts it is less plausible to suggest she was more active in house church leadership. Jewett, *Romans*, 955. Murphy-O'Connor suggests Prisca's prominence in the church; see Murphy-O'Connor, 'Prisca and Aquila', 42.

4.3.2. Contribution to the Pauline mission

The greetings are given due to the couple's devotion to the ministry and Paul himself. They are portrayed as his fellow workers, and are mentioned as having risked their lives for Paul. Both these descriptions require further elaboration.

4.3.2.1. Co-worker (συνεργός)

Paul begins the greetings in Rom. 16 by designating Prisca and Aquila as συνεργοί μου (my co-workers, v. 3). The personal pronoun 'μου' emphasises their relationship to Paul and is more significant than the collective ἡμῶν. The phrase 'my co-workers in Christ Jesus' seems to imply that they worked as colleagues with Paul. Additionally, they were mentioned accompanying Paul in Corinth and Ephesus, where they had resided when they were expelled from Rome due to Claudius' edict. They may have gone back to Rome by the time Paul composed the epistle to the Romans, and he perhaps lists them as the first of his acquaintances because they were early supporters of his ministry.

Paul used this title of his associates in Christian ministry elsewhere: Urbanus (Rom. 16.9), Timothy (Rom. 16.21), Titus (2 Cor. 8.23), Epaphroditus (Phil. 2.25), Euodia and Syntyche (Phil. 4.3), Philemon (Philemon 1), and others such as Tychycus, Onesimus, Aristarchus, Mark and Justus (Col. 4.11), Mark, Aristarchus, Demas and Luke (Philemon 24), and Paul himself (1 Cor. 3.9; 2 Cor. 1.24). According to Ollrog, συνεργός is a distinctive Pauline expression to denote 'one who labours together with Paul as commissioned by God at the shared work of mission preaching'.[113] He analyses the word in the light of its frequent use in the Pauline letters. It includes: (1) partaking in the divine commission (1 Cor. 3.5-9; 2 Cor. 1.24; 6.1-4; 1 Thess. 3.2); (2) working together with Paul in the activities of the congregation (1 Cor. 3.5-9; 15.4-8; 16.10; 2 Cor. 1.24; 6.1; 8.17, 23; Phil. 2.30; 1 Thess. 3.2); and (3) proclamation of the word (in close association with διάκονος and κοπιᾶν; 1 Cor. 3.8-9; 16.15-18; 1 Thess. 3.2). Jewett also suggests that this usage is unique to Paul as it is not found in any other early or later church writings. This reveals a 'distinctive Pauline approach to missional collegiality, referring both to himself and to others with this egalitarian term'.[114] Ellis argues that συνεργός is not used of believers in general, and that the qualifiers 'with God', 'in Christ', 'of Paul', and 'for the Christian community' indicate 'whose work it is, the sphere and company in which it is done, and those who receive its benefits'.[115]

As a co-worker with Paul, Prisca probably functioned as a colleague in his mission. Notably, Prisca is not denied the title συνεργός because she is a woman. Prisca may have been known as Paul's associate for undertaking tasks similar to him and those of Paul's male co-workers. Although she worked in

---

113   Ollrog, *Paulus und seine Mitarbeiter*, 67; see also Dunn, *Romans 9–16*, 892.

114   Jewett, *Romans*, 957.

115   Ellis, 'Paul and his Co-workers', 440. They are co-workers 'with God' (1 Cor. 3.9; 1 Thess. 3.2); in Christ (Rom. 16.3, 9; cf. 1 Thess. 3.2); of Paul (Rom. 16.21; Phil 2.25; Philemon 24); and for the Christian community (2 Cor. 8.23; cf. 1 Cor. 3.9; 2 Cor. 1.24). In 1 Cor. 3.9; 2 Cor. 1.24; 8.23, the co-workers are implicitly distinguished from the congregation.

friendly association with Paul, most of her work was independent of him.[116] It is evident from Acts that they both shared the same occupation (tent-making), but it is obvious that συνεργός referred to their effort and contribution to the Pauline mission. The phrase ἐν Χριστῷ Ἰησοῦ highlights their endeavour in the Christian mission.

4.3.2.2. Risking lives (τράχηλον ὑπέθηκαν)

The figurative language 'risked their lives for my sake' denotes some sort of sacrifice on their part to save Paul's life from a dangerous situation. The details of how they risked their lives (necks) is unknown, but there is a widely accepted view that they intervened to rescue Paul during the Ephesian crisis referred to in 1 Cor. 15.32 (cf. Acts 19.23-31). Jewett suggests that their ability to save Paul's life from a dangerous situation shows their 'patronal capacity', and it is supposed that they used their social status to negotiate with the authorities for Paul's release.[117] The expression used is a colloquialism for 'risking execution', and the particular verbal expression alludes explicitly to death by decapitation.[118] Although the phrase is used symbolically, it is possible that Prisca and Aquila might have risked their lives for Paul (cf. Acts 18.12-17; 19.23-41; 1 Cor. 15.32; 2 Cor. 1.8-10; 6.5; 8.2; 11.23).[119] Therefore, it seems that they acted as patrons or benefactors for Paul at some point (perhaps in Ephesus, cf. 1 Cor. 15.32), and with some amount of personal risk, to ensure his safety.

4.3.2.3. House church

It is interesting to note that the second object of the main verb 'greet' is 'the church in their house'. The subordinate clauses such as 'who risked their own necks for my life, to whom not only I give thanks, but also all the churches of the Gentiles' are sandwiched between the two objects of the main verb. The word ἐκκλησία means 'assembly' and denotes 'political as well as religious groups'.[120] In this context, it denotes religious groups.

Prisca and Aquila established and supported a church in their house wherever they lived. There is no clear evidence for the existence of special buildings used for churches until the third century CE.[121] Christians would have met in private houses.[122]

---

116   Ellis, 'Paul and his Co-workers', 439.
117   Jewett, *Romans*, 957. See discussion on the social status of Prisca, above 4.3.1.
118   Jewett, *Romans*, 957, 958. The form of quick execution was normally the privilege of Roman citizens, avoiding crucifixion, strangulation, burning at the stake, etc.
119   Dunn, *Romans 9–16*, 892.
120   Jewett, *Romans*, 958. Paul used 'church of God' (1 Cor. 1.2; 10.32; 11.22; 15.9; 2 Cor. 1.1; Gal. 1.13) and 'churches of God' (1 Cor. 11.16; 1 Thess. 2.14), which he did not use in Romans; however ἐκκλησία was used in order to denote the Christian congregations in Cenchreae (16.1), in Corinth (16.23), and in all other locations (16.4, 16).
121   J. M. Peterson, 'House-churches in Rome', *VC* 23 (1969), 264–72; Fiorenza, *In Memory of Her,* 179.
122   W. Sanday and A. C. Headlam, *A Critical and Exegetical Commentary to the Epistle to the Romans* (Edinburgh: T&T Clark, 1902), 420; Ziesler, *Romans,* 351.

The house church 'provided space for the preaching of the word, for worship, as well as for social and eucharistic table sharing'.[123] Women played an important role in founding and supporting the house churches.[124] Paul greeted Aphia 'our sister', who, together with Philemon and Archippus, was a leader of a house church in Colossae (Philemon 2). Prisca and Aquila were mentioned twice with 'the church in their house' (Rom. 16.4; 1 Cor. 16.19). Similarly, the epistle to the Colossians also highlights Nympha of Laodicea and 'the church in her house' (Col. 4.15). Women's involvement in the Roman church is evident from the number of women greeted (one-third of the entire greeting list) in the closing of the letter (Rom. 16.1-16).[125]

Prisca worked for the establishment and support of the house churches with her husband Aquila. Their tent-making trade helped them to support their ministry, effectively becoming financially independent from local churches.[126] Although they were Paul's co-workers, they worked independently.[127] Their house churches in Corinth, Ephesus, and possibly Rome, were centres for mission activity, where, it seems, Prisca was proficient in teaching (Acts 18.24-26).[128]

---

123   Fiorenza, *In Memory of Her*, 175. Fiorenza argues that the house churches presuppose that some wealthy citizens have joined the Christian movement, who could provide space and economic resources for the community. On the contrary, Meggitt suggests that wealth is not a deciding factor in antiquity for hospitality. See Meggitt, *Paul, Poverty and Survival*, 134, 135. See above 4.2.2.2. I think that the women who supported the Christian community with their resources were relatively wealthy.

124   Acts gives evidence that the church of Philippi began with the conversion of the businesswoman Lydia from Thyatira (Acts 16.15). It is possible to assume that women were also involved in the household conversions and house churches, along with men (cf. Acts 10.1ff.; 16.32f.; 18.8f.; 1 Cor. 1.14, 16; 16.15f.; Rom. 16.23). See A. Weiser, 'Der Rolle der Frau in der urchristlichen Mission', in G. Dautzenberg (ed.), *Die Frau im Urchristentum* (QD, 95; Freiburg: Herder, 1983), 158–81, at 166, 167; Klauck, *Hausgemeinde*; V. Branick, *The House Church in the Writings of Paul* (Wilmington: Michael Glazier, 1989), 58–97; D. C. Verner, *The Household of God: The Social World of the Pastoral Epistles* (SBLDS, 71; Chicago: Scholars Press, 1983), 127–80; Banks, *Paul's Idea*, 118–27; G. Dautzenberg, 'Zur Stellung der Frauen in der paulinischen Gemeinden', in *Die Frau im Urchristentum* (QD, 95; Freiburg: Herder, 1983), 193–221.

125   There are eight women mentioned by name in Romans 16, and two more women, the mother of Rufus and the 'sister' of Nereus, are mentioned in relational terms. Women may be included among the house of Aristobulus and Narcissus, and also among the 'brethren' or 'saints' in Rom. 16.15.

126   Klauck, *Hausgemeinde und Hauskirche*, 21–26; Fiorenza, *In Memory of Her*, 178.

127   Fiorenza suggests that Prisca did not stand under Paul's authority. Fiorenza, *In Memory of Her*, 178. 'Standing under his authority' is an unclear picture of Prisca's relationship with Paul, since we cannot see any conflict between their missionary strategies. Their relationship was governed by mutuality and there was also conformity in the mission agendas. The similarity between Paul and the missionary couple were that they had the same trade, supported their missionary activity by themselves, were Jewish Christians, travelled for the cause of mission, and suffered for the cause of the gospel.

128   There is an interpretation that Prisca's teaching role is not an official one, but one that was undertaken in private. See R. Schumacher, 'Aquila und Priscilla', *TGI* 12 (1920), 89–99; Fiorenza, *In Memory of Her*, 202. I suggest that her active leadership in the house church, and her role as co-worker, clearly show that she held the same roles as those of Paul's male co-workers.

The mission strategy of Prisca and Aquila differed from Paul's as they travelled as a pair and gathered converts together in house churches. This was done so that 'they did not divide the apostolic διακονία of the eucharistic table sharing that establishes community and the word that aims at conversion of individuals'.[129]

Furthermore, Prisca and Aquila's house churches shed light on the type of people who gathered to them; they were not just other family members (the *paterfamilias* or *materfamilias*), but were most likely made up of converts from other families. It should be stressed that the church that met at their house was not only made from members of their own household.[130] The gatherings at Prisca and Aquila's seems to be 'the community of Christians regularly meeting in their house, including, in addition to the Christian members of the household or *familia*, other Christians for whom it was convenient to meet for worship in their house'.[131]

House churches played a vital role in the development of the early Christian movement.[132] Whilst being co-workers of Paul, Prisca and Aquila seem to have an independent footing in mission. Prisca's role in the house church could include leadership, which would explain her fervour and significance in the Christian mission.

4.3.3. Mutuality

The greeting formula Paul uses to address Prisca and Aquila (ἀσπάσασθε) is combined with a thanksgiving formula (εὐχαριστῶ) in order to express Paul and the Gentile churches' (πᾶσαι αἱ ἐκκλησίαι τῶν ἐθνῶν) indebtedness. I will now elaborate on the greeting and thanksgiving formulas to explore Prisca and Aquila's involvement in the Christian mission. I will also assess Paul's rhetoric.

4.3.3.1. Greeting: ἀσπάσασθε

As discussed above, Prisca and Aquila had to be honoured and welcomed because they were fellow workers who risked their lives for Paul. The greeting directed to them serves to honour and welcome them and their church.

The second-person plural imperative form ἀσπάσασθε is used for the greeting, and it has some unique characteristics. Paul is not merely sending his own greetings, but is asking his recipients to greet them themselves ('you

---

Osiek identifies that some women taught mixed groups. Osiek, *Woman's Place*, 162. See also R. W. Gehring, *House Church and Mission: The Importance of Household Structures in Early Christianity* (Peabody: Hendrickson, 2004), 216; A. von Harnack, *The Mission and Expansion of Christianity in the First Three Centuries*, J. Moffat (trans.) (New York: Harper, 1962 [1908]), 222.

129   Fiorenza, *In Memory of Her*, 179.

130   Moo, *Romans*, 920.

131   Cranfield, *Romans*, 2.786.

132   See for more discussion, F. V. Wilson, 'The Significance of the Early House Churches', *JBL* 58 (1939), 105–12.

[plural] greet …').[133] In light of this, ἀσπάσασθε cannot be translated as 'I send greetings to …', as suggested by Gamble.[134] His assertion that 'the greeting verb functions here as a surrogate for the first person indicative form' is an unconvincing argument that diminishes the significance of the verb's rendering in the second-person imperative form. Therefore, ἀσπάσασθε is not merely the writer passing his greeting to the individuals mentioned, but rather ἀσπάσασθε asks the recipients to greet them themselves. This type of greeting is not intended as a 'one-off' greeting, but is intended to establish and strengthen a chain of close relationships. It is important to note that this greeting also serves to give recognition to the party being greeted. The recognition underlying the greetings in Romans 16 is a mutual recognition that Paul wants the recipients to carry to one another, including both men and women who toiled for the gospel or himself. In light of this, the greeting can be observed to possess several important functions: (1) it acknowledges the roles of those who are the key figures in the church; (2) it has a commendatory function, calling for mutual honour and recognition; (3) it establishes close relationships between the ones doing the greeting and its recipients, and also between Paul and the recipients.

Paul (group A) asked the believers in Rome (group B) to greet Prisca, Aquila and the church in their house (group C), which works as a direct greeting from group B to group C. This type of greeting is significant since it not only strengthens the relationship between B and C, but also that between A and C, and A and B, thus creating a mutual bond between all parties.

4.3.3.2. Thanksgiving: εὐχαριστῶ

The εὐχαριστῶ formula[135] used to communicate gratitude (Rom. 16.4) to Prisca and Aquila is noteworthy. This formula is found in an imperial inscription at Ephesus;[136] *1. Eph.* III. 961: εὐχαριστῶ σοι, κυρία ̈Αρτεμι ('I give thanks to you, Lady Artemis'). The Pauline method of thanksgiving parallels the thanksgiving of the patron–client system, which reminds us of the reciprocal relations between the parties: 'reciprocity governed the entire gamut of relationships – human and divine in antiquity'.[137]

---

133   ἀσπάσασθε is repeated sixteen times in the pericope (Rom. 16.3-16a). This form shifts to ἀσπάζονται (they greet) in v. 16b.

134   Gamble, *Textual History*, 93; Weima shares a similar view, Weima, *Neglected Endings*, 105, 108.

135   εὐχαριστῶ and εὐχαριστία are Hellenistic words, derived from χάρις, χαρίζομαι, εὐχάριστος, which were not in existence before 300 BCE. See P. Schubert, *Form and Function of the Pauline Thanksgivings* (Berlin: A. Töpelmann, 1939), 121. *BDAG*, 4I5, 416. εὐχαριστῶ carries meanings such as feeling obligated to thank, render, or return thanks. The references in the Pauline literature which express thankfulness to God are Rom. 1.8, 21, 7.25; 14.6; 1 Cor. 1.4, 14; 10.30; 11.24; 14.17, 18; 2 Cor. 1.11; Eph. 1.16; 5.20; Phil. 1.3; Col. 1.3, 12; 3.17; 1 Thess. 1.2; 2.13; 5.18; 2 Thess. 1.3; 2 Thess. 2.13; Philemon 4. See Moulton and Geden, *Concordance to the Greek New Testament*, 440.

136   G. H. R. Horsley, 'Giving Thanks to Artemis', *NewDocs*, 4.127–29, at 128.

137   J. H. Harrison, *Paul's Language of Grace in its Greco-Roman Context* (Tübingen:

Paul has given particular attention to his expression of thanks to Prisca and Aquila. The reason for his indebtedness may be because of at least two factors: for being his fellow workers, and for risking their lives to save his own. Moreover, all the Gentile churches were indebted to Prisca and Aquila. The reason for the Gentile churches' indebtedness is not specified in the passage, but Cranfield suggests that the Gentiles were thankful for saving the life of the 'apostle to the Gentiles'.[138] Jewett suggests that this view may direct the attention to Paul himself, which was against his intention since his aim was to honour Prisca and Aquila, for them to receive the Gentiles' recognition.[139] It is likely that Paul's indebtedness is because of the significance the couple had for the mission in Corinth and Ephesus, both in their own right and by patronising Paul in his mission process. Patronising the mission included devotion, commitment, and financial backing. These might have been the reasons the Gentile churches were to show gratitude to them.[140]

Paul's intention in conveying the Gentiles' thanksgiving to Prisca and Aquila bears significance for the rest of the epistle; the greeting echoes Paul's theme of unity between Jews and Gentiles (Rom. 14.1–15.13), and expresses a sense of mutuality between the two groups described in relation to the Jerusalem offering (Rom. 15.27).[141] Paul highlights this sense of unity and mutuality to the church, and also draws attention to what Prisca and Aquila have done for him personally. Here we can observe Paul's motives in extending the greeting, which is primarily to honour and acknowledge the couple's actions, but also to reciprocate their deeds of benefaction. Paul may also have been implying that in order to gain universal recognition and thanks from others, one should contribute to his mission through risk-taking and provision of aid.[142]

Moreover, it is striking that the praise and thanksgiving come from 'all the churches of the Gentiles'. It paints an image of churches from many different regions honouring the missionary couple with one voice. This implies Prisca and Aquila's influence and ability to win the recognition of all.

Mohr Siebeck, 2003), 320. In the Greco-Roman world, the rendering of honour and gratitude governed human–human as well as divine–human relationships. Schubert identified that one of Paul's purposes of thanksgiving is to honour the churches to which it is addressed and that Paul also gives thanks to God for grace on the house churches (1 Cor. 1.4). He suggests that the thanksgiving in Rom. 16.4 is 'at a colloquial, conversational level'. Schubert, *Form and Function of the Pauline Thanksgivings*, 83. Moreover, Paul's mode of thanksgiving reflects the Greco-Roman thanksgiving conventions. That is, there is a tone of public praise for his converts and co-workers; for example, Phil. 1.3, 5; 2 Cor. 8.16; 1 Thess. 2.13-15; Rom. 16.4. See Harrison, *Paul's Language*, 269.

138   Cranfield, *Romans*, 2.786.
139   Jewett, *Romans*, 958.
140   Ollrog, *Mitarbeiter*, 27; Jewett, *Romans*, 958.
141   Oster argues that τὰ ἔθνη in Rom. 16.4 denotes 'congregational religious culture more than congregational racial character'. R. E. Oster, 'Congregations of the Gentiles (Rom. 16:4): A Culture-Based Ecclesiology in the Letters of Paul', *RestorQuart* 40 (1998), 39–52, at 40.
142   Jewett, *Romans*, 958.

The believers in Rome also joined the thanksgiving, and the image is of a wide group (Paul, the Gentiles' churches, and the Roman church) giving thanks to Prisca and Aquila. This image enhances and strengthens the bond between those who have joined together in expressing their obligation to them. This sort of commendation has an implied agenda of refreshment and the establishment of new relationships, bonds, and friendships. The theme of mutuality is very much implied in the thanksgiving formula.

4.3.4. Rhetorical analysis

Paul presents Prisca and Aquila in a significant and rhetorically crucial manner. First of all, they are mentioned as associates of Paul by being described as making a remarkable contribution in their willingness to risk their lives for Paul. Paul then moves on to broaden their sphere of influence to all the churches of the Gentiles, which possibly included the Romans. It also seems to have an echo of Rom. 15.27, where Gentiles are mentioned as partakers of spiritual things. Prisca and Aquila's presentation in the greetings is as follows:

1. Prisca and Aquila were to be greeted by the Romans.
2. Prisca and Aquila were stated to be associates of Paul in Christ, and they risked their lives for him.
3. Paul and all the churches of the Gentiles thanked them.
4. The church in their house was also to be greeted by the Roman believers.

Paul's description of Prisca and Aquila as his associates (συνεργοί μου) who risked their lives for him obviously reveals their relationship with Paul. Paul wanted to give them thanks (εὐχαριστῶ) from himself and from all the Gentile churches. His use of πᾶσαι ('all') is significant as it envisages a wider community showing gratitude to Prisca and Aquila. Why did Paul use this type of implied inclusive language? I assume that he was using it to show that Prisca and Aquila's action benefited the Romans. Paul did not explicitly state that the Romans were on the receiving end of Prisca and Aquila's efforts, but it seems that there is an implied inclusion of the Romans in the phrase 'all the churches of the Gentiles'. Moreover, since the Roman church is predominantly a Gentile church, the Romans might be included in the wider group. At the same time, the role of Prisca and Aquila was not limited to the Romans. In a similar manner to Phoebe's description as the patron of many beneficiaries, Paul is introducing Prisca and Aquila in terms of universal recognition.

It seems as if Paul and all the Gentile churches made one group, and Prisca and Aquila, and their house church, formed another. The first group was indebted to the second because of their actions, and as a result the second group expected to be greeted and thanked. Paul gave reasons why the Romans should greet Prisca and Aquila, and he motivates them to do so. Thus Paul rhetorically created a sense of mutuality by giving instructions to greet, and by describing Prisca and Aquila's actions and association with himself and other churches.

Thus it is clear from the greetings to Prisca (and Aquila) that Prisca played a significant part in the Christian mission. Paul is acknowledging her commitment and accomplishments as his co-worker who was willing to support his ministry at all costs. Moreover, she may have been the leader of the church in her house and involved in teaching and preaching of the word. Her contribution was profound because she was beneficial to all the Gentile churches, which would have included both men and women. She was also gifted in equipping leaders for ministry (e.g. Apollos). Prisca and Aquila's 'missional collegiality' with Paul was remarkable in spite of their different strategies and methods. 'She was obviously a very important, well-travelled missionary and church leader whose work on occasion intersected with that of Paul.'[143]

Paul's presentation of the greeting is significant as it creates mutuality. He told the Roman believers that Prisca had influence in all the Gentile churches and, by implication, theirs too. The greeting formula and the thanksgiving formula highlight the theme of mutuality, which is one of the things that Paul wanted to cultivate in the Roman church.

4.4. The role of Junia (Rom. 16.7)

Ἀσπάσασθε Ἀνδρόνικον καὶ Ἰουνιᾶν τοὺς συγγενεῖς μου καὶ συναιχμαλώτους μου, οἵτινές εἰσιν ἐπίσημοι ἐν τοῖς ἀποστόλοις, οἳ καὶ πρὸ ἐμοῦ γέγοναν ἐν Χριστῷ.

Greet Andronicus and Junia, my relatives who were in prison with me; they are prominent among the apostles, and they were in Christ before I was. (NRSV)

Junia is a controversial figure among the recipients of Paul's greetings in Rom. 16.2-16. The controversy is due to the fact that she is the only woman who is called an 'apostle' in the New Testament. The four descriptive phrases used by Paul are significant to understanding Junia's role: she and Andronicus are συγγενεῖς μου ('my relatives'), συναιχμάλωτοι ('fellow-prisoners'), ἐπίσημοι ἐν τοῖς ἀποστόλοις ('prominent among the apostles') and πρὸ ἐμοῦ γέγοναν ἐν Χριστῷ ('in Christ before me') (16.7). The last two phrases used for Junia (and Andronicus) are especially significant, since such phrases are seldom used to describe Paul's co-workers. However, the discussion about Junia's role has revolved around two complex issues. One is the name–gender debate, and the other concerns her participatory role in the apostolic circles (if the name does actually refer to a woman).

The aim of this section is to show that the Junia greeted with Andronicus is a woman and that she is 'prominent among the apostles'. Therefore, this section attempts to discuss the controversial issues regarding Junia in order to deduce her role in the early Christian missionary movement in general, and

143   Bassler, 'Prisca', 136.

the Pauline mission in particular. The issues such as the name–gender debate, Bauckham's arguments on Joanna-Junia, and her relationship to the apostolic band will be discussed in the first section, while the other descriptions, which state her relationship to Paul, will be discussed in the second section; finally, the significance of Junia's contribution to the believers in Rome will be explored.

4.4.1. Junia or Junias? The name–gender debate

Differently accented Greek forms allow the possibility for the name of Andronicus' partner in Rom. 16.7 to be the feminine Ἰουνίαν (from Ἰουνία -ας, ἡ, 'Junia') or the masculine Ἰουνιᾶν (from Ἰουνιᾶς, -ᾶ ὁ, 'Junias') or Ἰουνίαν (from Ἰουνίας, -α, ὁ 'Junias').[144] The evidence shows that by far the most likely reading of Ἰουνιαν is Junia.

4.4.1.1. History of debate

Until the twelfth century, there was a consensus (with a few exceptions) that the name was feminine.[145] From the thirteenth century to the middle of the twentieth century, scholars were more inclined towards a masculine identification.[146] As Thorley writes:

> The universal view of the church fathers was that the name was Junia and she was a woman and the English *Authorized Version* of 1611 followed this in reading 'Junia', clearly a woman's name; and in fact 'Junias' became a man in English translations only in 1881 when the *Revised Version* was published. Luther, however, in his German translation of 1552 had already opted for 'den Juniam', and continental translations have since then mostly followed this masculine interpretation.[147]

---

144   Epp, *Junia*, 23. The masculine forms have been understood as the contracted forms of the Greek name Ἰουνιανός (Junianos) or the Latin name Iunianus.

145   Fitzmyer, *Romans*, 737, 738. Fitzmyer lists the patristic Fathers who agreed that Junia is a female character and identified reasons for her being qualified among the apostles. Those include Ambroisaster, Chrysostom, Rufinus, Jerome, Theodoret of Cyrrhus, Ps-Prismasius, Oecumenius, John Damascene, Haymo, Rabanus Maurus, Hatto, Lanfranc of Bec, Bruno the Carthusian, Theophylact, Peter Abelard, and Peter Lombard. The possible exception is Origen, who once reads a masculine name 'Junias' in Rufinus' translation of his commentary in Migne, *PG* 14, 1281B and 1289A in *In epistolam ad Romanos* 10.39. This is probably an error, because all the other witnesses to the same commentary offer 'Junia' and in *In epistolam ad Romanos* 10.21 he uses the feminine name. See Lampe, 'The Roman Christians of Romans 16', 223; Moo, *Romans*, 922. Epiphanius (c. 315–403 CE) cites the name as masculine although it is overlooked. However his opinion is unreliable since he calls Prisca a man too.

146   Giles (Aegidius) of Rome (thirteenth century CE) seems to be the first commentator to take both Andronicus and Julian (the variant reading) to be men, based on the assumption that only a man could be an apostle. Thus Junias the masculine name was preferred to the feminine name till the 1970s. See Bauckham, *The Gospel Women*, 167.

147   Thorley, 'Junia, A Woman Apostle', 18. Thorley argues that Junia is a woman and explored the reasons for the most probable feminine name on linguistic grounds. Junia was a woman until Luther opted for a masculine name, and its impact on recent translations could be

Many recent views favour the feminine name,[148] but the Greek texts, with their different accentuations of the name, do not help resolve this impasse.[149] Similarly, the translations[150] and the commentators[151] show disagreement regarding the name. The conflict regarding the name originated from the presupposition that no woman could be called an apostle and so the accusative form of the name must refer to a male name Junias or Junianus.[152]

4.4.1.2. Cases against the masculine form

According to the name-contraction theory, the shortened form Junias (masculine) is a 'Greek hypocoristic form' of the Latin name Iunianus.[153]

---

tainted with a 'chauvinistic' flavour. Thorley suggests that although Schulz arrives at the same conclusion, there are 'linguistically several imprecise arguments' in his article, which are clarified in his own article. See Thorley, 'Junia', 19; R. R. Schulz, 'Junia or Junias?', *ExpTim* 98 (1987), 108–10. Some continental translations restore the name Junia; see e.g. *Die Gute Nachricht Bibel*, ad loc. The *Authorized Version* of 1611 followed Tyndale's translation, reading Junia.

148   Burer and Wallace, 'Was Junia Really an Apostle?', 78. Thorley comments that recent commentators 'have asserted that there is no justification for a masculine interpretation of the name'; see Thorley, 'Junia', 19.

149   The Greek texts with masculine accentuation are the United Bible Societies 3rd (1975) and 4th (1993) editions and the Nestle-Aland 25th (1975), 26th (1979), and 27th (1993) editions. Those with feminine accentuation are *Textus Receptus* (Trinitarian Bible Society); Loch's (Ratisbonae, 1862); Tischendorf's 8th edition (Lipsiae, 1869–72); Westcott-Hort's (Macmillan, 1881); von Soden's (Göttingen, 1913); Souter's 2nd edition (Oxford University, 1947); and *The Majority Text* (edited by Z. Hodges and A. Farstad, Thomas Nelson, 1982). The Modern Greek translation of Vellas (United Bible Societies, 1967) has added the feminine article to the name, which explicitly specifies that the gender is feminine. For these details I am indebted to Cervin 'A Note Regarding the Name Junia(s) in Romans 16.7', 464, 465. Some of the manuscripts read Julia in Rom. 16.7, which is a feminine name and it occurs in 16.15. Julia is found in P[46] 6 it[ar, b] vg[mss] cop[bo] eth Jerome, which Metzger suggests is a clerical error. See B. M. Metzger, A *Textual Commentary on the Greek New Testament* (London: Deutsche Bibelgesellschaft/UBS, 2nd edition, 1994), 475, 476. See also U.-K. Plisch, 'Die Apostlein Junia: Das Exegetische Problem in Röm 16.7 im Licht von Nestle-Aland and der Sahidischen Überlieferung', *NTS* 42 (1996), 477–78.

150   The Revised Standard Version, New American Standard Bible, New American Bible, New International Version, German Version (*Die Heilige Schrift*, Philadelphia: National Bible Press, 1967), Norwegian version (*Biblen*, Minneapolis: Norske Bibekselskabs, 1898) assume the name to be masculine, while KJV, NKJV, NRSV, ESV, NET, TNIV, Latin Vulgate (*Nouyi Zavet'* United Bible Societies, 1959), Russian version (*Biblia*, United Bible Societies, 1989) assume that the name is feminine.

151   Modern commentators are divided on the gender of the name. Those who agree on the feminine gender include Jewett, Dunn, Sanday and Headlam, Cranfield, Schreiner, and H. Koester, whereas those who agree on the masculine gender include Barrett and Murray. There are also some who assume the gender to be 'problematic' and suggest that the issue cannot be resolved.

152   Cranfield, *Romans*, 2.788. He suggests that the possibility of the accentuation of the masculine name rests on 'conventional prejudice' and that the feminine name is ruled out by others for contextual reasons. Another notion is that the personal descriptions such as τοὺς συγγενεῖς μου, συναιχμαλώτος and ἐπίσημοι and the relative pronoun οἵτινες are all masculine. Cervin argues that the masculine gender is used here because in the plural it is the generic gender. In order to refer to a group of mixed gender, the masculine form must be used. For example, τοὺς συγγενεῖς μου means my relatives (masculine/feminine). See Cervin, 'Name Junia(s)', 470.

153   Bauckham, *Gospel Women*, 168.

The name Iunianus is derived from the form of name (*cognomina*) ending in -*anus* and from *gentilicia,* whereas the male names in Greek end in -ας (the examples in the New Testament are Epaphras from Epaphroditus, Antipas from Antipatros). The possibilities can be assessed by three factors: the occurrence of similar Greek names, the evidence for the contracted form, and the context of the whole passage containing Rom. 16.7.

The arguments against the masculine form of the name include the lack of evidence for the abbreviated form of Junias among Greek names from antiquity, and that Junius and Junianus are rare names even among Greek people. Cervin comments that 'this name does not occur in any extant Greek or Latin document of the New Testament milieu'.[154] So also Bauckham suggests that the name Junias is not attested, while Junia is 'well attested'.[155] In addition, the claim that the name Iunianus could be shortened to Iunias (or has been shortened at all) lacks evidence and is thus to be considered unwarranted.[156] Moreover, the general context of the passage does not exclude women's active participation in mission.

Therefore, it is unlikely that Andronicus' partner in Rom. 16.7 bears the masculine name ᾿Ιουνιᾶς or ᾿Ιουνίας.

4.4.1.3. Cases for the feminine form

Junia was a very common Latin name.[157] The typical Latin name has three parts, the *praenomen* (personal name), the *nomen* (name of the clan or gens), and the *cognomen* (family name). Other names were probably added as titles, honours, and by adoption. Latin *nomina* (clan names) often have the suffixes -*ius* (masc.) and -*ia* (fem). Women usually did not have a *praenomen* but were named with their gens. Cervin, in his analysis of the names has discovered a large number of Iunii in the Greco-Roman world.[158] Peter Lampe counts more

---

154   Cervin, 'Name Junia(s)', 466. See also Bauckham, *Gospel Women*, 168.

155   Bauckham, *Gospel Women*, 169.

156   Cervin, 'Name Junia(s)', 467. The theory of the contracted name Junias has serious difficulties. See Epp, *Junia*, 24.

157   Lampe, 'Roman Christians', 223; see Cervin, 'Name Junia(s)', 467. Lampe suggests slave origins in pre-Pauline apostles; P. Lampe, 'Iunia/Iunias: Sklavenherkunft im Kreise der vorpaulinischen Apostel (Röm 16 7)', *ZNW* 76 (1985), 132–34.

158   Cervin showed that the claim of J. Piper and W. Grudem that 'the name Iunia was not a common woman's name in the Greco-Roman world' is erroneous by referring to a large number of women named as Iunia. J. Piper and W. Grudem (eds.), *Recovering Biblical Manhood and Womanhood: A Response to Evangelical Feminism* (Wheaton, IL: Crossway, 1991), 80. Julius Caesar's murderer's sister is named as Iunia; the Iunia familia is found in Tacitus' (AD 1–2) *Annals* (3.24, 69; 15.35); in Livy's (1 BC–AD 1) *History of Rome* (2.5.7; 9.17.11); and in Cornelius Nepos' (1 BC) Lives (*Atticus* 18.3). Iunia Calvina (Vespasian 29.4) and Iunia Claudilla (Caligula 12.1-2) are mentioned in Suetonius' (AD 1–2) *Twelve Caesars* and also in Tacitus' *Annals*. Men are also mentioned in *Twelve Caesars*: Iunius Novatus (*Augustus* 51.1); Iunius Rusticus (*Domitian* 10.3) and L. Iunius Silvanus (Claudius 24.5). There are quite a few women mentioned in the Latin Anthology and Latin Inscriptions. Moreover a number of Greek authors are also mentioned by this name. For detailed analysis, see Cervin, 'Name Junias', 468.

than 250 instances of Junia in Rome alone.[159] The number of occurrences of the name Junia is one of the pieces of evidence for the feminine name.

The occurrence of the name pairs in Rom. 16.7 (Andronicus and Junia), and 16.3 (Prisca and Aquila, certainly a couple) shows the possibility of a feminine name, even though the names of the sisters or relatives Tryphaena and Tryphosa in 16.12 appear paired in the same way. It is likely that Andronicus and Junia were husband and wife.[160]

The gender-biased interpretation, which is based on the assumption that women could not be apostles, is unjustified because the general consensus favours the feminine name. The 'church tradition from the Old Latin, Coptic, Syriac and Vulgate versions and the early Greek and Latin fathers onwards affirms a female apostle'.[161] Moreover, Romans 16 contains significant indications that women were involved in active ministry at many different levels. As a result, the feminine name 'Junia' is the most likely translation of Ἰουνιαν.

4.4.2. Joanna–Junia: Bauckham's arguments

Bauckham opts for a sound-equivalence theory concerning the names Joanna and Junia.[162] This theory is based on the thought that 'the similarity in sound of Junia to the Hebrew name Joanna (Yehohannah or Yohannah) is quite close'. Because of this, he suggests that 'the Junia of Romans 16.7 is the same person as Luke's Joanna (Luke 8.3)'.[163] The custom of adopting a Greek name in addition to one's original Semitic name was in 'alignment with Roman political rule'. Bauckham built his argument on the presupposition that Andronicus and Junia were among the founders of the Jerusalem Christian community, and that Paul's description of her as 'prominent among the apostles' was observed in early Christian literature. An example of this is the reference to her in the Gospel of Luke.[164]

Bauckham argues his point with two possible scenarios. First of all, other early Christian missionaries also had a 'Greek or Latin sound-equivalent to their Semitic name and evidently preferred to use the former when working in the diaspora, since it was more culturally appropriate and user-friendly for non-Semitic speakers'.[165] Among these are Silas/Silvanus, John Mark, and Joseph/Justus Barsabbas; Joanna/Junia could be another example of this. Second, Joanna and her husband Chuza belonged to the Herodian aristocracy of Tiberias. Due to this, the name 'Junia' would have been an equivalent name used for her in a Palestinian context, and would have the appropriateness 'not

159   Lampe, 'Roman Christians', 226.
160   Cranfield, *Romans*, 2; 788; Sanday and Headlam, *Romans*, 422; Ziesler, *Romans*, 351.
161   Belleville, Ἰουνιαν ... ἐπίσημοι ἐν τοῖς ἀποστόλοις, 231, 232. Epp has come up with reasons for accepting the feminine name 'Junia', see for details Epp, *Junia*, 23, 24.
162   Bauckham, *Gospel Women*, 181–94.
163   Bauckham, *Gospel Women*, 184.
164   Bauckham, *Gospel Women*, 184.
165   Bauckham, *Gospel Women*, 184.

only of being a sound-equivalent of her Hebrew name but also of being a distinguished, aristocratic Roman name'.[166] Although Bauckham stated that he could not decide between the two possibilities, he took the second as more plausible. This was because Joanna would already have spoken Latin (as the wife of Herod's steward) and could therefore become a Christian missionary in Rome with ease. He also suggested that either the Greek name Andronicus could be the name adopted by Chuza, or that Andronicus would be Joanna's second husband since she was already widowed during Jesus' ministry.[167]

Winter mentions Bauckham's argument, but he does not reveal whether he thinks Bauckham's proposal is correct. Rather, Winter suggests possible inferences from Rom. 16.7:

> Junia is a married woman, who along with her husband has been a long-standing Jewish Christian. Together they have been imprisoned with Paul, presumably for their identification with his cause. ... They clearly have a considerable sphere of influence among Christians, and while Junia is unlike Phoebe in that she has a husband, both she and Andronicus are connected to the leading authorities in this movement.[168]

The evidence for arguing that Joanna was the same persona as Junia is very speculative. Although there is a little evidence for the name-change hypothesis, it is not explicit from the textual evidence and Bauckham cites no exact parallels to a potential equivalence between Joanna and Junia. However, she possibly belonged to one of the earliest Christian communities since Paul describes her as being in Christ before him.

It is also interesting to note Winter's discussion on the possibility of the Junia (of Rom. 16.7) being the same person as Junia Theodora.[169] (The similarities between Junia Theodora and Phoebe in Romans 16 have already been discussed above.[170]) However, the following arguments counter Winter's proposal: first, Paul's description of Junia being in Christ before him cannot be applied to Junia Theodora; second, there is no evidence in the inscriptions that Junia Theodora is married, whereas the Junia mentioned in Rom. 16.7 certainly was: 'the names Andronicus and Junia were linked by the connective "and", just as Prisca and Aquila were (Rom. 16.3), who according to Acts 18.2 are married'.[171]

4.4.3. Relationship to the apostolic band

Paul's description of Andronicus and Junia is very significant. The phrase ἐπίσημοι ἐν τοῖς ἀποστόλοις is translated and interpreted in two different ways: either as 'prominent among the apostles', or 'well-known to the

166 Bauckham, *Gospel Women*, 186.
167 Bauckham, *Gospel Women*, 186.
168 Winter, *Roman Wives*, 203.
169 Winter, *Roman Wives*, 201.
170 See above 4.2.2.3.
171 Winter, *Roman Wives*, 201, 202.

apostles'. The former depicts Junia as holding a position among the ranks of the apostles, while the latter excludes her from this sphere. The translation 'noteworthy among the apostles' implies that Andronicus and Junia were apostles, while 'esteemed by the apostles' or 'well-known to the apostles' implies that they were not apostles.

4.4.3.1. Exclusive approach

The exclusive view considers that Andronicus and Junia were 'well-known to the apostles' or 'esteemed by the apostles', but were not apostles themselves in any real sense. The assumptions of the exclusivists are: (1) Paul uses ἀπόστολος only 'in its strict, official sense'; (2) the article τοῖς 'seems to point out the definite, well-known class of persons almost exclusively so called';[172] (3) the term 'apostle' retains the meaning 'one commissioned and sent', and is never used concerning men (or women) who minister from their own choice, and Paul never uses it in the wider sense; (4) 'ἐν states *where* these two were considered illustrious: "in the circle of" the Twelve at Jerusalem ("by" is incorrect)';[173] (5) scripture would not be silent about Andronicus and Junia elsewhere if they were prominent apostles.

Burer and Wallace argue that 'the collocation of ἐπίσημος with its adjuncts shows that, as a rule ἐπίσημος with a genitive personal adjunct indicates an inclusive comparison ("outstanding among"), while ἐπίσημος with (ἐν plus) the personal dative indicates an elative notion without the implication of inclusion ("well-known to")'. They conclude that Junia was 'well-known to the apostles' rather than 'outstanding among them'.[174] Burer and Wallace accept Junia as a member of the apostolic group, but they question her apostolic status due to the following observations: ἐπίσημος does not just imply a comparative sense ('prominent or outstanding among'), but also an elative notion ('famous, well-known to/by'); the meaning of a term is linked with the context and 'the collocation of the word with its adjuncts'; in the comparative sense the 'substantival adjunct' should be personal.

Three critics, Epp, Bauckham, and Belleville, challenge this view.[175] Bauckham argues that their method of interpretation is ambiguous because of the minimal evidence to justify the arguments, whereas Belleville argues that in Greek, the primary usage of ἐν and the plural dative inside and outside (with

---

172   C. Hodge, *Commentary on the Epistle to the Romans* (New York: Hodder and Stoughton, 1983), 449; see also Burer and Wallace, 'Was Junia Really an Apostle?', 81.

173   R. C. H. Lenski, *The Interpretation of St. Paul's Epistle to the Romans* (Minneapolis: Augsburg, 1961), 906–907; Burer and Wallace, 'Was Junia Really an Apostle?', 81; See also Murray, *Romans*, 2.229–30; Romaniuk suggests the term ἀπόστολοι as an 'analogical' interpretation for Junia and Andronicus because they were not among the twelve disciples, which is vague in terms of Paul's other descriptions. Romaniuk, 'Was Phoebe in Romans 16, 1 a Deaconess?', 133.

174   Burer and Wallace, 'Was Junia Really an Apostle?', 76. In this article, they analysed the inclusive and the exclusive views and opted for the exclusive notion by picking up examples from biblical Greek, patristic Greek, papyri, inscriptions, classical and Hellenistic texts. See also Hutter, 'Did Paul Call Andronicus an Apostle in Romans 16.7?', 778.

175   Epp, *Junia*, 76–78; Bauckham, *Gospel Women*, 175–76; Belleville, 'Re-examination of Romans 16.7', 243–48.

exceptions) the New Testament is inclusive ('in'/'among') and not exclusive ('to'). Moreover, Burer and Wallace fail to offer one clear biblical or extra-biblical (Hellenistic) example of an exclusive sense of ἐπίσημος and a plural noun to convey 'well-known to'.[176]

Epp suggests that their statement that 'the genitive personal modifier was consistently used for an inclusive idea, while the (ἐν plus) dative personal adjunct was almost never so used' cannot be taken without 'very significant difficulty' depending on the evidence they supplied.[177] Greek grammatical rules state that the agent of the passive is expressed by ὑπό + genitive and not by ἐν + the dative case, which is used to denote impersonal instrument and means.[178]

The claim of the exclusivists that the term 'apostle' is used only in the 'technical sense' is incorrect on the basis of its usage elsewhere in the Pauline epistles.[179] The content and context of the passage show that the exclusive view is unlikely. Verse 7 cannot be taken as an independent pericope but as a part of 16.2-16. Women who are in leadership roles are greeted elsewhere in the greeting section. Translations that express exclusivism clearly misread the text. For example: (CEV) 'highly respected by the apostles'; (Amplified) 'they are men held in high esteem by the apostles'; (NET) 'well known to the apostles'.

4.4.3.2. Inclusive approach
The scholars who agree with the inclusive view argue that Junia was 'outstanding among the apostles', and there is a consensus that she was an apostle, although not in the technical sense of the word. The inclusive approach takes the term 'apostle' in a broad sense.[180] Patristic commentators[181] and modern translations[182] consider that Junia was part of the apostolic band.

---

176   Belleville, 'Re-examination of Romans 16.7', 244–45.

177   Epp found thirteen personal examples: eight ἐπίσημος + dative instances that are exclusive; no ἐπίσημος + genitive that are exclusive; three ἐπίσημος + genitive that are exclusive; and two personal cases that have ἐπίσημος + ἐν + dative but also are inclusive. See Epp, *Junia*, 77.

178   Cervin, 'Name Junias', 470.

179   Paul uses the term 'apostle' not only in the technical sense with a meaning of being 'sent and commissioned by God' (1 Thess. 2.6), but also with the meaning delegates of the churches (2 Cor. 8.23; cf. Phil. 2.25); preacher of the gospel and other roles related with the establishment and the administration of the churches (1 Cor. 9.5; 12.28; Eph. 2.20; 3.5; 4.11). See P. W. Barnett, 'Apostle', *DPL*, 45–51, at 47; H. D. Betz, 'Apostle', *ABD*, 1, 309–11, at 309, 310.

180   Barrrett, *Romans*, 283–84; Dodd, *Romans*, 240; Cranfield, *Romans*, 2.789; Käsemann, *Romans*, 414; Schreiner, *Romans*, 796; Fitzmyer, *Romans*, 739–40; Sanday and Headlam, *Romans*, 423; Dunn, *Romans 9–16*, 895; Moo, *Romans*, 923; Jewett, *Romans*, 963. Dunn argues that Andronicus and Junia belonged to the apostolic band in a short period following Jesus' resurrection.

181   See above 4.4.1.1.

182   The renderings are as follows: New International Version and New American Standard Bible as 'outstanding among the apostles'; New Revised Version and New American Bible as 'prominent among the apostles'; New Century Version as 'very important apostles'; KJV, ASV, RSV, NKJV as 'who are noted among the apostles'.

The adjective ἐπίσημος means marked out, distinguished, outstanding, and prominent, which compares the person or thing with other representatives of the same class and distinguishes it/them as prominent.[183] The notion of the apostle was much broader in the early church than merely the 'Twelve'. It is also used to designate 'messenger', 'missionary preacher', or 'itinerant missionary'. In the epistles, Paul strongly defends his apostleship: he claims to have had an encounter with the risen Christ (1 Cor. 9.1; Gal. 1.1, 15-17); says he has received a divine commission to proclaim the gospel (Rom. 1.1-5; 1 Cor. 1.1; Gal. 1.1, 15-17); refers to the 'acceptance and endurance of the labours and sufferings' connected with his ministry; and states that he has experienced 'signs, wonders, and mighty works'.[184] Epp rightly argues that unless Paul had found these criteria in Andronicus and Junia, he would not have hastily labelled them as apostles or even as 'outstanding among the apostles'. Although Paul does not mention whether Andronicus and Junia witnessed the resurrection, he points to the fact that 'they were "in Christ" before he was and they were in prison with Paul and therefore had suffered as he had for his apostleship'.[185] Presumably, these are the reasons why Paul acknowledges Andronicus and Junia as being 'outstanding among the apostles'.

Paul meets all the criteria of an apostle: he had seen the risen Christ, received a divine commission, suffered for the gospel, and worked signs and wonders. Paul probably expects any apostle to meet all four of these requirements. Andronicus and Junia could have met all four criteria but Paul does not spell this out. This type of apostleship is different from an 'apostle of churches' (2 Cor. 8.23), who did practical work or missionary work (Acts 13).

Paul does not specifically point out why Andronicus and Junia were honoured among the apostles, but the other descriptions imply their toil in Christian mission and place them in a privileged position.

Another question concerns the location of their apostolic ministry: were they related to any of the local congregations? Paul does not give any particular hint as to what the focus of their ministry might be, nor does he specify whether they were witnesses of the resurrection. Jewett suggests that they had functioned somewhere in the eastern mission during the time of shared imprisonment with Paul, and that they resided in Rome when the epistle was written.[186]

---

183   K. H. Rengstorf, 'ἐπίσημος', *TDNT* 7, 267.

184   Epp, *Junia*, 69–71. 'The apostles of Christ include Barnabas (1 Cor 9:6), the brothers of the Lord (Gal 1:19; 1 Cor. 9:5), probably Silvanus/Silas (1 Thess 2:7) and perhaps Apollos (1 Cor 4:9), as well as Paul himself'; Bauckham, *Gospel Women*, 180.

185   Epp, *Junia*, 69, 70.

186   Jewett, *Romans*, 964. Bauckham argues that they were missionaries in the 'Greco-Roman circles', which is one possibility, but not a certain one. Bauckham, *Gospel Women*, 181–203.

Junia's actual role is not specified, but the description of Paul 'shows that she had a role and it was not a case of Andronicus simply travelling with a wife who was an appendage (1 Cor. 9.5). She has shared imprisonment with him because she was identified as a significant player herself in the Christian cause. ... Junia had her sphere of influence in the circle in which she operated.'[187] Their apostolic status could be counted in the same way as that of Barnabas, Silas, and Apollos (1 Cor. 4.6, 9; 9.5-6; Gal. 1.19; 1 Thess. 2.1, 7). Since they were in Christ before Paul, it is likely they were members of the Jerusalem crowd who received a vision of the resurrected Jesus (1 Cor. 15.7).

Barrett does not support a 'second-grade apostleship' in Pauline letters, but argues for two well-defined categories such as 'apostles of Christ' (Paul and Peter) and envoys of churches.[188] Although the categorization of Junia's role is not explicitly stated, she may have been a representative of a church in the same way Paul and Barnabas were for the Antioch church (and not as 'apostles of the churches' [agents or messengers] with specific purposes such as practical duties like collecting money for the poor in the Jerusalem church [2 Cor. 8.23]). Andronicus and Junia might have adopted this role of missionary agent, acting as itinerant missionaries engaged in the work of the gospel with a particular focus on the Gentile mission.[189]

4.4.4. Other descriptions

4.4.4.1. Relatives (συγγενεῖς)
In Romans 16 Paul identifies three individuals as his kinspeople or relatives (συγγενεῖς μου) in Rome. He sends his greetings to these three people, and three other persons send their greetings to Rome from Corinth. The first group consists of Andronicus, Junia, and Herodion (Rom. 16.7, 11) and the second group is made up of Lucius, Jason, and Sosipater (Rom. 16.21).

συγγενής is not mentioned in any of the other Pauline epistles except Romans, and the term may have different connotations according to use. One potential meaning portrays family connections by referring to a common ancestry or descent, or perhaps literal 'relatives'.[190] The meaning is unlikely

---

187   Winter, *Roman Wives*, 203. Fiorenza suggests that the traditional role as 'wife' is not the matter of consideration, 'but rather their commitment to the partnership in the work of the gospel'. Fiorenza, *In Memory of Her*, 173.

188   C. K. Barrett, *The Signs of an Apostle* (London: Epworth, 1970), 47. Barrett argues for the translation of ἐπίσημοι ἐν τοῖς ἀποστόλοις as 'men of note among the apostles', which opposes my argument. Barrett identifies different categories of apostles (ἀπόστολος or *shaliah*). They are (1) the twelve; (2) the Supreme Apostles: Peter and John who belonged to the twelve, and James who did not; (3) apostleship of circumcision (Gal. 2.8); (4) John's work; (5) the agents of Jerusalem leaders (Gal. 2.4; 1 Cor. 15.7); (6) Paul's own apostleship; (7) subordinate apostles to the Jerusalem church (possibly including Andronicus and Junia); (8) apostles of the churches who were delegates or messengers (2 Cor. 8.23; Phil. 2.25). See Barrett, *Signs of an Apostle*, 71–73.

189   Fiorenza, *In Memory of Her*, 172. Betz also suggests that they could serve as a missionary apostle; see Betz, 'Apostle', *ABD*, 310.

190   Ellis, 'Paul and his Co-workers', 186.

to be the same as that of the ἀγαπητός, φίλος, which is a second reading.[191] Apart from familial relations and friendly connections, it describes people of the same tribe or race. It seems more likely that συγγενής in Romans 16 denotes Jewish ancestry. In other words, Paul is referring to Christians who are fellow Jews with him.[192]

Why is Paul especially interested in emphasising Jewish relations in Romans? Does this mean that special recognition of a few of his kinspeople categorises the rest of the people in the list as Gentile Christians?[193] Jewett suggests that this is 'Paul's effort to affirm the legitimacy of some of the Jewish Christians currently being discriminated against by the Gentile Christian majority in the Roman house and Tenement churches'.[194] Other than in Romans 16, the term is used in Rom. 9.3, where Paul says that 'I could wish that I myself were accursed and cut off from Christ for the sake of my brothers and sisters, my relatives according to the flesh' (τῶν συγγενῶν μου κατὰ σάρκα).[195] Paul's use of συγγενής is significant because it highlights the inclusion of Jews and Gentiles in God's plan of salvation (Romans 9–11).

4.4.4.2. Fellow prisoners (συναιχμάλωτοι)

Another significant description of (Andronicus and) Junia in Romans 16 is συναιχμαλώτους (fellow prisoners of Paul), and is used elsewhere in Col. 4.10 (Aristarchus) and Philemon 23 (Epaphras). The word 'prisoner' (αἰχμάλωτος) refers to a captive taken in a war.[196] It is interesting to note that Paul applies it very selectively to four people. The personal pronoun 'μου' along with 'σύν' ('with') indicates a 'shared experience'[197] or a joint venture.

It is clear from Col. 4.3 and Philemon 1, 10, 13, that Paul was imprisoned with others who were locked up with him.[198] Although the cause for Andronicus and Junia's imprisonment is not specific, it does not reduce the impact of their effort. Therefore, συναιχμαλώτους perhaps shows that they were imprisoned with Paul at some point. 'They are his "fellow prisoners" in the sense that they too had suffered imprisonment for their allegiance to

---

191   W. Michelis, 'συγγενής, συγγένεια', *TDNT* 7, 742. Fàbrenga suggests that συγγενεῖς denotes 'friend' and not 'fellow countrymen', suggestions that according to Lampe are based on 'shaky presuppositions'. See V. Fàbrega, 'War Junia[s], der hervorragende Apostel [Röm. 16, 7], eine Frau?', *JAC* 27/28 (1984/85), 47–64. Lampe, *From Paul to Valentinus*, 74.

192   Clarke, 'Jew and Greek', 112. See also Jewett, *Romans*, 962; Dunn, *Romans*, 894; Bauckham, *Gospel Women*, 170; Moo, *Romans*, 921; Belleville, 'Re-examination of Romans 16.7', 233; Schreiner, *Romans*, 795.

193   Lampe, *From Paul to Valentinus*, 74.

194   Jewett, *Romans*, 962. See also Watson, 'The Two Roman Congregations', 210. Watson suggests that Andronicus and Junia are linked with the earliest Jewish Christianity.

195   Cf. συγγενεῖς is used in Josephus, *Ant.* 1.276; 2.269, 278; 9.249; 11.341; 12.257, 338.

196   *LSJ*, 45; *MM*, 16.

197   Jewett, *Romans*, 962.

198   Luke refers to an overnight incarceration in Philippi (Acts 16.24-34), while Paul refers to many imprisonments (2 Cor. 11.23).

the gospel.'[199] Kittel argues that 'fellow prisoner' is used in a metaphorical sense,[200] which seems unlikely since Paul was imprisoned on many occasions (2 Cor. 6.5; 11.23).

4.4.4.3. In Christ before Paul (πρὸ ἐμοῦ γέγοναν ἐν Χριστῷ)
Paul's description of Andronicus and Junia as being in Christ before him suggests that they were early Jewish Christians. It follows that their conversion experience was before Paul's (prior to 34 CE), which probably attests to their apostolic status on the basis of being witnesses to the resurrection (since Paul refers to himself as the last of the series of witnesses to the resurrection [1 Cor. 15.8]).[201] It also indicates that they could have been present among 'the visitors from Rome' on the day of Pentecost (Acts 2.10); as the members of the Jerusalem church, they could in addition have been involved in the incidents mentioned in Acts (6.1; 11.19).[202] It seems that Paul wanted the Romans to acknowledge their long-standing service as missionaries.

Bauckham suggests that 'they were almost certainly Palestinian Jews (unless they were diaspora Jews converted while visiting Jerusalem) and probably members of the early Jerusalem church', that 'Andronicus and Junia may well have been involved in the founding or early growth of the Christian community in Rome', and that 'they must certainly have been leaders of considerable significance among the Roman Christians' as 'outstanding among the apostles'.[203] Although the expression is not explicit enough to draw a firm conclusion, it is plausible that 'this couple had functioned as Christian apostles for more than two decades before Paul wrote this letter to Rome requesting they be greeted by other believers in Rome, who evidently were not inclined to acknowledge their accomplishments and status'.[204]

4.4.5. The significance of Junia to the Roman church: Pauline motivation
Why is Paul asking the Romans to greet Junia and what is her significance to the Roman church? First, the purpose of constructing the greetings in the second-person plural serves to create relationships and bonds. Second, Paul acknowledges her toil in ministry, which also encourages others to suffer for the gospel.

---

199   Bauckham, *Gospel Women*, 172. The same opinion is shared by the majority of the scholars like Dunn, Jewett, Schreiner, and Moo. Sanday and Headlam suggest a different place and time of imprisonment and not the same as that of Paul, which is unlikely because the term implies the possibility of the same occasion as that of Paul. See Sanday and Headlam, *Romans*, 423; Cranfield, *Romans*, 788–89.

200   G. Kittel, 'συναιχμάλωτος', *TDNT* 1, 196–97.

201   Jewett, *Romans*, 964.

202   Jewett, *Romans*, 964.

203   Bauckham, *Gospel Women*, 181.

204   Jewett, *Romans*, 964. There is another possibility that Andronicus and Junia were members of the Antioch church, but Jewett considers this view as less plausible because of their early origin as Christian missionaries. See also Käsemann, *Romans*, 414.

Paul describes Junia and Andronicus as συγγενεῖς μου and συναιχμαλώτους, which gives insight into their relationship with Paul. These descriptions seem to imply an equal standing in mission with Paul and his co-workers. But the other two descriptions ἐπίσημοι ἐν τοῖς ἀποστολόις and πρὸ ἐμοῦ γέγοναν ἐν Χριστῷ explicitly state their relationship to the early Christian community and their significant contribution to the Christian mission. In fact, Paul's descriptions imply why they are remarkable to the Roman church. First, Junia is portrayed as an associate of Paul. She is not only an apostle (in the sense of co-worker) but also prominent among them. The reason for their distinctiveness is not specific, but one can postulate that the reasons might have included their toil (as fellow prisoners) and missionary zeal (as they were in Christ before Paul). Second, Paul's description of Junia as 'prominent among the apostles' seems to return the benefaction to Paul through the reputation of those who associate with him (cf. Rom. 16.3, 4). Third, it reveals the mutual obligation which comes about by being in Christ (cf. Rom. 12.5). The phrase 'in Christ' places the human relationships in a deeper context; i.e. we all belong together because we are in Christ/the Lord. Reciprocity in the actions of Andronicus and Junia is not as explicit in the text as it was with Phoebe (προστάτις of many as well as Paul) and Prisca (ἀσπάσασθε not only from Paul but also a large group from all the churches of the Gentiles). Rather, all are mutually obliged in the 'body of Christ'.

Paul wants to create a chain of relationships. It seems that Paul wants to establish and maintain relationships with the Roman believers on the basis of Junia's fame. He asks the Romans to greet Junia, who is a well-reputed figure among the apostles, which in turn helps Paul's relationships with the Romans. By greeting Andronicus and Junia, the Romans participate in the circle of those who recognise and honour them.[205]

In conclusion, it is highly plausible that Junia is a feminine name and that she was considered to be 'outstanding among the apostles'. Although her role is not explicitly stated, like Phoebe or Prisca's were, Junia's leading role in her house church paints a picture of her contribution to the early Christian mission. She is a Jewish Christian and the wife of Andronicus, and she was one of the leading members of the Christian community known as 'apostles'.

The greeting coupled with its descriptive phrases show Paul's intention to create and strengthen mutual relationships and bonds. These descriptive phrases shed light on Junia's significance and contribution to the Christian church. Her prominence among the apostles probably signifies her active leadership in ministry.

4.5. Hardworking members: Mary, Persis, Tryphoena and Tryphosa

The same descriptive phrase is used in relation to four of the women in the greeting list: Mary, Tryphoena, Tryphosa, and Persis (to labour κοπιάω, Rom. 16.6, 12): πολλὰ ἐκοπίασεν εἰς ὑμᾶς denotes Mary (v. 6); πολλὰ ἐκοπίασεν

---

205   Some textual variants (C* F G) read Ἰουνιαν for Ἰουλίαν (Rom. 16.15).

ἐν Κυρίῳ describes Persis (v. 12); κοπιώσας ἐν Κυρίῳ depicts Tryphoena and Tryphosa (v. 12). This term is used only for these four women, despite the list's length, and implies that these women's works need to be appreciated and acknowledged. These four women were not working as a team (excluding Tryphoena and Tryphosa), which indicates Mary and Persis had independent endeavours.

The verb is used elsewhere by Paul of himself (1 Cor. 15.10; 2 Cor. 6.5; 11.23, 27; Gal. 4.11; Phil. 2.16; Col. 1.29; 1 Thess. 2.9; 3.5; 2 Thess. 3.8); of himself and Apollos (1 Cor. 3.8); of apostles in general (1 Cor. 4.12); of the household of Stephanas, including Fortunatus and Achaicus, and of other individuals (1 Cor. 16.16; 1 Thess. 5.12); and as a characteristic that should be reflected in all believers (1 Cor. 15.58; cf. Eph. 4.28).

4.5.1. Mary (Rom. 16.6)

'Maria'/Mary in Romans 16 represents the pagan name of a Roman gens.[206] On the one hand, the name was very common among Jews,[207] but on the other hand, the name was also used among Gentiles,[208] which poses a difficulty in deducing her ethnicity. Lampe suggests that her ethnicity lies in her pagan status, since Paul does not identify her especially as a kinswoman.[209] Jewett opts for her possession of a strong Jewish background in Rome.[210]

However, her toil for the Romans is specially mentioned by Paul as ἐκοπίασεν εἰς ὑμᾶς 'she has laboured for you'. It seems that Mary functioned as a missionary in Rome, and that her work benefited the congregation, as Paul specifies her work 'for you'. The verb 'labour' occurs twenty-three times and the noun 'labour' occurs eighteen times in the early Christian sources. Harnack suggests that labouring is a technical meaning for missionary and congregational work.[211] Dunn argues that the term does not denote a leadership function because Paul recognises general devoted work on behalf of the church too (1 Cor. 16.16; 1 Thess. 5.12);[212] the willingness to meet the needs of a new congregation such as voluntarily submitting to undertake tasks. But this seems improbable, since one of Paul's purposes for the greetings in Rom. 16.2-16 seems to be to commend those who are in leadership roles, including women. The verb implies honourable toil for the sake of the gospel or the community

---

206   'The Latin-pagan "Maria" occurs 108 times in the Roman inscriptions of *CIL* VI. The Semitic "Maria" cannot be counted even 20 times in Rome.' Lampe, 'Roman Christians', 225.

207   Dunn, *Romans*, 893.

208   See Jewett, *Romans*, 960. She is likely a slave or former slave in the Marius family. Horsley suggests that whether Mary was 'a Jew or a Roman cannot be determined with certainty' by examining the other examples of this name. G. H. R. Horsley, 'Maria the διάκονος', *NewDocs*, 2: 193–95.

209   See Lampe, *Paul to Valentinus*, 176.

210   Jewett, *Romans*, 961.

211   A. von Harnack, 'κοπιᾶν (Οἱ Κοπιῶντες) im früchristlichen Sprachgebrauch', *ZNW* 27 (1928) 1–10; Jewett, *Romans*, 961. See also Ollrog, *Mitarbeiter*, 71.

212   Dunn, *Romans*, 893.

and is clearly a commendation.[213] The term as used elsewhere for Paul and his co-workers in denoting apostolic labours in fact throws light upon Mary's role in relation to the church.

The adjective πολλά ('much') denotes her hard work for missionary purposes and probably aims to emphasise a longer period of service. Murray suggests Mary as 'one of the earliest members of the church at Rome and its organization could have been largely due to her influence'.[214] Therefore, Paul is appreciating her hard work for the missionary cause on behalf of a congregation for an extended time. Her leadership might have helped the congregation to flourish in Rome.

4.5.2. Persis (Rom. 16.12)

Persis may be Gentile or Jewish. It is a typical name for a feminine slave, a name found six times in the Roman epigraphic and literary sources.[215] It is also interesting to note that Paul adds one more descriptive phrase τὴν ἀγαπητήν ('the beloved') for Persis along with one depicting her missionary task and toil as πολλὰ ἐκοπίασεν ἐν Κυρίῳ. 'In the Lord' could be seen as a further sealing of her hard work as a missionary for an extended period, as in the case of Mary.[216]

Paul often indicates his affection for his fellow Christians, by referring to them as 'my beloved [name]' (Rom. 16.5, 8, 9b, Epaenetus, Amplias, Stachys). 'The beloved Persis' reveals a close relationship that also implies a corresponding relationship to the Roman believers. ἀγαπητός in vv. 5, 8, 9, 12, denotes a 'warm personal relationship'.[217] The Pauline description of some individuals as ἀγαπητός is important since Paul emphasises the theme of ἀγάπη in Rom. 12.9-21; 13.8-10. Persis played a significant role in the congregation and her role probably needed to be appreciated; she is beloved by the Roman believers as well as Paul.

4.5.3. Tryphoena and Tryphosa (Rom. 16.12)

On the basis of the names found in the inscriptions, Lampe suggests that Tryphoena and Tryphosa were possibly Gentile Christians from a background of slavery.[218] Lampe does not think that they were sisters, while others argue that the similarity in names and the conjunction 'and' denote a sibling

---

213   Schreiber suggests community leadership of women with the use of the term κοπιάω (Rom. 16.6, 12); Schreiber, 'Arbeit mit der Gemeinde (Rom 16:6, 12)', 217. See also, A. L. Chapple, 'Local Leadership in the Pauline Churches: Theological and Social Factors in its Development. A Study based on 1 Thessalonians, 1 Corinthians and Philippians', PhD diss., University of Durham, 1984, 398–449.

214   Murray, *Romans*, 2.229.

215   P. Lampe, 'Persis', *ABD* 5, 244.

216   See the section on Mary, 4.5.1.

217   Dunn, *Romans*, 893. In v. 8, Amplias is described as Paul's 'beloved in the Lord', which shows Paul's relationship with him as well as his position in the church.

218   Lampe, *Paul to Valentinus*, 169, 183.

relationship.[219] They are described as labourers in the Lord κοπιώσας ἐν Κυρίῳ (v. 12), indicating their missionary work or roles as local church leaders. They too need to be honoured for their toil in mission.

4.6. Rufus' mother (Rom. 16.13)

Paul states that Rufus' mother was also a 'mother of mine' (v. 13). Although it is unclear what Paul really meant by this, it could be inferred that she might have helped him in a specific situation or ministered to him regularly at some point in his labours (as a mother).[220]

Meeks suggests that the language of familial affection (e.g. mother, father, brother and sister) was a characteristic of Pauline Christian groups, but was rare in other associations.[221] Members are unrelated in a literal sense but address one another in familial terms 'to express identity and feelings of belonging and community'.[222] As Horrell rightly suggests: 'Paul's labelling of Christians as ἀδελφός implies "role ethics", a set of expectations as to how behaviour and relationships should be structured which follow from a certain role-designation'.[223] It signifies the Pauline vision of a Christian community that upholds mutuality and harmony in relationships between one another.

4.7. Nereus' sister (Rom. 16.15)

Nereus' sister is also mentioned in a cluster of five names (v. 15) but is not given any particular designation. The term ἀδελφή denotes her relationship to Nereus as a sister in the literal sense.

Jewett suggests that Paul does not know Nereus' sister personally but may have heard about her due to her leading role in the church.[224] That may explain why Paul does not mention her name and only refers to her as the sister of Nereus. It is suggested that she and Nereus are the children of Philologos and Julia,[225] but there is no evidence in the text to support this. It is interesting to

---

219   P. Lampe, 'Tryphaena and Tryphosa', *ABD* 6, 669. Those who think that they were sisters include Käsemann, *Romans*, 414–15; Dunn, *Romans 9–16*, 879; Fitzmyer, *Romans, 741*; R. L. Omanson, 'Who's Who in Romans 16? Identifying Men and Women among the People Paul Sent Greetings to', *Bib Trans* 49 (1998), 430–36, at 433.

220   Schreiner, *Romans*, 793.

221   Meeks, *Urban Christians*, 31.

222   Harland, *Associations, Synagogues, and Congregations*, 33. Harland suggests that language of familial affection occurs in a number of associations, where the members are not literally related to the same family.

223   Horrell, *Solidarity and Difference*, 113. The term ἀδελφός when metaphorically used indicates that a sibling-like bond is expected from the two parties involved.

224   Jewett, *Romans*, 972.

225   Cranfield, *Romans*, 2.795; Fitzmyer, *Romans*, 742; Moo, *Romans*, 926; Dunn, *Romans*, 2.898 suggest this view only as a possibility.

note that she and Julia are among the leading members of the congregation, which is possibly a 'tenement church' since it is led by a group of leaders rather than by a 'single patron'.[226] It is possible to assume collective leadership in 'tenement churches', which may also be different in structure from the house church led by Prisca and Aquila.

4.8. Julia (Rom. 16.15)

Julia is likely a slave or a freedwoman. She is a part of a group of five members (v. 15).

Julia is connected with Philologus, which probably indicates that they were either a married couple[227] or brother and sister.[228] They are connected with καί ('and'), which suggests that she was married to him. Like Nereus' sister, Julia may perhaps be involved in the leadership of the tenement church as she is one of the five leaders mentioned by Paul to be greeted in v. 15. The greeting acknowledges her work for the church.

4.9. Conclusion

In this study of the roles of the women from Rom. 16.1-16, I have observed that some women clearly exercised leadership roles since their descriptive phrases indicated their fulfilling of different roles in the church. Phoebe is the διάκονος of the church of Cenchreae and προστάτις of Paul and many others. Prisca was a co-worker of Paul and was willing to support his ministry at all costs. Moreover, she may have been the leader of the church in her house. Her contribution was profound and she was beneficial to all the churches of the Gentiles, including both men and women. Junia is a feminine name belonging to a Jewish Christian and the wife of Andronicus. Both are described as being 'prominent among the apostles', which is indicative of their leading position of repute in the community. Mary, Persis, Tryphoena and Tryphosa were hardworking women and part of an appreciated team who supported Paul and his mission by various means. Rufus' mother was a 'mother' to Paul. Nereus' sister and Julia were possibly part of the leadership team of a tenement church.

Primarily, what we have deduced from these passages is that these women held roles that included leadership and active participation in the church and the Pauline mission.

Second, women were greeted and appreciated for their hard work, which gives us an insight into Paul's attitude to women church leaders. Paul refers

---

226   Jewett, *Romans*, 972.

227   Sanday and Headlam, *Romans*, 427; Cranfield, *Romans*, 2.795; Dunn, *Romans*, 2: 898; P. Lampe, 'Julia', *ABD* 3, 1125.

228   Jewett, *Romans*, 972. See also above, fn. 205: some textual variants (C* F G) read Ἰουνιαν for Ἰουλίαν (Rom. 16.15).

to women in various kinds of leadership positions without feeling the need to offer any kind of explanation or defence; their leadership is mentioned and honoured alongside that of men (or over men) without any special remark to suggest that it was unusual or controversial. The reciprocity Paul describes and creates disregards gender: he binds these women into webs of exchange with himself, his churches, and the Romans with mutual obligations that flow between all the parties. There are no special provisions, expectations, or limitations because they are women: they are treated like everyone else and can take part in the web of mutual exchange. Their hard work is honoured and reciprocated without reference to their gender.

The third but not the least important aspect of this passage is mutuality. Paul respects mutual relationships as he asks the Roman believers to greet others. The rhetoric of the passage envisages mutuality and encourages reciprocal relations between one another regardless of gender identity.

This aspect of mutuality is not an exclusive theme of Romans 16, but may be found more profoundly in the exhortation in Romans 12–15, where Paul repeatedly emphasises collective mutuality through thematic and linguistic links. This will be the subject of the next two chapters.

CHAPTER 5

THE BODY METAPHOR AND ἀλλήλους: A PARADIGM OF
MUTUALITY IN ROMANS 12, 13

5.1. Introduction

Women's ministry within the structure of mutualism, one of the important
aspects of the greetings (Rom. 16.1-16), was the focus of the preceding
chapter. Although Paul pinpoints mutual relationships between Jews and
Gentiles in Romans 1–11, it is apparent in chs. 12–15 that he wants to hold
the believers together to strengthen social relationships as 'one body in Christ'
(Rom. 12.5).[1] The body metaphor is also used by Paul's contemporaries such
as rhetoricians, philosophers, moralists, and historians. Although Paul uses
a similar rhetoric, he depicts it from a Christian communitarian perspective.

It is striking that Paul speaks about the mercies of God at the beginning of
chapter 12. This includes the whole story of the gospel and the love of God
(Rom. 12.1 cf. 5.5, 8; 8.39). This is not accidental: ἀγάπη is a subject that
runs throughout Romans 12–13. The theme of love (ἀγάπη) and the term
'one another' (ἀλλήλους) underscore mutual relationships that embrace the
community. Paul reminds the Romans that social existence and responsibilities
should go hand in hand with their personal devotion to God (Rom. 12.1, 2).

How does Paul describe mutual relations through the body politic and the
language of 'one another'? The aim of this chapter is to discuss the body
metaphor and the exhortations of Paul to enhance love and mutuality in order
to identify the Pauline mutuality model implied in Romans 12–13.

---

1   Apart from 1 Corinthians 12 and Romans 12, the body metaphor is used in the deutero-
Pauline epistles (Eph. 1.23; 2.16; 3.6; 4.1-16; Col. 1.8-24; 2.17-19; 3.15). Kim has recently
suggested that the different approaches to the conception of community as the body of Christ are:
'*boundary-protected* community' (ecclesiological organism); '*boundary-overcoming* community'
(the New Perspective on Paul as the matter of relationship); and the 'apocalyptic community'
(participating in the divine will). Kim, *Christ's Body in Corinth*, 11.

5.2. The body metaphor in the Pauline epistles

Paul uses the body metaphor in the context of the charismatic community (Romans 12; 1 Cor. 12; cf. Eph. 4.12; Col. 1.18). As Dunn suggests, 'The body imagery is actually an expression of the consciousness of community and oneness experienced by the first Christians as they met "in Christ".'[2] In the following sections, the discussion is focused on the body as a political metaphor in antiquity and its use by Paul in Romans.

5.2.1. The body as a political metaphor in antiquity

In the Greco-Roman world, the metaphor of the body is used as an expression of political and cosmic solidarity. Ancient literature witnesses the use of the metaphor for a social and political group. It is also used in *homonoia* (concord) speeches. The most important themes in the use of the body metaphor are unity, hierarchy, and interdependence.

5.2.1.1. Unity
Unity is a common topos in antiquity's use of the body metaphor. For example, Plutarch describes the unity of the Greek city-states with the same phrase used by Paul: ἕν σῶμα (one body).[3] In the speech of Menenius Agrippa, Aesop's widely known fables were used to exhort the plebs to stop their agitation and submit to the patricians; they compare the state to the human body and depict the revolt of some body parts against the stomach until they were starved and returned to their organic unity: 'they therefore conspired together that the hands should carry no food to the mouth, nor the mouth accept anything that was given it, nor the teeth grind up what was received'.[4]

Aelius Aristides compares political turbulence to a disease-like consumption, depicting a tearing apart of the body and to the folly of cutting off one's own feet.[5] The body image is widely used by the philosophical moralists, who were Paul's contemporaries. Seneca wrote:

> What if the hands should desire to harm the feet, or the eyes the hands? As all the members of the body are in harmony one with another ... so mankind should spare the individual man, because all are born for a life of fellowship, and society can be kept unharmed only by the mutual protection and love of its parts.[6]

---

2   Dunn, *Romans 9–16*, 724.

3   Plutarch, *Philopoemen*, 8, cited by E. Schweizer, 'σῶμα κτλ.', *TDNT* 7 (1971), 1041.

4   See Livy, *History of Rome* 2.32; Aesop *Fables* 132; Dio Chrysostom, *Discourses* 33.16; Epictetus, *Dissertationes* 2.10.4–5.

5   Aelius Aristides, *Orations* 17.9; 23.31; 24.18, 38-39; 26.43. See also R. F. Collins, *First Corinthians* (Collegeville: Liturgical Press, 1999), 459.

6   Seneca, *Anger* 2.31. See Collins, *1 Corinthians*, 458.

Dio Chrysostom used the metaphor in his speeches.[7] Delivered in Tarsus around the beginning of the second century, they point to the *polis* (the city-state), as a body, and strife, discord, or civil disturbance as a disease that must be eradicated from it.[8] Discord affects the whole body politic.[9] These *homonoia* speeches use the body metaphor to argue for unity or concord.

5.2.1.2. Hierarchy

It is also significant to observe the hierarchy of society affirmed by *homonoia* speeches. It is assumed that the 'body is hierarchically constituted and that illness or social disruption occurs when that hierarchy is disrupted'.[10] In relation to class conflict, the speeches reflect the social situation of ancient political thought as opposition between the two groups in the ancient city: rich and poor, or upper class (the 'haves') and lower class (the 'have-nots'). Examples include Aelius Aristides' admiration of Solon, the quasi-legendary Greek forefather and lawgiver: 'He was most of all proud of the fact that he brought the people together with the rich, so that they might dwell in harmony in their city, neither side being stronger than was expedient for all in common.'[11] Dio speaks in Tarsus to the *demos*, the main body of citizens as opposed to the small ruling class.[12] The strong and the weak classes of society were in conflict with each other.

To some extent, the main aim of *homonoia* speeches is the alleviation of conflict by affirming society's hierarchy. The political hierarchy of the city is related to the hierarchical model of the cosmos, as each entity knows its position in the whole galaxy.[13]

---

7   Dio Chrysostom, *Discourses* 9.2; 33.44; 39.5; 40.21; 41.9; 50.3. He also used the body metaphor to refer to friends. See *Discourses* 3.104–107; cf. 1.31–32. See also Collins, *1 Corinthians*, 458.

8   Dio Chrysostom, *Discourses* 34.17, 20, 22; 38.12; 48.12; Aelius Aristides, *Orations* 24.16, 18. Dio compares the citizens of the state to different aspects of the body such as eyes, with which to see the city's interest, ears to hear and tongues to advise, with some as the minds (*Discourses* 39.5). It is said by the rhetoricians that strife in the political body is the same as the illness caused by the improper working of the internal parts of the body. See Isocrates, *On the Peace* 109. See also Martin, *Corinthian Body*, 38.

9   Dio Chrysostom, *Discourses* 34.20. The speeches urging for unity are called *homonoia* speeches (*concordia* in Latin). In times of crisis, these speeches are delivered calling for unity or concord. 'Within "deliberative rhetoric" – that is, rhetoric urging a political body toward some course of action – a popular topic was concord or unity.' Martin, *Corinthian Body*, 38. Cf. 1 Cor. 1.10 'I encourage you brothers … that you all agree and that you allow no schisms to exist among yourselves'; 12.25 'that there be no schisms in the body': Paul's major concern is the unity of the church, Christ's body. M. M. Mitchell categorises 1 Corinthians as a letter with the topoi of *homonoia* speeches, since Paul's main intention is the unity of the church. M. M. Mitchell, *Paul and the Rhetoric of Reconciliation: An Exegetical Investigation of the Language and Composition of 1 Corinthians* (Tübingen: Mohr, 1991), 65–66.

10   Martin, *Corinthian Body*, 40.

11   Aelius Aristides, *Orations* 24.14.

12   Dio Chrysostom, *Discourses* 34.16, 21, 23.

13   Aelius Aristides, *Oration* 23.77.

Dio refers to the heavenly bodies and the elements of the cosmos that represent concord.[14] However, it is interesting to note that the topos of the cosmos related to the city could work in the reverse direction. Pseudo-Aristotle refers to the elements of the cosmos by appeal to commonplaces regarding concord, noting that the opposite classes could work together for unity-maintaining hierarchy.[15] Since it is assumed that 'the opposites are necessary for each other's existence, it would appear that the weak and poor are necessary to balance the strong and rich – in the city as well as the cosmos'.[16]

In another topos of *homonoia* speeches the idea of the state as a household is followed; the different members do their own duty with mutual respect but with submission to those superior to them in their families.[17] However, interdependence between the family members does not imply equality.

Homonoia speeches have a familiar theme of working together for the common good by denying personal interest and yielding to others. The upper class should honour the interests of the lower in order to maintain concord and the common good. Aelius Aristides calls forth the opposite classes to follow the pattern of the household, fathers to their sons, and masters to slaves; that is, on the one side, the ruling class should renounce some of their authority and, on the other side, the inferior class are to be led by accepting the decisions of their superiors.[18]

In contrast to *homonoia* speeches, conservative ideology in the Greco-Roman world may be referred to as a benevolent patriarchalism which 'maintained the social hierarchy by urging the lower class to submit to those in authority and the higher class to rule benevolently and gently'.[19] In other words, the upper class continues to exercise its rule without any reversal of position.

14   Dio Chrysostom, *Discourses* 38.11; air, earth, water, fire and ether are hierarchically arranged; see Philo, *On Joseph* 145; *1 Clement* 20; Marcus Aurelius, *Meditations* 5.30; Aelius Aristides, *Oration* 24.42; 27.35.

15   Pseudo-Aristotle, *On the Cosmos* 5.396b.

16   *Contra* Mitchell, who considers that the purpose of the whole political body is to make all members strong. Martin observes, 'Homonoia is not aimed at equality or strength for all the members but the preservation of the "natural" relation of strength to weakness'. Mitchell, *Paul and Rhetoric of Reconciliation*, 127; Martin, *Corinthian Body*, 41.

17   Dio Chrysostom, *Discourse* 24.24; 38.15; Aelius Aristides, *Oration* 24.7; Martin, *Corinthian Body*, 41.

18   Aelius Aristides, *Oration* 24.32–33. See also Dio Chrysostom, *Discourse* 40.34; Demosthenes, *Epistle* 3.45; Mitchell, *Paul and Rhetoric of Reconciliation*, 130–32.

19   Martin, *Corinthian Body*, 42. Martin renamed Paul's 'love patriarchalism' (proposed by Theissen) as 'benevolent patriarchalism'. See Theissen, *Social Setting of Pauline Christianity*, 107–10; D. B. Martin, *Slavery as Salvation: The Metaphor of Slavery in Pauline Christianity* (London: Yale University Press, 1990), 26–30, 88–91, 126–29. Martin states that benevolent patriarchalism is used by Greco-Roman writers; see Philo's *patēreunous*, *On Joseph* 67–69. Benevolent patriarchalism falls between democracy (excessive freedom of the masses and the enslavement of the upper class to the lower) and tyranny (harsh dictatorship that does not listen to the desires of the masses).

Dio, when dealing with the conflict between the powerful city of Tarsus and the smaller neighbouring towns (*Discourse* 34.47–50), advises Tarsus to yield to the smaller towns without reversal of their status.[20] In a second speech, he addresses Nicomedia (*Discourse* 38) insisting that they achieve the title of 'the first city' by being benefactor to the smaller cities in their area and surpassing Nicea in benefaction, with whom they are in conflict and dispute. He accepts the natural hierarchy because he thinks that it is not wrong for a man to seek recognition or to attain the first rank.

5.2.1.3. Diversity and interdependence

Apart from the aspects of unity and hierarchy, the community members' different gifts, and how they are employed for the benefit of the community, are the other significant feature of the body metaphor in Greco-Roman literature. In the Sophist doctrine of society, Dionysius of Halicarnassus (c. 20 BCE) compares the state to a body with interdependent members.[21] Epictetus (c. 55 CE–c. 135 CE) wrote:

> What, then, is the profession of a citizen? To treat nothing as a matter of private profit, not to plan about anything as though he were a detached unit, but to act like the foot or the hand, which, if they had the faculty of reason to understand the constitution of nature, would never exercise choice or desire in any other way but by reference to the whole.[22]

There is evidence in Plato's *Republic* and Cicero's *On Duties* about the different functions of members of the body.[23] Plutarch also comments that, because of the law of nature, the different members are 'for mutual preservation and assistance, not for variance and strife'.[24] Another tradition by Orphics and Stoics considers the universe as the body of God.[25]

It is important to note the reference of Seneca to the pantheistic tradition, where humans are a part of the world body:

> all that you behold, that which comprises both god and man, is one – we are the parts of one great body. Nature produced us related to one another, since she created us from the same source and to the same end. She engendered in us mutual affection, and made us prone to friendships.[26]

---

20   Dio, *Discourse* 34.6–7; Martin, *Corinthian Body*, 46.
21   Dionysius Halicarnassus, *Antiq. Rom.* 6.86.1; see Jewett, *Romans*, 743.
22   Epictetus, *Discourses* 2.10.4–5.
23   Plato, *The Republic* 370A–B; Cicero, *On Duties* 3.5.22–23; 3.6.26–27.
24   Plutarch, 'On Brotherly Love', *Moralia*, 478D.
25   E. Schweizer, 'σῶμα κτλ.', 1037–38.
26   Seneca, *Epistulae Morales,* 95.52; see J. N. Sevenster, *Paul and Seneca* (NovTSup 4; Leiden: Brill, 1961), 170–71. See Jewett, *Romans*, 743.

Seneca also expresses the difference between 'a composite body' and 'a separate body' in the social sphere.[27] The first-century Jewish authors Josephus[28] and Philo[29] referred to the body metaphor too.

The study of the body politic in the Greco-Roman world is useful as we move to discuss Pauline rhetoric of the body. Paul's rhetoric shares some of the common topoi found in antiquity as both aimed to create unity. The question that faces us now is whether Paul sought to attain this unity by maintaining the social hierarchy and status classes that prevailed in society. What is the special dynamism in the Pauline rhetoric of the body politic?

5.2.2. Romans 12.3-8: exegetical analysis

Romans 12.4-5 seems to be a shorter exposition of 1 Cor. 12.12-27;[30] this may be because the Romans were already familiar with the description of the body being used as a metaphor in communal rhetoric. Although it seems that Paul addresses the same type of audience as in Corinth (he also writes from Corinth) – 'pneumatics', 'Christians who overvalued certain more evident or spectacular manifestations of the Spirit' – his emphasis is probably on 'the way in which gospel was to transform the lives of Christians'.[31] Romans 12.1-2 seems to be an introduction to the following verses (Rom. 12.3f.) and signifies the complete devotion of a believer to God.[32]

5.2.2.1. Sober-mindedness (12.3)

Devotion to God manifested in commitment to the community is the main focus of Rom. 12.3-8. Verse 3 highlights the need for sober-mindedness (σωφροσύνη) as an essential characteristic in the life of a Christian.[33] Paul

27   Seneca, *Epistulae Morales*, 102.6; see E. Schweizer, 'σῶμα κτλ.', 1034f.; See Jewett, *Romans*, 743.

28   Josephus wrote, 'As in the body when inflammation attacks the principal member all the members catch infection, so the sedition and disorder in the capital gave the scoundrels in the country free licence to plunder.' Josephus, *Bell* 4.406–407; cf. 1.507; 2.264; 5.277–79.

29   Philo, *Special Laws* 3.131; cf. *Dreams* 1.27–28. See Collins, *1 Corinthians*, 459.

30   Paul uses the body metaphor to deal with the Corinthians' erroneous view of spiritual gifts that upset their social harmony (1 Cor. 12.12-31). It is an elaborate exposition, more descriptive than in Romans, and helps to identify the different emphases in Romans. However, in Romans he explores its implications in a lucid way.

31   Moo, *Romans*, 759.

32   Cranfield, *Romans*, 2.611; Schreiner, *Romans*, 650; Moo suggests that the 'call to Christian humility and unity is certainly one important manifestation of the transformation in thinking that should characterize the believer'. Moo, *Romans*, 759. However, Käsemann regards the passage (12.3f.) as breaking from the preceding verses, since λέγειν suggests an imperative mood designating Paul's charisma – 'through the grace which has been given to me' (cf. 15.15; 1 Cor. 3.10; Gal. 2.9) and it has a theme σωφρονεῖν, which is indirectly related to vv. 1-2: Paul borrowed this term from popular philosophy (Aristotle, *Nicomachaean Ethics*, 1117b.13); and Christianised it. See Käsemann, *Romans*, 322.

33   The repeated usage is notable: ὑπερφρονεῖν (to think proudly) .... φρονεῖν (to think) .... φρονεῖν ... σωφρονεῖν (to think sensibly). σωφρονεῖν (qualifies φρονεῖν) states the way in which one should think (cf. 12.16; haughtiness prevents one from associating with the lowly).

admonishes each member of the community about their perspective and relation to others. Käsemann suggests, 'Paul characterizes that soberness as the criterion which resists over-evaluating oneself'; while Jewett says, 'Paul defines "sober-mindedness" as the refusal to impose the standard of one's relationship with God onto others.'[34] Over-evaluating oneself results in the destruction of relationships and leads to judging others on the basis of one's own spirituality. As Schreiner notes, 'Believers are not to be proud but to have a sober, sane, sensible, and realistic estimate of themselves.'[35]

Here it seems that Paul cautions against haughtiness and the improper evaluation of one's own gift (cf. 1 Corinthians 12); however, 'prominence is given to the functions which no community can be without and which obviously already enjoy special prestige'.[36] The exhortation is addressed to each member of the community (παντὶ τῷ ὄντι ἐν ὑμῖν) as each has been given a measure of faith[37] in accordance with which they make their evaluation. In this case, faith does not denote a special gift to perform miracles (1 Cor. 12.9 cf. 13.2), but rather the trust each believer has in God; it indicates the 'measure of reliance on God which enables χάρις to come to expression in χάρισμα. It is the confident trust in God which recognizes that all faith and grace is from God which prevents the misjudgement of ὑπερφρονεῖν.'[38]

The other usages in Romans are 8.5; 11.20; 8.6, 7, 27 (the cognate noun), 11.25 (adjective). The Pauline corpus uses σωφρονεῖν (cf. also 2 Cor. 5.13) and its cognates σωφρονίζω (Tit. 2.4), σωφρονισμός (2 Tim. 1.7), σωφρονῶς (Tit. 2.12), σωφροσύνη (2 Tim. 2.9, 15), and σώφρων (1 Tim. 3.2; Tit. 1.8; 2.2, 5), which denotes 'a steady, clear-headed understanding of the believer and his or her world that recognizes the truth of the gospel'. Moo, *Romans*, 760 (fn. 12). φρονεῖν was one of the primary virtues in the Greek world. See U. B. Luck, 'σωφρονεῖν κτλ.', *TDNT* 7, 1098–100; R. M. Thorsteinsson, 'Paul and Roman Stoicism: Romans 12 and Contemporary Stoic Ethics', *JSNT* 29 (2006), 139–61, at 149.

34   Käsemann, *Romans*, 334. Jewett suggests, 'Christian soberness makes use of all the opportunities being aware of the limits and boundaries, for one's own existence, and that of others and the given situation.' Jewett, *Romans*, 742.

35   Schreiner, *Romans*, 651, 652. Ziesler notes, 'It stands for balance, clarity of vision, and good sense.' Ziesler, *Romans*, 652.

36   Käsemann, *Romans*, 332.

37   μέτρον πίστεως is interpreted in different ways. μέτρον is defined as standard of faith as Jesus Christ; those who agree with this view are Cranfield, *Romans*, 2.614; Ziesler, *Romans*, 296; Fitzmyer, *Romans*, 646; cf. Moo, *Romans*, 761; Morris, *Romans*, 438 or as the gospel (Stuhlmacher, *Romans*, 192); and those who agree with 'measure' or 'quantity of faith' are Schlatter (A. Schlatter, *Romans, The Righteousness of God* [Peabody: Hendrickson, 1995], 231); Murray (*Romans*, 118–19); Michel (O. Michel, *Der Brief an die Römer*, 14th edn [Göttingen: Vandenhoeck & Ruprecht, 1978], 296–97); Leenhardt (F.-J. Leenhardt, *The Epistle of St. Paul to the Romans: A Commentary* [London: Lutterworth, 1961], 308–309); Dunn (720); Schreiner (653); Jewett (741). The latter seems to be more likely as the verb ἐμέρισεν with the noun suggests the measure of something (cf. 1 Cor. 7.17; 2 Cor. 10.13). As Schreiner notes, 'the phrase relates to the apportioning of an amount of faith instead of apportioning "the standard of faith"'. Schreiner, *Romans*, 653.

38   Dunn, *Romans 9–16*, 722. As Dunn suggests, χάρις is 'the divine commissioning and enabling which comes to concrete expression in Χάρισμα' (720). The self-understanding of faith as a gift from God helps a person to rid themselves of their pride. 'What prevents pride from

5.2.2.2. One body, many members (12.4)

The soberness of one's own faith was a way for the church to function as one body; that is implied from γάρ in v. 4 ('for just as in one body … do not have the same function'). It is notable that the usage of καθάπερ … οὕτως ('just as … so'; vv. 4, 5) also appears in 1 Cor. 12.12, where v. 4 denotes the basis for the comparison, while v. 5 refers to the conclusion.[39]

The body metaphor communicates Paul's desire to create unity amongst diversity: the body has many members, but all the members do not have the same function. As Jewett comments:

> the two premises Paul sets forth are indisputable from the perspective of everyday experience: that a body has 'many members, but all members do not have the same use'. The formulation of these premises moves beyond any universal definition of the 'we' that are joined together ἐν ἑνὶ σώματι ('in one body/in a single body').[40]

The use of πρᾶξις (v. 4) in Romans is significant (it is not used in 1 Corinthians), since it conveys practical action (cf. Rom. 8.13; Col. 3.9), and implies continual effort will help the body function healthily.

Although it is not clear whether the passage refers to the universal or local church, it is probable that the local church is in view. After all, the Christian community addressed in Romans 16 met in several house churches.[41]

5.2.2.3. One body in Christ (12.5)

How does Paul develop the body metaphor in Romans? Although it seems that Paul is influenced by the use of body as a political metaphor in antiquity, one needs to look carefully at the distinction between a political metaphor and an ecclesiological one. First Corinthians 12 and Romans 12 move beyond the Greco-Roman political model of the body, to equating the body with Christ ('body of Christ' and 'body in Christ').[42] Jewett comments that while Paul is speaking about one body in Christ (Romans 12), his sense is metaphorical rather than a 'realistic identification of the Christian community with Christ'. Stuhlmacher regards this as 'not merely a metaphor but a reality which has been established for believing Christians by the crucified and resurrected Christ'.[43]

---

cropping up is a sober estimation of one's faith, and this sober estimation is based on the truth that God apportioned to each one a measure of faith.' Schreiner, *Romans*, 653.

39   Moo, *Romans*, 762. 'In classical rhetoric, a *similitudo* (similitude) is a type of argument drawn from everyday experience, as contrasted with an *exemplum* (example) drawn from history or literature.' Jewett, *Romans*, 742. See also Cranfield, *Romans*, 302; D. M. Coffee, 'The Function of Homeric Simile', *AJP* 78 (1957), 113–32.

40   Jewett, *Romans*, 743.

41   Moo, *Romans*, 763.

42   See R. Jewett, *Paul's Anthropological Terms: A Study of their Use in Conflict Situations* (AGJU, 10; Leiden: Brill, 1971), 249.

43   Jewett, *Romans*, 743. P. Stuhlmacher, *Paul's Letter to the Romans: A Commentary*, S. J. Hafemann (trans.) (Westminster: John Knox, 1994), 191. The phrases with the preposition ἐν

It is important to note that uniformity in Christ does not diminish the importance of the individual: 'the unity of the members of the body for all their diversity, a unity brought about by the fact that they are all in Christ, a unity that does not reduce them all to a drab uniformity'.[44] Christ is the unifying matrix among the diversified members of the church ('one body in Christ'), which calls for unity and solidarity between different congregations. Schreiner suggests, 'Paul surprises the reader by emphasizing unity rather than the diversity of the body of Christ.'[45] Unity and diversity are important to the body's proper function, as Dunn suggests, 'without that diversity the body would be a monstrosity'.[46]

Unity in Christ is achieved by interdependence between the members ('each one is a member of others': τὸ δὲ καθ' εἷς ἀλλήλων μέλη). The expression τὸ δὲ καθ' εἷς 'each one, individually' denotes that 'each Christian is actually an interdependent "member" along with all others'.[47] This unity is characterised by the 'in Christ' relationship. The corporate dimension of the body of Christ is emphasised; in Christ the different churches and members of the community are joined together to become one entity. As Jewett rightly affirms, 'Christ is the larger reality within which the various congregations and individual members are to find their unity.'[48]

How is this expression (τὸ δὲ καθ' εἷς ἀλλήλων μέλη) different compared to its use in 1 Cor. 12.27? In 1 Corinthians the 'members of the body of Christ' is used in a collective sense, but in Romans, it specifies and signifies the members of the body as the members *of one another*. The notion of the church being members of one another is expressed in Rom. 12.9f. and 13.8f.[49] In Romans Paul recommends a more intense form of interdependence in comparison with 1 Corinthians: in being the members of one another (not

---

('in') with Christ and the Lord (including 'in him') as the object are used 165 times in the Pauline letters. The function of the phrase 'in Christ' points to a new communal identity that holds the believers together in unity. This formula shows the belonging-togetherness 'in the Lord', which implies that the existence of the community is grounded in Christ. For more discussion, see J. D. G. Dunn, *Theology of Paul the Apostle* (London: T&T Clark, 2003), 396–400.

44   Morris, *Romans*, 439.

45   Schreiner, *Romans*, 654.

46   Dunn, *Romans 9–16*, 725. The unity of the body does not imply equality of gifts and faith among the members. See Schreiner, *Romans*, 654.

47   Jewett, *Romans*, 744. See A. J. M. Wedderburn, 'Some Observations on Paul's Use of the Phrases in Christ and with Christ', *JSNT* 25 (1985), 83–97. Members have no meaning unless they are part of a body that 'one cannot be a "member" of nothing'. Morris, *Romans*, 439. It is also significant that Paul wants each believer to be members of 'someone else'. B. Wannenwetsch argues that being members of one another works in 'the representation of *Charis* and ministry' of others. I think he focuses on one of the aspects of being members of one another. B. Wannenwetsch, '"Members of One Another": *Charis*, Ministry and Representation: A Politico-Ecclesial Reading of Romans 12', in C. Bartholomew et al., *A Royal Priesthood? A Use of the Bible Ethically and Politically, A Dialogue with Oliver O'Donovan* (The Scripture and Hermeneutics Series, vol. 3; Grand Rapids: Zondervan, 2002), 197–220, at 220.

48   Jewett, *Romans*, 744. See also Thorsteinsson, 'Paul and Roman Stoicism', 150, 151.

49   Refer below 5.3.1.and 5.3.7.

just of something else they all contribute to), their very identity as a body is composed of the contribution of others. 'So we many are one body in Christ' suggests a common belonging to Christ that marks a new unity formed by an individual being 'in Christ'. 'They are not each one individually, but as a corporate unity, all together in him.'[50]

5.2.2.4. Differing grace to differing charismatic gifts (vv. 6-8)

The use of the body metaphor is explained in the context of correctly using charismatic gifts. The grace is apportioned differently so that the gifts are also differently distributed. Dunn suggests that vv. 6-8 is a continuation of the body metaphor in vv. 4-5,[51] implying the task or function each gift has in the church. It is not appropriate to think that the gifts are apportioned between the office holders alone, since the use of the participle 'having', the reference to the body with many members, the use of 'the many' and 'each' (12.5), and the mention of 'the grace given to us' (12.6) suggest that each person in the church had a charismatic gift (χάρισμα). The different gifts were to be used with regard to one another so that the specific purposes of the gifts could be fulfilled. Each Christian was a recipient of grace (χάρις), and charismatic gifts (χαρίσματα) are the expressions of the grace's reception. Jewett observes, 'this rhetorically effective wordplay between χάρις and χαρίσματα, ... resulting in a shift of emphasis away from the more spectacularly ecstatic manifestation such as glossolalia to the sober expressions of the congregational leadership mentioned in Romans'.[52] The gift of 'tongues' is meant for one's own spiritual edification (1 Corinthians 14), while other gifts ('tongues' is not mentioned in Romans) work with one another.

Having discussed the body metaphor's purpose in illustrating the value of mutuality within the community, I shall now examine other ways in which Paul sought to express his exhortation to communal mutuality (Romans 12–13).

5.3. Love enhancing mutuality in Romans[53] *(Rom. 12.9-13; 13.8-10)*

Paul's strategies to bring forth mutuality in the community are very obvious in Romans as he repeatedly uses key words such as ἀγάπη and ἀλλήλους, followed by the body metaphor. In Romans ἀγάπη (Rom. 5.5, 8; 8.35, 39; 12.9; 13.10a, 10b; 14.15; 15.30) is used nine times; ἀγαπάω (Rom. 8.28, 37; 9.13, 25a, b; 13: 8a, b, 9) is used eight times; and ἀλλήλους (Rom. 1.12, 27;

---

50   H. Ridderbos, *Paul: An Outline of His Theology*, J.R. De Witt (trans.) (Grand Rapids: Eerdmans, 1977), 371.

51   Dunn, *Romans 9–16*, 725.

52   Jewett, *Romans*, 745.

53   Love can enhance mutuality and vice versa. Love increases mutuality and mutual relationships increase love. Since Paul considers love as an essential ingredient in the Christian life, claiming that it should guide all actions (1 Corinthians 13; Romans 12, 13), the gifts and charismata are irrelevant without it.

2.15; 12.5, 10a, b, 16; 13.8; 14.13, 19; 15.5, 7, 14; 16.16)[54] is used fourteen times (nearly all uses of ἀλλήλους occur in Romans 12–16). The core of the message Paul conveys is to honour others more than oneself through genuine love. Thus ἀγάπη shows the character of real love as the 'love of the higher lifting up the lower', and is seen in giving oneself wholly to others.

In Rom. 12.9-21; 13.8-10, love is the prominent theme as Paul launches into a series of exhortations on the internal life of the Christian community and its relation to the outside world.[55] The following sections focus on selected issues such as genuine love, brotherly affection, honour, generosity and hospitality, identifying love, harmonious living, and obligatory love.

5.3.1. Genuine love (12.9)

Paul exhorts that love should be genuine (12.9), which seems to be the caption of the entire pericope[56] (cf. 2 Cor. 6.6; cf. 1 Pet. 1.22); in other words, 'love (is) without pretense'. Romans 12.9a describes the practical implication of vv. 1-8. Wilson notes that 12.9 has a gnomic form that defines love rather than insisting on its performance.[57] Wilson notes that the individual's devotion to God, as a result of the gift of salvation, is the foundation of the charismatic ethic (12.1, 2) and it is built upon 'the love' (v. 9).[58] It is likely that Paul has in mind the love already present in the Roman churches: love among believers. Most scholars agree that the term ἀγάπη is used more by early Christians than other contemporary writers.[59] Dunn relates the use of the term ἀγάπη

---

54   Although it is used elsewhere in the Pauline letters, it is not used as extensively in Romans (1 Cor. 7.5; 11.33; 12.25; 16.20; 2 Cor. 13.12; Gal. 5.13, 15a, b, 17, 26a, b, c; 6.2; Phil. 2.3; 1 Thess. 3.12; 4.9, 18; 5.11, 15; 2 Thess. 1.3; cf. Eph. 4.2, 25, 32; 5.21; Col. 3.9, 13; Tit. 3.3). Lowe notes, 'the ἀλλήλων reciprocal pronoun ... acts as a call to functionalize the theological truth in concrete relationships and behaviours'. S. D. Lowe, 'Rethinking the Female Status/ Function Question: The Jew/Gentile Relationship as Paradigm', *JETS* 34 (1991), 59–75, at 70.

55   The pericope in 12.9-21 seems to be similar to the love hymn in 1 Corinthians 13: both are preceded by the exposition on the body metaphor. Moreover, both portray the different dimensions and implications of love in the day-to-day life of a Christian. However, mutual relationships are emphasised more in Romans.

56   Dunn, *Romans 9–16*, 739; M. Black, *Romans* (NCBC; Grand Rapids: Eerdmans, 1989), 15; W. T. Wilson, *Love without Pretense: Romans 12.9-11 and Hellenistic-Jewish Wisdom Literature* (Tübingen: Mohr, 1991), 142, 150; Stuhlmacher, *Romans*, 195; Jewett, *Romans*, 758. Käsemann does not agree that the section has love as its heading. He suggests, 'It is simply one mode of behaviour among others, not the criterion and true modality of all the rest.' Käsemann, *Romans*, 343.

57   Wilson, *Love without Pretense*, 150–51. As Wilson notes, 'let love be without pretense', is the traditional translation of v. 9a. The gnomic form has only a noun and adjective and does not necessarily need an imperative verb, which seems to be the same in 12.9a 'ἡ ἀγάπη ἀνυπόκριτος'. He cites the famous Delphic maxim as verbless and nounless: μηδὲν ἄγαν 'Nothing to excess', see Jewett, *Romans*, 758. He lists the similar sayings in Cleobulus *Epig.* 1; Thales *Epig. ded.* 11–13; Pittacus *Epig.* 11; Periander *Ep.* 11.

58   Wilson, *Love without Pretense*, 155. The use of the definite article implies the particular nature of love, as a 'well known virtue' (Moo, *Romans*, 775) and to avoid other unwanted interpretations.

59   V. Warnach, *Agape. Die Liebe als Grundmotiv der neutestamentlichen Theologie*

to the social context of the love feast among the Roman believers.[60] This love is not limited to believers, but should be offered to strangers and persecutors (12.13-14). Love is the root of all the rest and 'such love is poured into the heart (5.5) of each member of the community (1.7), to be both spontaneous and indiscriminately generous'.[61]

Paul labels love as genuine and without pretence rather than as 'sincere' or 'unhypocritical'.[62] Why does Paul use the adjective ἀνυπόκριτος? Since the adjective is derived from ὑποκρίτης ('actor'), he might have foreseen the possibility of a deceptive and corrupt love. A similar saying envisaging friendship (a different word is used by Paul) is found in Prov. 27.5 and among the pre-Socratic philosophers.[63] In 2 Cor. 6.6, Paul used the same word ἀγάπη ἀνυποκρίτῳ ('with genuine love') in contrast to the false apostles who used their gifts for the sake of power and status. Why does Paul mention 'genuine' love? It is likely that he wishes the love to be genuine because of his struggles with the opponents (2 Cor. 6.6).[64] 'To remain "genuine" in love requires a disciplined commitment to honesty and respect to limits, as the rest of the passage will demonstrate.'[65]

Paul advises the Romans that genuine love 'hates (ἀποστουγοῦντες) what is evil and holds fast (κολλώμενοι) to what is good' (9b-c). Although the connection between 9a, 9b, and 9c has been debated recently, denying its logical connection, it is possible that there is a link between them on substantive and grammatical grounds.[66] As Morris notes, 'True love involves

---

(Düsseldorf: Patmos, 1951), 106–44; Ceslas Spicq, *Agape dans le Nouveau Testament. Analyse des Textes, EtBib* (Paris: Gabalda, 1958–59) 1.208–315; 2.9–305; V. P. Furnish, *The Love Command in the New Testament* (London: SCM, 1973), 102–11; John Piper, *Love your Enemies: Jesus' Love Command in the Synoptic Gospels and the Early Christian Paraenesis* (SNTS 38; Cambridge: Cambridge University Press, 1979), 4–18, 102–108; Wilson, *Love without Pretense*, 151.

60   Dunn, *Romans 9–16*, 739. Jewett thinks that Dunn is the only commentator to mention the agape meal in the early churches' use of the term. See Jewett, *Romans*, 758.

61   Jewett, *Romans*, 758. Käsemann defines love as 'being for others' and genuine love is 'whole hearted and disinterested service'. Käsemann, *Romans*, 345.

62   U. Wilckens, 'ὑποκρίνομαι κτλ,' *TDNT* 8 (1972), 559–71. He thinks 'genuine' is an appropriate translation since the psychological connotation of 'insincerity' or 'hypocrisy' is not used by pre-Christian users.

63   The maxim in Prov. 27.5 is: 'open rebukes (are) better than disguised love'. Among the pre-Socratic philosophers, the maxims are: 'many who seem to be friends are not, and many who do not seem to be are'; 'it is difficult for an enemy to deceive his foe, Cyrnus, but easy for friend to deceive friend'. See *Gnomologium Democrateum* 97; Theognis *Eleg.* 1219–20. See also Jewett, *Romans*, 759.

64   See Georgi, *Opponents*, 258–64, 315–19. The point here is people can pretend to be nice and kind but lack genuine love. See Schreiner, *Romans*, 663.

65   Jewett, *Romans*, 759. See also Jewett, *Christian Tolerance*, 92–120.

66   ἀποστουγοῦντες (abhor, KJV) is a strong word for hatred; commentators suggest that ἀπο- gives emphasis to the verb. κολλώμενοι refers to the marriage relationship elsewhere (1 Cor. 6.16, 17; cf. Mt. 19.5). Barrett argues that the participles (ἀποστουγοῦντες, κολλώμενοι) are imperatival; by contrast, Fitzmyer suggests they are not imperatival. See Barrett, *Romans*, 221; Fitzmyer, *Romans*, 653. Cleaving to good is elaborated in vv. 10-16 and abhorring evil in vv. 17-21.

a deep hatred for all that is evil, for evil can never benefit the beloved.'[67] Love not only hates evil but also has 'a strong affinity for what is good, so that they seek it fervently and cling to it no matter what the cost'.[68] The genuineness of love can be tested with evil actions because sincere love is always committed to the good of others (cf. Rom. 12.21; overcoming evil with good).

5.3.2. Brotherly affection (φιλαδελφία 12.10a)

Paul continues to emphasise that love equates to mutual responsibility in v. 10a: 'love one another with brotherly affection'. Genuine love is necessary for practising φιλαδελφία. In 1 Thess. 4.10, Paul used this term in a sense of emotional and material sharing. Brotherly love appears to be a uniquely developed notion among Christians; the idea was so strong that it was as if they were members of a natural family bound by a special sense of love.[69] In Romans, Paul focuses this sense of love's importance on interpersonal actions and attitudes.

Verse 10 can be considered as a pair of admonitions which are related to one another. The two parts of v. 10 form a structured parallelism and can be interpreted on the basis of each other.[70] Paul moves from the individual focus to the congregational focus, which is evident in the word εἰς ἀλλήλους ('one another'). Aasgaard observes that Paul is speaking about brotherly love in general, and that the mutual obligation among Christians is expressed without bias.[71]

It is also striking that φιλαδελφία is used with φιλόστοργοι; both terms have a φιλο- stem, and φιλόστοργοι occurs only once in the whole New Testament. Paul speaks about 'family affection' (φιλόστοργοι) and also uses the term φιλαδελφία to convey an attitude of brotherly and sisterly love.[72]

---

67   Morris, *Romans*, 444.

68   Schreiner, *Romans*, 664.

69   The idea of brotherly love is common among the Jews (which Christians took over), and it is also common among Essenes (it is used for fellow countrymen, members of the religious society, and for friends; see H. F.von Soden, φιλαδελφία, *TDNT* 1, 146). The sense of one family united in love with God as their Father is significant among the Christians, as this sense of familial relationship existed only among the members of the natural family. Morris, *Romans*, 444. See also Moo, *Romans*, 777; Schreiner, *Romans*, 664; Dunn, Jewett, Cranfield, Barrett also agree with this view.

70   Aasgaard regards the second part of the verse to be interpreted as the explanation of the first part, and that the two verse halves form a 'synthetic parallelism'. Aasgaard, *My Beloved Brothers and Sisters*, 171.

71   Irrespective of groups or persons, love should be given to all. The repetition of ἀλλήλους: εἰς ἀλλήλους (v. 10a) and ἀλλήλους (v. 10b) strongly highlights the aspect of mutuality; εἰς ἀλλήλους is significant since it focuses on brotherly love as an internal obligation. See Aasgaard, *My Beloved Brothers and Sisters*, 172. Aasgaard also suggests that the element of reciprocity is more evident in Romans than 1 Thessalonians, possibly because of the internal strife in the Roman church.

72   The Christian identity as ἀδελφός and ἀδελφή designates the familial language, which has its influence in the early Christian communities, to depict their relationship as that of siblings; this implies 'role ethics' that determines the pattern of behaviour. See Horrell, *Solidarity*

He compares the church to a natural family, suggesting that their love for one another should be like a natural family's love because all members of the church are brothers and sisters in Christ.

5.3.3. *Honouring one another (*τῇ τιμῇ ἀλλήλους προηγούμενοι *12.10b)*

The interpretation of τῇ τιμῇ ἀλλήλους προηγούμενοι has divided scholars into two groups: one group has come up with the meaning 'to lead the way ...' or 'be the first in conferring honour on others',[73] and the other group interprets the phrase on the basis of Phil. 2.3: 'in humility preferring others as more excellent than yourselves'.[74] I suggest that the more viable translation of v. 10b (τῇ τιμῇ ἀλλήλους προηγούμενοι) is 'taking the lead in honouring one another'.[75] The two exhortations in v. 10 are related to each other. The prefix προ- signifies or intensifies the verb ἡγέομαι ('lead').[76] This verse can be understood best in the context of social honour in the Mediterranean world, where public recognition was the mark of personal identity.[77] Moxnes notes

and Difference, 113. Aasgaard highlights the emotional element evident in φιλόστοργοι, as φιλ- is repeated, where Paul emphasises that our attitudes should be affectionate. See Aasgaard, *My Beloved Brothers and Sisters*, 173.

73   Those who agree with this view are Dunn (741); Fitzmyer (654); Stuhlmacher (195); Moo (777–78), NRSV, RSV.

74   The difference between the two views is narrow since the verbal root ἡγεῖσθαι is used. Those who agree with the second option are J. Calvin, *Commentaries on the Epistle of Paul to the Romans,* J. Owen (trans.) (Vol. XIX; Grand Rapids: Baker House, 1993), 465; Sanday and Headlam, *Romans*, 361; Barrett, *Romans*, 221; Käsemann, *Romans*, 346; Schreiner, *Romans*, 664. Wilckens, *Römer*, 3.20; Cranfield, *Romans*, 2.632, 633; KJV, NIV.

75   Jewett, *Romans*, 761. Τιμή is used elsewhere in Romans (2.7; 9.21; 13.7). The related terms are glory (δόξα [2.7; 3.7; 4.20; 5.2; 8.18, 21; 11.36]), dishonour (ἀτιμία [1.26; 9.21]), boast (καύχημα/καύχησις [3.27; 4.2; 15.17]). See also J. Schneider, 'τιμή κτλ.,' *TDNT* 8 (1972) 169–80.

In an article entitled 'The Relationship with Others: Similarities and Differences between Paul and Stoicism', T. Engberg-Pedersen notes there are two types of honour in Stoicism; 'τιμή and δόξα. 'τιμή is to 'be given to others' δόξα is 'one that gets for one's own'. He argues that Paul's argument of 'other-regardingness' is completely one-sided: 'forgetting completely about oneself, thinking instead and only of the others' and Paul missed out the other aspect of Stoicism: 'the wise man ... also remains an individual bodily being'. It is purposefully omitted by Paul that 'Paul wished to make his image of the fully committed Christ-believer as radically onesided as at all possible' (Arius, SVF III, 112). T. Engberg-Pedersen, 'The Relationship with Others: Similarities and Differences between Paul and Stoicism', *ZNW* 96 (2005), 35–60, at 56, 57. See also T. Engberg-Pedersen, *Paul and the Stoics* (Edinburgh: T&T Clark, 2000).

As P. H. Esler notes, 'Paul's paramount concern with the nature of face-to-face contacts between Christ-followers, who treat one another with ἀγάπη and put the interest of others ahead of their own, is so radically different from anything in the stoic thought that he brings into sharp focus his distinctive vision of moral life in Christ.' P. H. Esler, 'Paul and Stoicism: Romans 12 as a Test Case', *NTS* 50 (2004), 106–24, at 124.

76   See *BDAG*, 864; *LSJ* 1480. It is a compound verb and it is used only once in the New Testament; 'take the lead in honouring' or 'be a leader in honouring'.

77   See B. J. Malina, *The New Testament World: Insights from Cultural Anthropology* (Louisville: John Knox Press, 2001), 25–50; R. Jewett, 'Honour and Shame in the Argument of Romans', in A. Brown, G. F. Snyder, and V. Wiles (eds.), *Putting Body and Soul Together: Essays*

that in antiquity honour was displayed in 'due balance' among those of the same honour status, and thus there was a balanced mutuality.[78] But in Paul the standard of honour reverses or 'even transcends the given order': others are to be honoured higher than oneself. It is important to note the Hebraic idiom mentioned by Michel, 'the virtue of taking the lead in greeting others'.[79] Here it has some effect on the congregational situation in Rome, as there is lack of acceptance in their love feasts (see below in chapter 6 on Romans 14, 15). Paul mentions this strategy of honouring others in v. 3, 'not to think of yourself more highly than you ought to think', and more explicitly in v. 16, 'associate with the lowly' (τοῖς ταπεινοῖς, which refers to what lacks honour).

The re-evaluation of one's values takes place in the form of 'honouring others higher than oneself'. If each one takes the lead, then there will be 'sharing' of honour, by honouring others higher than oneself. Thus one can demonstrate genuine love and the competition to gain honour as a way to give honour to others. Moxnes comments, 'In the transformation of values, Paul claims that honour is now freely to be granted on the basis of love, regardless of status and merit.'[80] It implies that 'the standards are to be changed, and the tables turned upside down'[81] and that the interests of Christian siblings are to be honoured by renouncing one's own.

---

in Honour of Robin Scroggs (Valley Forge: Trinity Press International, 1997), 257–72. See also H. Moxnes, 'Honour and Righteousness', *JSNT* 32 (1988), 61–77, at 73–74.

78   H. Moxnes, 'The Quest for Honour and the Unity of the Community in Romans 12 and in the Orations of Dio Chrysostom', in T. Engberg-Pederson (ed.), *Paul in his Hellenistic Context* (Edinburgh: T&T Clark, 1994), 203–30, at 211–13, 220–23. See also Moxnes, 'Honour and Righteousness', 74.

79   O. Michel, *Der Brief an die Römer* (KEK, 4; Göttingen: Vandenhoeck & Ruprecht, 1978), 384. In P. *'Abot* 4.15 Rabbi Eleazar ben Shammua said: 'Let the honour of your disciple be dear to you as the honour of your associate, and the honour of your associate as the fear of your teacher, and the honour of your teacher as the fear of heaven.' In *'Abot* 4.20 the second-century rabbi Mattia ben Harasch taught, 'Be first in greeting every man …'. Jewett, *Romans*, 762, fn. 39.

80   Moxnes, 'Honour and Righteousness', 74–75. Moxnes observes that Paul relates the internal relations and behaviours of the community to the question of honour and recognition, since Paul instructs them 'to outdo in honouring one another' (12.10), and that honour is not to be awarded on merits and status but only on the basis of 'brotherly love'. Society's way of honouring those of higher status is reversed in Paul, and those of lower status should be the recipients of honour from those of the same level or higher. He also notes that Paul's argument is similar to that used in chs. 3–4. 'Behaviour among Christians should reflect God's free granting of honour.' It implies re-evaluation of values for the benefit of others.

81   Aasgaard, *My Beloved Brothers*, 173, 4. Aasgaard disagrees with Moxnes that the honour codes of Paul work in the framework of the honour shame system of the city. Rather he notes that the language of Christian relations employed by Paul is from the context of the family and siblingship. See Aasgaard, *My Beloved Brothers*, 175.

5.3.4. Generosity and hospitality (12.13)

Genuine love has its expression in sharing (κοινωνοῦντες) rather than merely contributing (μεταδοῦντες; 12.8). The verb κοινωνοῦντες in Paul's letters (Rom. 15.26, 27; 2 Cor. 8.4; 9.13; Gal. 6.6; Phil. 1.5; 4.15; cf. 1 Tim. 6.18; Heb. 13.16; cf. Acts 2.44; 4.32) carries a sense of making financial contributions and sharing resources. It is unlikely that Paul has the Jerusalem collection in mind,[82] since the Romans were not asked to contribute to the project; rather, Paul reminds the believers that sharing the needs[83] of the saints (all believers) is a mark of the Christian life. As Schreiner notes, 'Paul certainly believed that all those in financial distress should be provided with help, but he assigned priority to those in the believing community (Gal 6:10), in the same way that one should financially assist family members before giving to others (1 Tim 5:4, 8).'[84]

Paul links the practices of hospitality and sharing with the exhortation to be the first in meeting the requirements of others (v. 10b). The use of the participle διώκοντες indicates the initiative in helping with hospitality, and could be understood as another form of sharing resources, i.e. by opening one's own house for a guest or stranger so that they are fed and comfortable.[85] It is widely agreed that the term φιλοξενία can be translated as 'hospitality'. Moreover, Morris clarifies that, 'Paul is not advocating a pleasant social exercise among friends, but the use of one's home to help even people we do not know, if that will advance God's cause.'[86] However, Paul is mindful that hospitality should

---

82   Dunn, *Romans 9–16*, 743; Cf. T. Zahn, *Der Brief des Paulus an die Römer* (Kommentar zum Neuen Testament 6; Leipzig: Deichert, 1910). This view is opposed by Cranfield.

83   There is a textual variation over whether χρείαις or μνείαις is used (needs or remembrances). Most scholars reject the term 'remembrances' but accept 'needs'. The evidence for μνείας (D* F G) is not negligible, but χρείας fits the context better, and μνεία is not used in plural in the New Testament. The notion of remembering the saints as outstanding Christians is not convincing; rather it is more likely to mean to help those who are needy by being one with them. The early church was deeply concerned about the poor, whose situation was desperate. See L. Morris, *The Epistle to the Romans* (Grand Rapids: Eerdmans, 1988), 448; other scholars like Moo, Cranfield, Barrett, and Jewett accept the same view. Käsemann notes that assistance is to be given to widows, orphans, prisoners, and the needy (see Käsemann, *Romans*, 346), which gives a picture of those who are at a particular social level of the society. I think that 'needy' does not denote a particular social group as such, but it could be used as an inclusive term to denote people with different needs.

84   Schreiner, *Romans*, 666.

85   Ancient society highly regarded the virtue of providing hospitality to strangers; the people of Israel were sojourners in Egypt (Lev. 19.34; Deut. 10.19), Abraham was a model of hospitality (Genesis 18); likewise, hospitality was a key feature of Jesus' ministry (Mk. 1.29-31; 14.3; Lk. 10.38-42) as well as the early missions (Acts 16.15; 18.3). Dunn, *Romans 9–16*, 743, 744. See for more discussion J. Koenig, *New Testament Hospitality: Partnership with Strangers as Promise and Mission* (Philadelphia: Fortress, 1985), 61–65. The idea of hospitality resonates in Paul's admonition to welcome one another (Romans 14, 15), in greetings (Rom. 16.2-16) and Phoebe's welcome as she needs to be welcomed as is worthy of the saints (Rom. 16.1, 2).

86   Morris, *Romans*, 448. The missionaries lack money to pay for lodging, so the need of hospitality was urgent in Paul's days and their travel depended on hospitality; cf. Heb. 13.2; 1 Pet. 4.9; *1 Clem* 1.2; 10.7; 11.1; 12.1; *Herm Man* 38.10.

be practised, not only with regard to evangelistic purposes, but also with an obligation for the well-being of the whole community. Christian life has its fruits in communal sharing, caring, and supporting.

The practical value of preferring one another will take its form in hospitality and support offered to travelling leaders (Rom. 12.13; 15.24; 16.2, 23; cf. 1 Cor. 16.6, 11; Philemon 22),[87] which implies their universal significance. A local church is a prototype of the larger family in its broader context. It is not *a* body of Christ but *the* body of Christ (1 Cor. 12.27).[88]

5.3.5. Identifying love (12.15)

Relations in the community[89] are very well expressed as Paul admonishes the believers to be one with those who rejoice and with those who weep (v. 15). The infinitives χαίρειν (to rejoice), κλαίειν (to weep) are used in an imperative sense. Showing solidarity with others is a real expression of love in the Christian community.[90] This is total identification, or in other words, being one with others, i.e. being members of one another (12.5). It is more difficult to rejoice with others than weep with those who suffer. Chrysostom notes that the admonition to rejoice comes first because it is difficult to put into practice,[91] since envy could prevent its genuineness. Here Paul wants the believers not only to be indifferent to the happiness and sorrowfulness of others but also to share with them.

5.3.6. Harmonious living (Rom. 12.16)

Paul states that the believers should live in harmony with one another (τὸ αὐτό εἰς ἀλλήλους φρονοῦντες) v. 16a cf. 1 Cor. 12.25 (τὸ αὐτό ὑπὲρ ἀλλήλων);[92] Käsemann suggests this means that the community was expected to be of one mind.[93] Translations could be rendered as follows: 'live in harmony with one another' (NIV); 'thinking the same to one another' (literal Greek).

---

87   Meggitt, *Paul, Poverty, and Survival*, 163.

88   Banks, *Paul's Idea of Community*, 63.

89   Cranfield thinks that those outside the church are not in view. By contrast, Dunn suggests here the community implies a wider perspective including those outside the church. See Cranfield, *Romans*, 2.674f.; Dunn, *Romans 9–16*, 756.

90   Schreiner, *Romans*, 668. I disagree with Morris as he uses the term 'sympathy' to denote the sense of feeling to others (v. 15), since I suggest 'identifying' is more meaningful here in relation to the body metaphor. Morris, *Romans*, 449; cf. Barrett, *Romans*, 222.

91   Chrysostom, *Homilies on Romans*, 7.

92   The use of the proposition εἰς is notable in this verse, since it is not used with the phrase (τὸ αὐτό ... ἀλλήλους) elsewhere in the Pauline epistles (Rom. 15.5: ἐν ἀλλήλοις is used after τὸ αὐτὸ φρονεῖν). Calvin, Wilckens (*Der Brief an die Römer*, 3. EKKNT, 6. Neukirchen-Vluyn: Neukirchener Verlag, 1978–82), Moo, Dunn, and Jewett interpret this verse as referring to the relationship of Christians with one another, and not to outsiders; *contra* Cranfield, Leenhardt. It could be assumed that the 'same' attitude among the Christians could also be presented towards all other people irrespective of their status; TEV: 'the same concern for everyone'. Moo, *Romans*, 783.

93   Käsemann, *Romans*, 347.

As Moo rightly suggests,

> The 'one-another' language of v. 15 picks up the same theme from v. 10, while the use of the root φρον- ('think') in all three admonitions in this verse reminds us of Paul's demand for the right kind of 'thinking' among Christians in v. 3. … He is calling us to a common mind-set. Such a common mind-set does not mean that we must all think in just the same way or that we must think exactly the same thing about every issue, but what we should adopt an attitude toward everything that touches our lives that springs from the renewed mind of the new realm to which we belong by God's grace (v. 2).[94]

The phrase implies that the whole community has the same goal, to 'be of the same mind', and to achieve it they work together, which perhaps implies a common attitude of humility to one another. This has a lot to do with respect and honour that works in both directions as the preposition εἰς with ἀλλήλους (towards one another) signifies.

The other mark of a Christian noted in v. 16b is not to think highly about oneself, μὴ τὰ ὑψηλὰ φρονοῦντες (cf. v. 3 to avoid super-mindedness).[95] The biggest obstacle to unity is pride (Phil. 2.2-4) and that can be overcome by associating with the 'lowly' (τοῖς ταπεινοῖς συναπαγόμενοι). ταπεινοῖς refers to 'lowly people', 'the outcasts, the poor and the needy'.[96] Here it means that haughtiness strains relationships between people: especially towards those of lower status. Therefore, Paul is very keen to instruct that a believer should associate with 'all', irrespective of their position and status.

The final exhortation in v. 16 is not to be wise in one's own thinking (μὴ γίνεσθε φρόνιμοι παρ' ἑαυτοῖς). It is striking that Paul uses the φρον- root ('thinking')[97] and 'the person who is φρόνιμος is characterized by "thinking" and is therefore "wise"… it becomes negative only when the standard by which we judge our wisdom is our own'.[98]

---

94   Moo, *Romans*, 782.

95   The Greek neuter plural ὑψηλά could mean 'high positions'. However, here the phrase τὰ ὑψηλὰ φρονοῦντες hardly refers to high positions rather the same meaning of ὑψηλὰ φρόνει in Rom. 11.20. This view is accepted by Cranfield, Dunn, Fitzmyer, Moo, and Jewett.

96   Moo, *Romans*, 783. ταπεινοῖς is regarded as masculine by Godet, Cranfield, Käsemann, Fitzmyer, Schreiner, Jewett. *Contra* Sanday and Headlam, Murray, Michel, Schlier who think that ταπεινοῖς is neuter in connection with the neuter τὰ ὑψηλά; TEV 'accept humble duties'. Morris, Barrett, and Dunn accept both neuter and masculine options.

The Greek verb συναπάγω (used with the dative) has no instrumental meaning in Rom. 12.16. Rather, it has an 'associative' sense of meaning. However, it does have an instrumental meaning in two other New Testament occurrences (Gal. 2.13; 2 Pet. 3.17; cf. Exod. 14.6). See *LSJ*, *BDAG*, Moo, *Romans*, 784.

97   Romans 12.16 uses φρονοῦντες twice and the noun φρόνιμοι once. These terms are used by Paul to caution against haughtiness: Rom. 11.20, 25; 12.3; 15.5; 1 Cor. 13.4, 5; Phil. 2.2, 5; 4.2.

98   Moo, *Romans*, 784. Wise in a positive sense is used in Mt. 7.24; 10.16; 24.45; 25.2, 4, 8-9; Lk. 12.42; 16.8; 1 Cor. 4.10; 10.15; 2 Cor. 11.19.

Mutual relations are hindered by pride, and haughtiness springs from high personal esteem. Paul urges the Romans to avoid this danger by associating with the lowly, which creates a 'mental equality that might allow people to work with each other'.[99]

5.3.7. Obligatory love (13.8, 9, 10)

In Rom. 13.8, 9, 10, the noun and the verb forms from the ἀγαπ- root are used five times: ἀγαπή (13.10a, b), ἀγαπᾶν, ἀγαπῶν, and ἀγαπήσεις are used in 13.8a, b; 9. The ἀγαπ-root noun and verbs are used with ἀλλήλους (v. 8a), τὸν ἕτερον (v. 8b), and πλησίον (vv. 9, 10) showing the sphere in which love needs to be demonstrated. ἀλλήλους seems to encompass fellow believers alone (v. 8); however, it is doubtful whether Paul puts boundaries on those to whom the church should extend love, since it seems that Paul is widening the circle to the 'other' and 'neighbour' as well. Morris regards 'the other' as 'any other person with whom I have to do'.[100] In 13.8-10, the objects of love are, primarily, fellow believers, but non-believers are not excluded.[101]

Paul reminds the believers not to owe (ὀφείλετε) anything to others but to love one another (v. 8). The theme of obligation begins in v. 7, where Paul asks the believers to render to all what is owed (taxes, customs, respect, and honour). Paul urges them to clear off all debts so that believers can give themselves 'to love one another'.[102] Jewett suggests regarding 'the social context of Paul's formulaic obligation', 'That Paul has in mind the new obligation to love the members of one's house or tenement church as new fictive family in which believers are embedded is strongly indicated by the wording of this verse and close parallels elsewhere in the Pauline letters (1 Thess 3:12; 2 Thess 1:3; 4.9; Gal 5:13).'[103] As Dunn states, this is 'not merely an obligation but a responsive obligation, an obligation which arises from what those addressed have received' (from God).[104]

The obligation of love towards one another fulfils the law; 'the one who loves the other, has fulfilled the law' (v. 8b cf. Gal. 5.14).[105] Paul has in mind

---

99   Jewett, *Romans*, 770.

100   Morris, *Romans*, 468. *Contra* Jewett, who suggests that 'neighbour' denotes a Christian neighbour of any cultural background who is a member of house church or tenement church. The 'other' belongs to 'another congregation'. Jewett, *Romans*, 813.

101   Dunn, *Romans 9–16*, 781. Murray, Cranfield, and Fitzmyer agree that the 'neighbour' cannot be confined to a believer. See Murray, *Romans*, 160, Cranfield, *Romans*, 2.675; Fitzmyer, *Romans*, 678–79.

102   ᾽Αλλήλους ἀγαπᾶν ('to love one another') has parallels in Greek, Jewish, and Apocalyptic literature (T. *Zeb* 8.5; T. *Sim* 4.7; CD 6.20–21). In v. 8 'one another' refers to fellow believers as suggested by Zahn (562), Lietzmann (112), Lagrange (315), (M.-J. Lagrange, *Saint Paul: Épître aux Romain* [Études Bibliques; Paris: Gabalda, 1931]), Wilckens (3.68), and Jewett (806). *Contra* Dunn (776), who suggests 'all with whom the Roman Christians would come in contact'; see also Fitzmyer (678).

103   Jewett, *Romans*, 807.

104   Dunn, *Romans 9–16*, 776.

105   Jewett, *Romans*, 808. Verse 8b poses a translation problem as it translates: 'the one

'not the theology of love or love that fulfils the divine intent, but love as practised among the members',[106] emphasising the relevance of genuine love in the community of believers (12.9f.).

Loving one's neighbour as oneself 'sums up' (ἀνακεφαλαιοῦται)[107] all the commandments (v. 9). Love is the essence of the Christian life and all laws and commands should be made out of love, avoiding the danger of legalism.[108] The Pauline ethic focuses on love as its centre, and not merely on outward expressions. 'Love does no evil to the neighbour' (13.10a) echoes Paul's exhortation to overcome evil with good (12.21 cf. Ps. 15.3) and his claim that love is 'the fulfilment of the law' (v. 10), i.e. by loving, one puts the law into practice. This does not mean that love is 'the full content' of law; rather Paul considers that love and law are compatible in a wider way as they belong together.[109] Therefore, Paul's admonition to love one another raises a strong awareness of mutual responsibility. As Jewett summarises, 'the command to love aims at mutuality, with each aiming to meet the needs of others as well as oneself'.[110]

5.4. The Pauline emphases

As stated in the Introduction, Paul urges the Romans to conduct themselves from a Christian perspective. As one body in Christ, each one's behaviour affects the total behaviour of the community; each believer is interrelated with his/her fellow believers in Christ. The unity contributes to mutual interdependence and mutual interdependence contributes to unity, implying genuine love and harmony. This model of communal relationship works with the help of the grace apportioned to each one 'in Christ', which helps them serve one another as if serving the Lord (Rom. 12.11) and having the same mind as Jesus (Phil. 2.5).

Paul alters the hierarchical model towards that of equalisation, where no one is permanently in a superior or inferior position as each person is promoting the other by the reversal of positions: one takes the position of the other, puts his or her neighbour before him or herself. Thus, there is a process

---

who loves the other' or one who loves, fulfils the other law'. The 'other law' translation alludes to the Mosaic covenant, after the Roman law in 13.1-7, and some others assume it to be the Jewish Torah (Cranfield [2.675], Michel [409], Wilckens [3.68], Dunn [2.776-77]). Paul uses law in a generic sense and πληρόω has the sense to 'do' and 'perform' or 'to accomplish its original intent and purpose'; see Jewett, *Romans*, 808, 809.

106   Jewett, *Romans*, 809.

107   ἀνακεφαλαιόω is rarely used in secular Greek and other literary sources and only once used elsewhere in the New Testament (Eph. 1.10).

108   Schreiner, *Romans*, 692.

109   Schreiner, *Romans*, 693. Love as the fulfilment of the law shows the 'performance' or the pragmatic significance of the law and not in the sense of completion; Dunn, *Romans 9–16*, 780, 781; see also Stuhlmacher, *Romans*, 210.

110   Jewett, *Romans*, 813.

of reciprocal relationships, a repeated process of change in position. As Alain Badiou suggests, this may be 'the reversibility of an inegalitarian rule' such that there is a subsequent symmetrisation.[111]

Paul urges believers not to become proud but to stand in awe (Rom. 11.20), which could be interpreted in terms of mutuality of honourable status, i.e. constantly sharing honour, which is paradoxical as there was fierce competition for honour in the ancient world (the notion of superiority). If one is honoured, then the other is jealous of him and wants to achieve more honour than him. It is difficult to be first in honouring (προηγούμενοι 'to take lead', Rom. 12.10b); rather, it is easier and more comfortable to be honoured than to honour others. To be a leader and at the same time to honour others calls forth an interchange in status. Nonetheless, here Paul urges believers to take the first chance to honour others. Jesus took the form of a slave (Philippians 2) and became poor to make others rich (2 Cor. 8.9). Taking the place of others in order to honour them is the most significant expression of love the world has ever seen. Christ took the place of sinners and died on the cross for their sins. Christ has become a model par excellence in honouring others irrespective of their lower status or position (Rom. 15.1, 2). Genuine love helps to maintain relationships in the Christian community.[112] In 1 Corinthians it is the greater gift (12.31), while in Romans it is the fulfilment of the law (13.10). The body cannot function properly without the exercise of love; love that circulates all over the limbs and organs helps the body to act in mutuality, to keep intact, and to avoid division.

The hierarchical ordering of gifts in 1 Corinthians is subverted by the different gifts according to the grace given through serving the least (Rom. 12.3-8; 9f.). Another significant development of interdependence is the more clear-cut expression of being 'members of one another' (τὸ δὲ καθ' εἷς ἀλλήλων μέλη Rom. 12.5 cf. μέλη ἐκ μέρους 1 Cor. 12.27). Reciprocal relations are emphatically expressed in Romans by the repeated usage of ἀλλήλους/ἀλλήλων; self-sufficiency through ignoring others is unwarranted.

Paul calls for an attitude of sober-mindedness that creates 'other'-mindedness, and leads to being the 'body in Christ' and 'members of one another'. Harmony in the community can be maintained by overcoming evil with good (vv. 17-21). Paul applies the Christian value of forgiveness that not only forgives others but also rewards them with good. He redefines positive reciprocity as not simply repaying good for good, but also overcoming evil with good and, resultantly, triumphing over it. It seems that this type of nature would have been difficult to practise without the grace of Christ.

111   A. Badiou, *Saint Paul: The Foundation of Universalism* (Stanford: Stanford University Press, 2003), 104. The rule looks and is inegalitarian, but it can be and is reversed, so that what is unequal in one direction is made equal in another, resulting in a process of symmetry (what he calls symmetrisation).

112   Christian life is the practical expression of one's relationship to Christ, reflecting Christ's 'present sovereign dominion in the life of a Christian', implying solidarity, affection, and mutuality between the people of the community. Fitzmyer, *Paul and his Theology*, 90.

5.5. Conclusion

Paul develops his ethic of mutuality from the fundamental idea of mutual interdependence in body politics to 'the body in Christ', where relationships are based on genuine love towards one another. He points to being in Christ: the belonging-togetherness of the Christian community that holds together people of different status, gender, and ethnic origin. As Barclay suggests concerning Paul and multiculturalism:

> The foundation of Paul's gospel and the basis of its relativization of all cultures, is his radical appreciation of the grace of God which humbles human pride and subverts the theological and cultural edifices which flesh constructs. ... The church exists not for its own sake but to bear witness to the grace of God.[113]

The Christian experience is an apparent expression of the grace of God received. It is not only an individual experience, but has social and ethical aspects that are derived from incorporation into the body of Christ. The grace believers receive from God is not something Paul would think should be kept as one's own possession, but rather something to be passed on to others.

The ideals of the kingdom of God such as justice, peace, joy, and fellowship uphold the theological significance of mutuality as they involve relationships with others (cf. Rom. 14.17). The ethical implications of the Christian life are further explicated in Romans 14–15, which asks the question: how should we evaluate one another? This is the focus of the following chapter.

---

113   J. M. G. Barclay, 'Neither Jew nor Greek: Multiculturalism and the New Perspective on Paul', in M. G. Brett (ed.), *Ethnicity and the Bible* (Leiden: Brill, 1996), 197–214, at 213.

CHAPTER 6

RECEIVING ONE ANOTHER: A PARADIGM OF MUTUALITY IN
ROMANS 14, 15

6.1. Introduction

In the preceding chapter the discussion focused on Paul's encouragement of
mutual interdependence and its implications for the practical Christian life. Both
the individual and communal dimension of the believer was illustrated through
the body metaphor (Romans 12, 13; cf. 1 Corinthians 12, 13). This chapter
focuses on Paul's instruction to the Roman community concerning the particular
circumstances in which mutual respect and acceptance need to be practised.

Romans 14.1–15.13 stresses the need for unity amongst the community, and
reinforces the need for mutual relations and acceptance. Mutual relations are a
significant theme in Romans, and it manifests in Rom. 14.1–15.13 as an instruction
to welcome others. It seems that differences and diversity in a person's cultural
practice may hinder welcoming, and that may be why Paul strongly urged the
Roman Christians to love one another irrespective of position or status. Chapters
14 and 15 seem to be a continuation of the exhortations in chs. 12 and 13, and
provide a crucial link to the long list of greetings in Romans 16.

The paradigm of mutuality is obvious in Romans 14–15: the section starts
with an exhortation to 'receive one another' (14.1) and reaches its climax in the
statement: 'receive one another as Christ has welcomed us' (15.7). The present
chapter discusses Paul's rhetorical strategy to cultivate mutuality in three sections:
the social context; an exegetical analysis of mutual welcome; and the Pauline
ethos of mutuality.

6.2. The social context: the weak/strong dichotomy

6.2.1. Issues in group conflicts

Paul mentions two subgroups, 'the weak in faith' (ἀσθενοῦντα τῇ πίστει; 14.1;
15.1) and 'the strong' (οἱ δύνατοι; 15.1), who seem to be divided on issues of
food, wine, and days (the eating of meat, the observance of days, and the drinking
of wine) (14.2, 5, 21).

The first matter of dispute concerns eating habits: the strong person eats all things, while the weak eats only vegetables. The weak in faith probably avoid meat due to their respect for the Jewish law and the unavailability of kosher meat in their pagan environment.[1] Another point of disagreement between the strong and the weak is on the matter of days. It is implied that the weak believer prefers some days to others, while the strong believer considers each day to be the same. It is not certain whether the pagan environment of 'lucky' and 'unlucky' days, or the Jewish observance of specific days, is in Paul's mind. However, it is more likely that Paul was dealing with issues related to the Jewish law; the observance or non-observance of the law is the key issue. As Barclay suggests:

> these verses refer to Jewish scruples (which could be held by Jews or Gentiles) concerning the consumption of meat considered unclean and the observance of the Sabbath and the Jewish feasts or fasts; the wine, if it is relevant, is also a matter of Jewish concern, relating to its use in 'idolatrous worship'.[2]

6.2.2. The groups identified

The different possibilities regarding the identity of the strong and the weak are:[3]

1. The 'weak' were mainly Gentile Christians who abstained from meat (and perhaps wine), particularly on certain 'fast' days under the influence of certain pagan religions.[4]

---

1   There are some scholars who disagree that Jewish Law is the subject of dispute. E.g. Reasoner thinks that vegetarianism is the issue between the groups. See Reasoner, *The Strong*, 103f; See also J. P. Sampley, 'The Weak and the Strong: Paul's Careful and Crafty Rhetorical Strategy in Romans 14:1–15:3', in L. M. White and O. L. Yarbrough, *The Social World of the First Christians: Essays in Honour of Wayne A. Meeks* (Minneapolis: Fortress, 1995), 40–52 at 41, 42. Kosher laws required the blood to be properly drained from the animal (Lev. 3.17; 7.26-27; 17.10-14; Deut. 12.16, 23-24 cf. Acts 15.20, 29). One matter of consideration is the Claudius expulsion of Jews in 49 CE, which might have caused the fear of availability of food not tainted with idolatry. Josephus speaks of the Jewish priests imprisoned in Rome as they 'had not forgotten the pious practices of religion and supported themselves on figs and nuts'. Josephus, *Life* 14. See Dunn, *Romans 9–16*, 801. In addition, Watson thinks that Jewish Christians were not probably welcomed in the Jewish shops. F. Watson, *Paul, Judaism and the Gentiles: A Sociological Approach* (SNTSMS 56; Cambridge: Cambridge University Press, 1986), 95. I suggest what is at stake is not the availability or unavailability of kosher meat in Rome, but conflict on the issue of the food offered in a Christian's house, i.e. whether it was pure in the sight of those observing the Jewish purity laws. See Barclay, 'Do We Undermine the Law?', 291; Cranfield, *Romans*, 2.695. W. Schmithals, *Der Römerbrief: Ein Kommentar* (Gütersloh: Mohn, 1988), 103–104.

2   Barclay, 'Do We Undermine the Law?', 289. The majority of scholars agree that the main issue under consideration is the Jewish observance of the law. Minear, *Obedience of Faith*, 8–10; Cranfield, *Romans*, 2.690–98; Wilckens, *Der Brief an die Römer*, 3.109–15; Watson, *Paul, Judaism and the Gentiles*, 88–96; Wedderburn, *The Reasons for Romans*, 30–35; Dunn, *Romans 9–16*, 795–806.

3   For these classifications, I am indebted to Moo, *Romans*, 828, 829.

4   Käsemann, *Romans*, 367–68; Lagrange, *Saint Paul: Épître aux Romains*, 335–40; Reasoner, *The Strong*, 103. Orphism or Neo-Pythagoreans avoided anything with a soul. Some later Gnostics also avoided eating flesh (Irenaeus, AH 1.24.2; Eusebius, H. E. 4.29).

2.   The weak were Christians, perhaps both Jewish and Gentile, who practised asceticism.[5]

3.   The weak were mainly Jewish Christians who observed certain practices derived from the Mosaic Law out of their concern to establish righteousness before God.[6]

4.   The weak were mainly Jewish Christians who followed a sectarian asceticism in expressing their devoutness (due to syncretistic tendencies).[7]

5.   The weak were mainly Jewish Christians who refrained from eating meat sold in the marketplace, thinking that it was polluted by idolatry.[8]

6.   The weak were mainly Jewish Christians who refrained from certain kinds of food and observed certain days out of continuing loyalty to the Mosaic Law.[9]

Paul's categorisation of the strong and the weak seems to reflect the Roman usage of the categories that denotes the differences of status, position, and power.[10] The strong were a group of believers who had a higher status, whereas the weak held lower status in the Roman churches. This difference probably reflects their socio-economic and political status rather than differences in spiritual superiority.[11] Paul uses the same word 'strong' οὐ πολλοὶ δυνατοί

---

5   Lenski, *Interpretation of St. Paul's Epistle to the Romans*, 812–13; Murray, *Romans*, 2.172–74; P. J. Achtemeier, *Romans: Interpretation A Bible Commentary for Teaching and Preaching* (Atlanta: John Knox, 1985), 215.

6   Barrett, *Romans*, 256–57.

7   H. A. W. Meyer, *Critical and Exegetical Handbook to the Epistle to the Romans*, J. C. Moore (trans.) (Edinburgh: T&T Clark, 1876), 2.296–98; Hodge, *Romans*, 417; P. Althaus, *An die Römer übersetzt und erklärt* (NTD 6; Göttingen: Vandenhoeck & Ruprecht, 1966), 138; Black, *Romans*, 190–91. Paul confronts syncretistic false teachers in Colossae and Ephesus, which is apparently a mixture of Judaism and incipient Gnosticism. Colossian heretics advocated abstinence from food and drink, and advocated observance of certain days (Col. 2.6, 21), while Ephesians insisted on the avoidance of foods (1 Tim. 4.3), which may have influenced Timothy to stop drinking wine (1 Tim. 5.23). Jewish sectarian asceticism can be found in the 'Therapeutae', who were vegetarians and drank only 'spring water' (see Philo, *The Contemplative Life* 37), and some early Jewish Christians like James the brother of the Lord (cf. Eusebius, H.E. 2.23.5) and Ebionites (Epiphanius, *Haer*.30.15) who abstained from eating flesh.

8   A. Nygren, *Commentary on Romans*, C. C. Rasmuussen (trans.) (Philadelphia: Fortress Press, 1975), 422; Ziesler, *Romans*, 323–26.

9   This view has become the most widely accepted. See Wilckens, *Der Brief an die Römer* 3.79, 111–13; Cranfield, *Romans*, 2.694–97; Dunn, *Romans 9–16*, 799–802; A. F. Segal, *Paul the Convert: The Apostolate and Apostasy of Saul the Pharisee* (New Haven: Yale University Press, 1986), 231–33; P. J. Tomson, *Paul and Jewish Law: Halakha in the Letters of the Apostle to the Gentiles* (CRINT, Vol. 1; Minneapolis: Fortress, 1990), 236–58; Watson, *Paul*, 94–95; Watson, 'The Two Roman Congregations: Romans 14.1–15.13', in Donfried (ed.), *The Romans Debate*, 203–15; Wedderburn, *Reasons*, 31–35; H.-W. Bartsch, 'Die antisemitischen Gegner des Paulus im Römerbrief', in *Anti judaismus im Neuen Testament*? in P. W. Eckert, N. P. Levinson, and M. Stöhr (eds.), *Abhandlungen zum christlich-jüdischen* (Dialog; Munich: Kaiser, 1967), 33–34.

10   Reasoner, *The Strong*, 200–20.

11   O. Michel, *Der Brief an die Römer* (KEK, 4; Göttingen: Vandenhoeck & Ruprecht, 1978), 443; Dunn, *Romans 9–16*, 837; H. W. Schmidt, *Der Brief des Paulus an die Römer* (THKNT, 6; Berlin: Evangelische Verlagsanstalt, 1963), 237. Romans 15.27 suggests that the Gentiles are recipients of the spiritual blessings from the Jewish Christians.

(not many powerful, 1 Cor. 1.26) to indicate the social status of the believers in Corinth. Theissen agrees with this, noting that 'powerful' denotes the influential people in society.[12]

The weakness of the 'weak' connotes a deficit in both theological and social dimensions.[13] The reference to the 'weaker members' in 1 Cor. 12.22 denotes the social aspect in relation to honour (12.23-26). It indicates inferior status, power, and wealth in comparison with the so-called strong. The Epistle to Diognetus (10.5) states: 'For Happiness does not consist of domination over neighbours, nor in wishing to have more than the weak [i.e. the poor] nor in being wealthy, and having power to compel those who are below you.'[14] Paul makes use of the honour and shame language of the Roman world to suit his theological purpose of honouring one another in the Roman churches irrespective of their status.

For the reasons noted above, it seems that the 'weak', whom Paul refers to here, are those who observe the purity laws and the Sabbath (who consider their lifestyle is 'in honour of the Lord'; Rom. 14.6), whereas the 'strong' do not. It is not accurate to label the two parties as 'Jewish' and 'Gentile' because Paul, a Jew himself, claims to belong to the 'strong' group (Rom. 15.1). Moreover, there may be some Gentile Christians who uphold the Jewish laws. Additionally, there is an indication in the letter itself that Roman Christian communities are ethnically mixed, consisting of both Jews and Gentiles (e.g. the persons greeted in Romans 16).

---

12   Theissen, *Social Setting*, 72. Josephus used the same word to refer to 'the leaders complaining to Roman authorities about Herod's activities': 'the powerful among the Jews' ('Ιουδαίων οἱ δυνατοί). Josephus, *Bell* 1.242. The 'powerful' is an expression of social and political prominence. Thucydides, *Hist*.1.89.3. See also Jewett, *Romans*, 876.

13   Josef Zmijewski, 'ἀσθενής κτλ.' *EDNT* 1 (1990) 171; Reasoner, *The Strong*, 218–19. The terms used by Paul to describe the groups seem to parallel Latin terms such as 'inferior', 'tenuis', 'invalidus' and 'potens', 'firmus', 'validus', etc. From the perspective of honour/shame in Roman society, the weak were people of lower status compared to the strong who had higher status. The weak/strong dichotomy can also be seen in the realms of a person's 'mental and ethical standards'; in the philosophical schools such as that of the Epicurean Philodemus (110–40/35 BC), there was an educational programme to develop the '"weak" students into mature ones' so that they might bring moral improvement to groups and individuals. Other Hellenistic writers also made use of the topos of the weak and the strong, e.g. Aristides *Or.* 24.14; Dionysius of Halicarnassus, *Ant. Rom.* 4.26.1; Ps-Arist. *Mund.* 6.396B; Philo *Abr.* 216; Philo *Spec.* 2.141; Plutarch *Arat.* 24.5. See also Aasgaard, *My Beloved Brothers*, 180–83.

14   Translation by Jewett, *Romans*, 877. See 1 Clement 10.2. Job 5.11, 15-16 refers to God as the powerful saviour for the powerless; 'the one who (raises) the weak ones to the heights … (and) the powerless one escapes from the hand of the powerful. But there is hope for the powerless ones, but the mouth of the unjust will be stopped.' The term 'powerful' indicates the powerlessness of the opposite group.

6.2.3. General or specific instruction?

The reason for Paul's inclusion of these issues in the epistle could lie in his awareness of a specific issue of division among the strong and the weak. However, several scholars refuse to accept this explanation on the grounds that:[15]

1.　Romans 12.1–15.13 is a general paraenesis, an outline of the gospel ethic that is engendered by the gospel itself and not by the needs of a particular community.
2.　The impressive number of verbal and conceptual parallels with 1 Corinthians 8–10 confirms that 14.1–15.13 is a generalised version of Paul's advice to the Corinthians about their disputes over idol meat.
3.　The difficulty in pinning down the precise religious motivations for the practices of the weak suggests that Paul is not describing a specific state of affairs but an idealised situation.

However, it is likely that Paul is addressing specific issues in the Roman community, and that Rom. 12.1–15.13 is not a general paraenesis as there is coherence in his arguments.[16] Although the parallels between this passage and 1 Corinthians 8–10 are clear,[17] there are also obvious differences between the two.[18]

15　　Moo, *Romans*, 827. These reasons are from R. J. Karris, 'Romans 14.1–15.13 and the Occasion of Romans', in *Romans Debate*, 65–84; W. A. Meeks, 'Judgement and the Brother: Romans 14.1–15.13', in G. F. Hawthorne with O. Betz (ed.), *Tradition and Interpretation in the New Testament: Essays in Honour of E. E. Ellis for his 60th birthday* (Grand Rapids: Eerdmans, 1987), 290–300; F. Vouga, 'L' Épiître aux Romains comme document ecclésiologique (Rom. 12–15)', *ETR* 61 (1986) 489–91; Furnish, *Love Command*, 115; Leenhardt, *Romans*, 344–46.

16　　The similarities are explained by some scholars on the basis of the problems being similar in nature (see Cranfield, *Romans*, 692f.; Wilckens, *Der Brief an die Römer*, 3.109–15; W. Schmithals, *Der Römerbrief. Ein Kommentar* [Gütersloh: Mohn, 1988], 494). Aasgaard suggests that Paul is presenting his arguments parallel to those in antiquity by using 'a standard pattern for how to relate to conflicts of various kinds'. Aasgaard, *My Beloved Brothers*, 180.

17　　The parallels are found in Karris, 'Romans 14.1–15.13', 73–75; Wilckens, *Der Brief an die Römer*, 3.115; Cranfield, *Romans*, 2.692–93; Reasoner, *The Strong*, 29–39; H. J. Klauck, *Herrenmahl und Hellenistischer Kult. Eine religionsgeschichtliche Untersuchung zum ersten Korintherbrief*(Münster: Aschendorff, 1982), 281–83.

　　　　Aasgaard included the following terminological and thematic similarities between 1 Cor. 8.1-11 and Rom. 14.1–15.13. They are: (1) the disagreement between two groups (Rom. 14.1; 15.1; 1 Cor. 8.9, 11); (2) one group as the 'strong' or 'free' (Rom. 15.1; 1 Cor. 8.9; 1 Cor. 9.1, 3); (3) the other group as 'weak' (Rom. 14.1f.; 15.1; 1 Cor. 8.7, 9-12; cf. also 11.30); (4) use of relational terms such as 'brother' or 'neighbour' (Rom. 14.10, 13, 15, 21; 1 Cor. 8.11, 12, 13; (5) exhortations to shun offending (Rom. 14.13, 20f.; 1 Cor. 8.9, 13; 10.32; Rom. 14.15; 1 Cor. 8.12); (6) admonition to avoid doing damage to another (Rom. 14.15; 1 Cor. 8.11); (7) the expression denoting Christ's redemptive action (Rom. 14.15; 1 Cor. 8.11); (8) the metaphor of building up (Rom. 14.19, 15.2; 1 Cor. 8.1; 10.23 cf. Rom. 14.20 destroy a building); (9) an idea of not pleasing oneself (Rom. 15.1f.; 1 Cor. 10.24, 33). See Aasgaard, *My Beloved Brothers*, 178, 179.

18　　Meeks, 'Judgment and the Brother', 291–93; Reasoner, *The Strong*, 34f., 312–17; B. Witherington, *Conflict and Community in Corinth: A Socio-Rhetorical Commentary on 1 and 2 Corinthians* (Grand Rapids: Eerdmans, 1995), 187; T. Söding, *Das Liebesgebot bei Paulus: Die Mahnung zur Agape im Rahmen der paulinischen Ethik* (NTAbh, 26: Münster: Aschendorff, 1995), 229f.; Reasoner, *The Strong*, 35–37.

For example, the issue of idolatry is not mentioned in Romans, while it is the main issue of 1 Corinthians.

Karris and others suggest that in Rom. 14.1–15.13, Paul generalises the situation in Corinth.[19] They consider that there was no strife in the Roman community, and this paraenesis is addressed to a problem that might arise in any community. But there are others who strongly disagree with this argument and suggest that the differences reflect the specific situation in Rome.[20] From the personal details of the leaders of the Roman congregations in Romans 16, we can infer that Paul would have known about the situation in Rome, otherwise he would not have included such detailed exhortations. Moreover, if Rom. 14.1–15.13 was a general exhortation, Paul would not have emphasised it as much as he did. He would have been in receipt of the news regarding the situation in Rome through Prisca and Aquila, Epaenetus, the mother of Rufus, Andronicus and Junia, etc.

As Barclay rightly suggests, the fact that Paul omitted some specific issues in the Corinthian community (reference to εἰδωλόθυτα), and added relevant issues to the Roman community such as the eating of vegetables (Rom. 14.2) and the observance of days (14.5), attests that Paul is offering relevant instruction; the detailed description of the theme of welcoming each other, the reference to the two groups, the prominence of the passage at the end of the 'paraenesis', and Paul's siding with the strong group (15.1) all indicate that Paul knew the circumstances in Rome.[21] In line with this argument, Reasoner observes that the strong and the weak titles might have been common in Rome and Paul would have known about them.[22] It is difficult to categorise the religious practices of the weak in the passage, but the themes in the chapters imply that Paul is addressing a specific problem in the Roman community.

6.3. Mutual welcome: exegetical analysis of Paul's exhortations

6.3.1. Welcome (προσλαμβάνω)
The core message of Romans 14–15 can be seen in the repeated usage of the term προσλαμβάνεσθε: Rom. 14.1 (προσλαμβάνεσθε); 14.3 (προσελάβετο); 15.7 (twice: προσλαμβάνεσθε; προσελάβετο). It is saturated with meanings that are significant in relationships between individuals, and assists in mutual

---

19   Karris thinks that the seven imperatives in the first-person plural or third-person singular (as opposed to six in the second-person plural) reveal the general nature of the material. See Karris, 'Romans 14.1–15.13', 73–77; Meeks, 'Judgment and the Brother', 292–93.

20   Wedderburn, *Reason for Romans*, 30–35.

21   Barclay, 'Do We Undermine the Law?', 289. Horrell suggests that Romans 14–15 is 'a carefully constructed and extended piece of argumentation'. Horrell, *Solidarity and Difference*, 167.

22   Reasoner, *The Strong*, 58.

up-building.[23] The 'one-another' relationship not only strengthens the personal bond but also facilitates the growth of the community. Paul urges his addressees to exercise the practice of welcoming.

6.3.1.1. Receive the weak in faith (14.1)

Paul's exhortation to 'receive the weak in faith' places the weak as the object of his exhortation and implies that the strong are the leading members of the Roman church. To receive means to 'receive or accept into one's society, home, circle of acquaintance',[24] which connotes more than mere acceptance into church membership, but also accepting others as brothers and sisters into the close fellowship of the people of God.[25] The verb in the present imperative possibly suggests a continuing attitude of acceptance. Jewett suggests that the home in the early Christian era may refer to the house or tenement church, but most likely to the love feast, 'since this was the format of the assembly that turned the secular space of a house or portion of a tenement or shop into an arena of sacred welcome'; this solid context is more helpful for understanding than hazy statements of 'mutual welcome'.[26]

Who are the 'weak in faith' to be received? The term implies a group, or number of groups, in Rome. The verb ἀσθενέω is used for physical illness, social or economic inferiority, and powerlessness of any kind.[27] The term has a moral connotation in Epictetus' warning: 'the reason is that usually every power that is acquired by the uneducated and weak is apt to make them conceited and boastful over it'.[28] As noted above, the Latin adjectives *tenuis* and *infirmis* denote a low economic, social, and political status.[29] In Horace's witty depiction of a man who declares that he is weak and could not speak on the Sabbath, we observe both social and religious inferiority: 'Certainly you know more than I do … I am a small man of weakness, one of many (*sum paulo infirmior, unus multorum*). Pardon me, we'll speak another time.'[30] Reasoner

---

23   προσλαμβάνω has different meanings: (1) 'to take something that needs a personal need, *take, partake of* food', Acts 27.34; (2) 'to promote one's own ends, *exploit, take advantage of*'; (3) 'to take or lead off to oneself, *take aside*', Mt. 16: 22; Mk. 8.32; Acts 18.26; (4) 'to extend a welcome, receive in(to) one's home or circle of acquaintances', Rom. 14.1; 15.7a; 14.3; Philemon 12; (5) to take or bring along ... with oneself as companion or helper', Acts 17.5. See *BDAG*, 883.

24   *BDAG*, 883; See also Esler, *Conflict and Identity*, 347.

25   Cranfield, *Romans*, 2.691. Dunn, *Romans 9–16*, 798. Barrett, *Romans*, 236: 'receive him into the Christian family'.

26   Jewett, *Romans*, 888. Jewett thinks that most of the commentators have neglected this social context. Dunn terms this 'mutual acceptance'; Murray as 'acceptance of believers'; Morris as 'whole hearted acceptance'; Stuhlmacher, 'accept one another'. Some others have regarded the common meal as the background of this welcome. See Michel, *Der Brief an die Römer*, 447; Black, *Romans*, 200.

27   *BDAG* 142; G. Stählin, 'ἀσθενέω κτλ.' *TDNT* 1 (1964), 490–93.

28   Epictetus, *Dissertations* 1.8.8–9.

29   Reasoner, *The Strong*, 49–55.

30   Horace *Sat.* 1.9.67–72, cited by Reasoner, *The Strong*, 53–54. See also Jewett, *Romans*, 834.

suggests this as a parallel to 14.1, since it shows that 'the person excessively observant in a foreign religion who matched the "weak" caricature was known to Horace's audience'.[31] The term implies an 'ethical-religious weakness' in the New Testament, since strength shows honour and weakness invokes contempt in the Roman world.[32] The title 'weak in faith' implies the other group is in the dominant position and finds fault with the faith of the inferior group (15.1).[33] Paul is here attesting the fact that the 'faith' of the weak meets the criteria for membership in church activities and communal meals.

The word 'faith' is significant in his description of welcome since he uses it to describe the disputes between the two groups: 14.1, 2 and 14.22, 23. As seen throughout Romans, 'faith', or to 'believe', conveys a person's response to the gospel (1.5, 8, 16, 17; 3.22, 25-30; 5.1, 2). It is less probable that Paul talks about a person's weak faith in Jesus as saviour and the Lord; rather, he is condemning the undesirable implications of their faith in Christ. This does not mean Paul challenges weakness per se, since elsewhere he thinks weakness is the opportunity for divine grace (2 Cor. 4.7-11; 11.30; 12.5, 9-10). As Moo suggests, 'he is criticizing them for the lack of insight into some of the implications of their faith in Christ'.[34] Those who cannot accept that faith in Christ is liberation from the Old Testament and Jewish regulations are weak in faith compared with those who have freedom from them. Paul wants to lift the 'weak' in faith into the status of the 'strong' by having the former accepted by the latter. 'Paul wants the "strong" to receive the "weak" into full and intimate fellowship, something that could not happen if the "strong", the majority group, persist in advancing their views on these issues, sparking quarrels and mutual recrimination.'[35]

6.3.1.2. 'For God has received ...' (14.3)

Negative attitudes to one another could control the freedom of Christians, even to the point of rejection from the fellowship of Christ. In principle they must receive those whom God has received. Paul's thinking here is that God receives sinners in spite of their actions or attitudes, and so the responsibility

---

31 Reasoner, *The Strong*, 58–61.

32 See Reasoner, *The Strong*, 58–61.

33 Wilckens, *Der Brief an die Römer*, 3.81; Käsemann, *Romans*, 369; T. H. Tobin, *Paul's Rhetoric in its Contexts: The Argument of Romans* (Peabody: Hendrickson, 2004), 408, 409.

34 Moo, *Romans*, 836. Barrett and Cranfield think that to be 'weak in faith' means lack of trust in God (cf. 4.19), which is less likely. Barrett suggests, 'The weak are *weak in faith*; they are weak, but they have faith; they have faith, but they do not draw from it all the inferences that they should draw.' Barrett, *Romans*, 236; Cranfield, *Romans*, 2.700. However, Dunn suggests that 'the weakness is trust in God *plus* dietary and festival laws, trust in God *dependent* on observance of such practices, a trust in God which leans on the crutches of particular customs and not on God alone, as though they were an integral part of that trust.' Dunn, *Romans 9–16*, 798. Dunn also considers that 'Paul's counter emphasis on faith (14:1, 2, 22-23) is not at all surprising and fits into the overall argument of the letter far more closely than has usually been perceived.' Dunn, *Romans 9–16*, 800.

35 Moo, *Romans*, 837.

is on other believers to extend the same grace. Those whom God has accepted became righteous; those who are made righteous have a change of status. The same term used for welcome here is also used in v. 1a, reinforcing the fact that the welcome extended to others should be the same as that given by God.

Jewett suggests:

> welcome to the banquet is the crucial issue here, and Paul probably relies on the widely shared tradition of Christ as the host of the Lord's Supper, the master of the love feast, acting in behalf of God to welcome the faithful into the messianic banquet in fulfilment of the ancient prophecies.[36]

Jewett and Käsemann consider that the recipient of this welcome is 'him' (αὐτόν), which seems to be a general reference to both the weak and strong. But Dunn makes a pertinent observation: the 'exhortation here (v.3c) is a rebuke particularly to the condemnatory attitude of the weak (vv.3b, 4): the one with the much tighter understanding of what is acceptable conduct for God's people would think that God has *not* accepted the other'.[37] The immediate object of the welcome here is the 'strong'. Paul's wording is similar to that of the Psalms: (LXX Ps. 26.10; cf. 64.4; 72.24) ὁ δὲ κύριος προσελάβετο με ('the Lord has welcomed me'). This acceptance in the worship context is described in the context of the Christian love feast (Rom. 12.13; 13.10; 14.1).[38]

6.3.1.3. Receiving one another (15.7a)

The entire exhortation on the weak and the strong beginning from 14.1 has its climax in 15.7, which begins with διό (therefore)[39] to urge them to 'receive one another as Christ has welcomed you' (προσλαμβάνεσθε ἀλλήλους, καθὼς καὶ ὁ Χριστὸς προσελάβετο ὑμᾶς). The admonition to the strong to accept the weak in faith (14.1), and the reference to God welcoming the strong (14.3), is broadened to welcome 'one another' (15.7), which is an interesting shift of focus. The recipients fall into two groups: the strong and the weak; they need to welcome one another irrespective of their status. This is similar to the command not to judge 'one another' (14.13) and to strive for edification for one another (14.19); both groups are expected to invite and welcome others. If only one group decided to welcome others there would be an imbalance of proper behaviour. As Jewett rightly suggests, 'The hostility cannot be overcome if only one side participates in this breaking down of barriers, and the barriers themselves can most effectively be dismantled by sharing in

---

36   Jewett, *Romans*, 841.

37   Jewett, *Christian Tolerance*, 129. Käsemann, *Romans*, 369; Meeks, 'Judgment and the Brother', 295. Dunn, *Romans*, 803. It is also significant that Paul is describing God rather than Christ. In these two chapters 'God' and 'Christ' are used with differing emphasis: God as the final authoritative figure (14.6, 10, 18, and 15.6), whereas Christ is the subordinate figure (14.3, 6, 10-12, 17-18, 20, 22; 15.5-6). See Dunn, *Romans 9–16*, 803.

38   See Jewett, Romans, 841.

39   διό sums up the preceding discussions and indicates a concluding statement. Cranfield, *Romans*, 2.739; see *BDAG*, 250.

sacramental love feasts in which Christ's inclusion of insiders and outsiders is recalled and celebrated.'[40] Therefore, the task of receiving is relevant for both groups as they welcome one another.

6.3.1.4. 'As Christ has welcomed ...' (15.7b)

The use of καθώς is significant since the Romans' welcome should be similar in manner to Christ's: 'just as Christ has welcomed you'. It means more than 'tolerating' or giving 'official recognition'.[41]

> What Paul has in mind is not simply the fact of Christ's acceptance, but the manner of it (διάκονος v.8): it is precisely the humbling of oneself to a position where one's own opinions do not count and may not be thrust on another (one's master!), which both weak and strong, Gentile and Jew, need to practice.[42]

Paul points to Christ as a model of how to welcome others – even if they are enemies. Christ was the host in the love feasts, and his death for sinners shows that the members of the congregations have received an undeserved welcome. This is clear in 15.3 and 15.8f., where Jesus did not please himself but loved those who rejected him and killed him; 'the reproaches of those who reproached you fell on me' (15.3). This is similar to Christ's welcome of sinners during his earthly ministry (Mt. 9.9-11; cf. Mk. 2.13-17; Lk. 5.27-32)

It is striking that the same verb προσλαμβάνομαι is used here to describe the redemption of Christ as well as the welcoming attitude to one another in the congregations (15.7a, b). This implies his love shown to sinners on the cross by sacrificing his life. A Christian has to follow Christ in loving others without pleasing themselves, yet also bearing the scruples of the weak (15.1). Christ's welcome is irrespective of ethnic, social, and theological barriers. There is an echo of inclusivity in ὑμᾶς as it encompasses various groups in Rome. Jewett suggests that 'it is an ethic of obligation anchored in the ancient views of reciprocity', as he quotes Reasoner who comments, 'Christ's acceptance of the believer forms the basis for the obligation to accept a fellow member.'[43] However, I would suggest this is not 'obligatory' behaviour, but that the self-giving of Christ acts as a pattern of conduct for accepting a fellow member. It is an outlook with which believers need to bring their character in line. The ultimate aim of welcoming others is to glorify God, i.e. to praise God with one mind and one mouth (15.7c cf. v. 6).

---

40   Jewett, *Romans*, 888; Jewett, *Tolerance*, 29. Paul possibly emphasises the main aim of the letter, i.e. the privilege of the Jews and the inclusion of the Gentiles within the promise of God. It is more likely that the point is mutual acceptance irrespective of different practices rather than converting the Jewish congregation to Paulinism as suggested by Watson. See Watson, *Paul*, 97–98; Dunn, *Romans 9–16*, 846.

41   Moo, *Romans*, 874.

42   Dunn, *Romans 9–16*, 846.

43   Jewett, *Romans*, 889; Reasoner, *The Strong*, 194.

6.4. Judging as hindrance to welcoming

Judging is the main issue Paul deals with as having negative control over relationships. Since his rebuke of judging follows his instruction on the act of welcoming, it implies that welcoming is hindered or blocked by being judgemental of others.[44] Paul's language shows that he strongly dislikes and condemns the destructive judgemental attitude. Paul seems deliberately to parallel this section on judgement with earlier reproofs of judging (κρίνειν) others (2.1-3; 14.3-4, 10); this perhaps serves as a reminder that God holds the ultimate authority to judge (2.16; 14.10-12).[45]

6.4.1. 'Who are you who are judging ...?' (14.4)

The section on judging opens with a rhetorical question (v. 4): 'Who are *you* who are judging ...?' It is in a diatribe style marked by the colloquial expression σὺ τίς εἶ (who are you?).[46] Here it may mean, 'Who do you think you are, you who are putting yourself in the position of judge over another believer?'[47] Each believer is answerable to his own master, who is responsible for the members of his own household. This gives a picture of the master–slave relationship of the Greco-Roman world. The phrase ἀλλότριος οἰκέτης, which is translated as 'someone else's slave or servant', overlooks the difference between οἰκέτης and δοῦλος.[48] Jewett suggests, 'the former denotes a normally inalienable member of the household, including slaves, who function almost as family members, whereas the latter is ordinarily limited to slaves and hired servants, whether in the household or in other service'.[49] The household motif was used elsewhere by Paul to describe his recipients, e.g. 'beloved of God' (1.7), 'children of God' (8.16), 'heirs of God ... joint heirs with Christ' (8.17), 'the elect of God' (8.33), 'the children of the promise' (9.8). Probably, the use of the term suggests that his aim is 'not to undermine the status of members of the Roman house and tenement churches but to establish their equality with each other in relation to the authority of their κύριος ("Lord/Master")'.[50] Paul argues that no believer has the right to judge because each is a household slave belonging to another. It is to his master (κύριος) that he stands or falls. κύριος

---

44 κρίνω has meanings such as (1) to select, prefer, e.g. Rom. 14.5a; (2) to pass judgement upon the lives and actions of other people, Mt. 7.1a, 2a; Lk. 6.37a; Rom. 2.1, 3; 14.3f., 10, 13a; Col. 2.16; 1 Cor. 4.5; (3) to think, consider, look upon, Acts 13.46; 2 Cor. 5.14; 1 Cor. 11.13; (4) to reach a decision, Acts 3.13; 20.16; 25.25; 1 Cor. 2.2; 5.3; Tit. 3.12; Rom. 14.13b; 2 Cor. 2.1; (5) to engage in the judicial process; and (6) to ensure justice for someone; *BDAG*, 567–69.

45 Meeks, 'Judgment and the Brother', 296.

46 S. K. Stowers, *The Diatribe and Paul's Letter to the Romans* (SBLDS, 57; Chicago: Scholars Press, 1981), 115.

47 Moo, *Romans*, 839.

48 See also Dunn, *Romans 9–16*, 803; Moo, *Romans*, 839; Cranfield, *Romans*, 2.698; Jewett, *Romans*, 841. οἰκέτης is used only once in Paul. There is some distinction between οἰκέται and δοῦλοι.' Ἀλλότριος is more emphatic than using ἕτερος.

49 Jewett, *Romans*, 842.

50 Jewett, *Romans*, 842.

is used with the same secular meaning as 'master'. This title is significant to the theological argument of vv. 4-9; it is used nine times in this passage, including with the verb 'lord it over', and as an interchangeable name for God (Θεός) and Christ (Χριστός).[51]

The ideal of the Christian community is different from a Jewish community, since the evaluation of a Christian should be in connection with Christ. The basis of the Christian commitment does not lie in written laws that judge those who do not observe them, but is instead found in 'mutual tolerance' even if one does not observe the rules. 'The mutual tolerance demanded by Paul in the Roman churches requires that neither side allow their strongly-held convictions to determine the contours of Christian commitment.'[52]

He directs his words not only to one group since he is aware that both are at fault in their attitude to their fellow brothers and sisters. The one who eats should not despise the one who does not eat, and the one who does not eat is not to judge the one who does (14.3). In this context, 'despise' means disdainful judgement.[53] Paul states that mutual judgement is not valid as long as 'God has received him'. The metaphorical use of the terms 'stand' or 'fall' shows the relationship of the slave to the master; it is the Lord that every Christian should please. Moo rightly remarks that, 'Paul here expresses confidence that the "strong" believer will persist in the Lord's favour. Perhaps Paul's intention is to suggest to the "weak" believer that the Lord's approval is attained not by following rules pertaining to food but by the Lord's own sustaining power':[54] 'is able' (δυνατεῖ) 'points both to the possibility and the power of grace'.[55]

---

51   Verse 3c '*God* has received him'; v. 4 'to his own *Lord* he stands or falls'; 'the *Lord* will cause him to stand'; v. 6 'observes the day to the *Lord*; eats to the Lord; give thanks to *God*'; 'does not eat to the *Lord*'; 'give thanks to the *Lord*'; v. 8 'we live to the Lord'; 'we die to the Lord'; 'we belong to the Lord'; v. 9 'Christ died and came to life, in order that he might also be lord over both the dead and the living'; v. 10 'we must all appear before the judgment seat of God'; v. 11 'as I live, says the Lord'; 'every tongue will praise God'; v. 12 'give account to God'.

The theological reasons for not judging are given in terms of a believer's relationship to God (interchangeably using the title 'Lord'). Every believer is related to another believer through God, who is the ultimate authority of the community as well as each believer. The freedom in relation to others is not to be used in destroying others, but in constructively up-building since each one needs to be accountable for his/her actions. The basic model of actions is the welcoming pattern of God (and Christ; 15.7). The fact that everyone belongs to God, and each one lives or dies to the Lord, implies accountability of his or her conduct towards God: a fellow believer is someone for whom Christ died (14.15). 'The relation of believers to their Lord takes precedence over any difference of opinion between believers. ... Life and death are much more important differences than disagreement over diet and days; and not even they disturb the relation between believers and their Lord.' Dunn, *Romans 9–16*, 808.

52   Barclay, 'Do We Undermine the Law?', 302.

53   *BDAG*, 352.

54   Moo, *Romans*, 841.

55   Käsemann, *Romans*, 370.

6.4.2. *'Who are you to judge your brother?' (14.10)*

The vv. 10-12 of the pericope begins, like v. 4, with a challenging question: σὺ δὲ τί κρίνεις ('But who are you to judge?'). This is intended to challenge the habitual judgement present in the Roman community.[56] The use of δέ (but) and σύ (you) explains the emphasis Paul is giving in this argument, since his main point from v. 4f. is to avoid mutual judgement. This verse probably has the same emphasis as v. 3, since the Romans' two major mistakes are indicated as judging and despising (κρίνω and ἐξουθενέω): 'Who are you to judge your brother? ... Who are you to despise your brother?' ἐξουθενέω conveys a strong feeling of contempt, and this is used to depict how the strong view the weak; κρίνω means to 'make a judgment regarding', and emphasises the act of condemning another party; in Rom. 14.10, the weak are seen to be condemning the strong.[57] κρίνειν is used eight times in ch. 14 (14.3, 4, 5 [twice], 10, 13 [twice], 22), and denotes the condemnatory judgemental behaviour of the weak. 'Christian judgment of *things* is valid and indeed essential (v.5), but judgment of *people* must give place to the judgment of God (vv.10-12).'[58]

The repeated use of 'brother' is striking, since it is used here in v. 10 after 12.1 and is also followed in vv. 13, 15, and 21; Paul's concern is that the fellow brother is being mistreated, and his use of the term 'brother' implies 'brother/sister in Christ'. The metaphor applies to both parties (cf. v. 13) as Paul does not label which side is placing an obstacle or trap before the other.[59] Paul instructs them to avoid judging or despising a brother/sister as it could result in their 'sibling's' ruin (14.15, 21). The verse wishes to communicate that the believer should maintain 'mutual loyalty' in order to build up their brother/sister instead of putting a stumbling block before them.[60] The repeated use of the 'brother' metaphor emphasises Paul's point; that the Romans belong

---

56   See Käsemann, *Romans*, 372; Schlier, *Der Römerbrief*, 410; Stowers, *Diatribe*, 115.

57   ἐξουθενέω has the same connotation in 2 Kgs. 19.21; 2 Chron. 36.16; Ezek. 22.8; Wisd. Sol. 4.18; Lk. 23.11; so also κρίνω in Rom. 2.1, 3, 12, 27; 3.7; 14.4, 10, 22; 1 Cor. 5.3, 12-13; 11.31; 2 Thess. 2.12 cf. Col. 2.16. See Dunn, *Romans 9–16*, 802.

58   Dunn, *Romans 9–16*, 808. James 4.12 has a similar argument: σὺ δὲ τίς εἶ, ὁ κρίνων τὸν πλησίον; ('But who are you that judges your neighbour?', which is also somewhat similar to Mt. 7.3: τί δὲ βλέπεις τὸ κάρφος τὸ ἐν τῷ ὀφθαλμῷ τοῦ ἀδελφοῦ σου ...; ('Why do you see the speck that is in your brother's eye ... ?').

59   Aasgaard, *My Beloved Brothers*, 214. 'He uses the metaphor in order to further the interests and prerogatives of one party in the face of the other party; no one should be made to fall, whether they are "weak" or they are "strong".' This clearly emphasises mutual responsibility towards others.

60   Aasgaard, *My Beloved Brothers*, 210. 'It is especially wrong to pass judgment on someone who is a Christian sibling.' Although Paul elsewhere advises making judgements (1 Thess. 5.14a; 1 Cor. 5.5, 12; 6.5; 2 Cor. 2.6), his aim is to avoid judgements that hinder unity and solidarity between one another.

Paul's use of the brother metaphor parallels the expectation of behaviour to a sibling in antiquity. Terence's *Adelphoe* illustrates the 'dynamics and strength' of the fraternal relationship (cf. Plutarch 6.7). Aasgaard, *My Beloved Brothers*, 70, 210.

to the Lord and all are members of the 'spiritual brotherhood of believers'.[61] It is noteworthy that the metaphors Paul uses to challenge the Romans move from depicting house slaves (14.4) to brothers and sisters (14.10). The first challenge is directed to the weak who judge others for not following the laws concerning food and days, whereas the second challenge is aimed at the strong who despise the weak.

6.4.3. 'Let us not judge one another' (14.13)

The admonition in v. 13 is directed at both groups: the strong and the weak. The present hortatory subjunctive κρίνωμεν is used to show that an activity that has been continued must no longer (μηκέτι) be continued.[62] The verb's object, ἀλλήλους (one another), makes it clear that the object of the exhortation concerns both groups.

Since κρίνειν is used in the aorist second-person plural, Barrett argues that the second clause ἀλλά τοῦτο κρίνατε μᾶλλον (v. 13) describes the judgement that both sides make on each other.[63] Calvin Roetzel argues that, in the first clause of v. 13, Paul is eager to bring the condescending and derisive judgements to an end and to encourage 'a new concern for the brother'.[64] κρίνειν here means 'to decide' not to put an offence (in this case a 'stumbling block') in a brother or sister's way. The use of πρόσκομμα ('stumbling block') and σκάνδαλον ('hindrance') (both words are used in connection with idolatry in Jewish thought but probably not here) explains how judging can be a destructive force in the way of a brother/sister.[65] Christ is referred to as the stone of stumbling (Rom. 9.32-33), a citation of Isa. 8.14. σκάνδαλον refers to 'cause of ruin' or 'occasion of misfortune' in the LXX.[66] What is the stumbling block in this instruction? Presumably, Paul is concerned about putting an end to negative evaluation of the sibling, i.e. by 'taking care not to place in his way anything that might cause him to fall from his Christian faith and practice'.[67] In sharing common meals, if one group forces the other to go against their conviction, then it would be a stumbling block as far as the second group is concerned.

---

61   H. Freiherr von Soden, 'ἀδελφος κτλ.', *TDNT* 1, 145; Cranfield, *Romans*, 2.709.

62   *BDAG*, 568.

63   Barrett, *Romans*, 262.

64   C. J. Roetzel, *Judgment in the Community: A Study of the Relationship between Eschatology and Ecclesiology in Paul* (Leiden: Brill, 1972), 134.

65   πρόσκομμα and σκάνδαλον are used in 1 Cor. 8.9 and 1 Cor. 8.13.

66   G. Stählin, 'σκάνδαλον, σκανδαλίζω', *TDNT* 7 (1971), 339.

67   Barrett, *Romans*, 241, 242.

6.5. Cost and effect of welcoming

6.5.1. Obligation: bearing the scruples (15.1a)

The strong are obliged to take the initiative in welcoming at the cost of bearing the scruples of the weak: ὀφείλομεν δὲ ἡμεῖς οἱ δυνατοὶ τὰ ἀσθενήματα τῶν ἀδυνάτων βαστάζειν. The language of obligation is characteristic of Romans but remains unused in 1 Corinthians.[68] Obligation is defined in the Roman legal context as follows: *Obligationum substantia non in eo consistit, ut aliquod corpus nostrum aut seruitutem nostram faciat, sed ut alium nobis obstringat ad dandum aliquid uel faciendum uel praestandum* ('The essence of obligations does not consist in that it makes some property or a servitude ours, but that it binds another person to give, do, or perform something for us').[69]

Paul declares that he is obliged to 'Greeks and Barbarians' (1.14), whereas the believers are obliged to love one another (13.8) and to live as the Spirit wants them to (8.12). Why are the strong obliged to bear the weak? Probably because Paul numbers himself among the strong and wants the strong to take the initiative in a manner that reverses the Greco-Roman system of obligation (where the weak submit to the strong). The Pauline system of obligation undermines the obligation culture by assuming that the strong are obliged to bear (βαστάζειν) the weaknesses of the weak.[70] It implies that the strong group act first to honour the weak group and put Paul's earlier exhortation to outdo one another in honouring (Rom. 12.10) into practice. Carrying another person's weaknesses implies placing one's strength in the place of the other's weaknesses and placing oneself in their position. 'Accept as our own burden'[71] has a sense of identifying with their struggles and weaknesses.

68   ὀφείλω is used in Romans 1.14; 8.12; 13.8; 15.1. Obligation functioned through the patronage system of Corinth; see J. K. Chow, *Patronage and Power: A Study of Social Networks in Corinth* (JSNTSup 75; Sheffield: JSOT Press, 1992) and is part of an 'ethic of reciprocity', since it controls the moral behaviour of many cultures. 'Ethic of reciprocity' is used by R. P. Saller, and is quoted by Reasoner and Jewett. See R. P. Saller, *Personal Patronage under the Early Empire* (Cambridge: Cambridge University Press, 1982), 19; Reasoner uses the term 'ethic' in the sense of 'moral code'. See Reasoner, *The Strong*, 176; Jewett, *Romans*, 876.

69   Digest of Justinian (ed. Theodor Mommsen and Paul Krueger; trans. and ed. Alan Watson; Philadelphia: University of Pennsylvania Press, 1985), 44.7.3, cited by Reasoner, *The Strong*, 181. It marks the interpersonal relationship and is a dynamic behind patronage. The Roman moralist speaks about 'gradations of duty' as 'our first duty is to the immortal gods; our second, to country; our third, to parents; and so on, in descending scale, to the rest'. Panaetius, according to Cicero, *Off.* 1.160, cited by Reasoner, *The Strong*, 182.

70   βαστάζω has a sense of bearing and enduring; 'bear patiently, put up with: weakness', *BDAG*, 171. In Gal. 6.2 it is said to 'bear one another's burdens and fulfil the law of Christ' (ἀλλήλων τὰ βάρη βαστάζετε καὶ οὕτως ἀναπληρώσετε τὸν νόμον τοῦ χριστοῦ). Another parallel is Mt. 8.7 as a quotation of Isa. 53.4: 'He took our weaknesses and bore our diseases.'

71   Cranfield, *Romans*, 2.731; Dunn, *Romans 9–16*, 837.

It is interesting that Paul balances the obligation to 'each of us' with pleasing 'the neighbour for good' (v. 2). But how and why are the 'strong' obliged to the weak? Jewett suggests, 'having received the supreme gift of salvation, granted freely to the undeserving, each recipient has the reciprocal obligation of gratitude to the divine giver and of passing on the gift with the similar generosity to others who are equally undeserving'.[72] Conclusively, Paul taught that the strong ought to help the weak by bearing their scruples and weaknesses.

6.5.2. Serving the interests of the other (15.2, 3)

The obligation to bear the weakness of the weak has a qualification in doing so: 'not to please ourselves' (καὶ μὴ ἑαυτοῖς ἀρέσκειν; 15.1). The verb ἀρέσκω implies accommodating oneself to someone.[73] Paul reverses the order of pleasing just as he overturns the obligatory system prevalent in Roman patronage; the cultural principle is that the superior class have the capacity to please themselves while those in the lower level lack ability; 'slaves and members of the urban underclass' always work to please their masters.[74] Paul's concept of pleasing assumes that in Christ those who are able should serve the powerless by refusing to please themselves. This exhortation looks back to Paul's earlier encouragements, e.g. 'not destroying the work of God' (14.15, 20), pursuing peace and mutual up-building (14.19), and stopping anything that offends others (14.21).

Although Paul sides with the strong, and counter-culturally places the responsibility of the weak on their shoulders, he broadens his vision of obligation in the Christian community by sharing the responsibility between both sides – weak and strong – with the formulation 'each of us'. Paul's concept of community envisioned all the members equally participating in mutual promotion of the other (12.3-8), and again stands in contrast with the assumptions of the society they inhabited.

Fulfilling the law through loving one's neighbour is referred to in 13.9-10, where Paul speaks of his apostolic strategy 'to please all people in all he does' (1 Cor. 10.33). Neighbour (πλησίον) has the broader definition of 'one's fellow human being',[75] which could imply all those with whom the Romans associate.

---

72   Jewett, *Romans*, 876. The obligation is defined as a duty that ought to be done as a result of receiving the 'new life in Christ', which is derived from 'faith in the gospel, the gift of the spirit, and membership in the community of faith'.

73   *BDAG*, 129. Rom. 15.1 cf. Gal. 1.10; 1 Thess. 2.4; 1 Cor. 10.33. Epictetus refers to pleasing oneself: 'Make it your wish then to please your own self, and you will be pleasing to god!' Epictetus, *Dissertations* 2.18.19. In *Assumption of Moses*, pleasing oneself is given in the negative sense: 'deceitful men, self-pleasing, hypocrites in all their affairs'. *Assumption of Moses: A Critical Edition with Commentary*, Johannes Tromp (trans.) (Leiden: Brill, 1993), 16–17.

74   Jewett, *Romans*, 877.

75   Klaus Haacker, 'πλησίον', *EDNT* 3 (1993), 113.

The pattern of Christ's acceptance of others without pleasing himself is the fundamental model in relationships to one another. It reveals that the redemptive action of Christ has not been fulfilled in our righteous effort, but in our undeserving and unrighteous character. The aorist verb ἤρεσεν implies Jesus' selfless attitude in his entire ministry (Phil. 2.3-5).[76] Christ did not please himself, but as it is written 'the reproaches of those who reproached you fell on me' (Rom. 15.3, cf. Ps. 69.9). Paul quotes the Psalmist as if it were Jesus speaking about the reproaches (ὄνειδος means disgrace, scandal, abuse, shame, etc.)[77] that fell on him. 'Christ died the most shameful of deaths in behalf of the shamed.'[78] In the context of Romans 15, Paul wants to maintain a 'mutually accepting attitude between the strong and the weak', which 'has the stunning implication that contempt and judging going on between the Roman congregations add to the shameful reproach that Christ bore on the cross for the sake of all'.[79] The two groups should work for mutual honour and integrity by pleasing others rather than judging and despising them.

6.5.3. Christian community ideals

If one does not care about others and holds to selfish ideals regarding food, they fail to act in love (14.15a) and could break down relationships in the community by offending others;[80] the theological rationale Paul gives for this is that continual offence could destroy one for whom Christ has died (14.15b). Christ's death for all was mentioned in Rom. 5.6, 8, and the inclusive character of his earthly ministry implies the worth of each individual before God.

Sigfred Pederson notes that not 'walking according to love' is a sin because 'the love of God through Christ' has not thus accomplished the objective of establishing 'a new eschatological reality' in this world of sin.[81] Love can be seen as the opposing force against destruction, and as the way to strengthen individuals and communities. I agree with Jewett's suggestion that 'when people are impelled to act in violation of their individual conscience, no matter how it has been formed in their familial and cultural tradition, they lose their integrity and their capacity to act as moral agents'.[82]

---

76   Barrett, *Romans*, 296; Cranfield, *Romans*, 2.732.
77   Johannes Schneider, ὄνειδος κτλ., *TDNT* 5 (1967), 238.
78   Jewett, *Romans*, 880.
79   Jewett, *Romans*, 880.
80   'Walking' (περιπατέω) is a distinctive Pauline metaphor that denotes one's actions and life. Georg Bertram and Heinrich Seesemann think that he has adapted it from the LXX usage (e.g. Prov. 8.20). See Georg Bertram and Heinrich Seesemann, πατέω, κτλ., *TDNT* 5 (1967), 544. Paul used to urge the congregations 'to walk worthily of God' (1 Thess. 2.12; cf. 2 Cor. 4.2; Phil. 3.17).
81   S. Pederson, 'Agape – der eschatologische Hauptbegriff bei Paulus', in S. Pederson (ed.), *Die Paulinische Literatur und Theologie* (Göttingen: Vandenhoeck & Ruprecht, 1980), 159–86, at 167. The consequence of not 'walking in love' leads to the ruin of the sibling. 'The person is being destroyed' is a metaphorical expression that emphasises the continual effect.
82   Jewett, *Romans*, 862. 'To act without regard to one's own conscience is to enter into destruction through the dissolution of the self' through the loss of 'personal unity' and 'integrity'.

Paul encourages the believers to have the same mind (τὸ αὐτὸ φρονεῖν) as that of Christ (15.5). τὸ αὐτὸ φρονεῖν is used (12.16) to communicate harmony between the groups and to allow solidarity by associating with the lowly instead of promoting oneself. It acknowledges the same Lordship without eradicating their cultural differences. Groups with diversities and differences have a Christological motivation for creating unity between them: 'let each of us please his neighbour for his good, to edify him' (15.2). For Jewett, 'This produces a distinctive form of same-mindedness because the focus is no longer on achieving unanimity in doctrine or practice but rather on bearing abuse for each other and pleasing each other as Christ did.'[83] Having the same mind as Christ helps to glorify God with one mind and one voice (15.6).

Paul goes on to speak of what characterises the reign of God (14.17); it is not characterised by eating and drinking, which are temporary and limited, but it is instead constituted by righteousness, peace, and joy in the Holy Spirit, which are everlasting principles. On the one hand, Paul wants to say that the reign of God is not present in the destructive behaviour and offensive disposition displayed towards one another. On the other, he wants to emphasise the fruit of the Spirit (Gal. 5.22) that aids the growth of the community. Holding a balance between the three community principles of righteousness, peace, and joy in the Holy Spirit, echoes Ps. 84.4 and describes the desirable attitudes the community should aspire to with the Holy Spirit's help. For Murray, these three significant terms 'should be taken as the rectitude and behaviour of the believer within the fellowship of Christ'.[84]

The expression 'pursue peace' in 14.19 echoes the righteous man in Ps. 34.14 (LXX 33.14), ζήτουσον εἰρήνην, καὶ δίωξον αὐτην ('seek peace and pursue it'). εἰρήνην διώκειν is an idiom in early Christian speech (2 Tim. 2.22; Heb. 12.14; 1 Pet. 3.11) and may have been based on Ps. 34.14 (as is clear in 1 Pet. 3.11).[85] Käsemann defines 'peace as openness toward everyone'.[86] The God-given and corporate dimensions of peace are seen in 14.17, 18; the kingdom of God is not eating and drinking but righteousness, peace, and joy in the Holy Spirit, thereby indicating that this conduct is pleasing to God. The plural formulation of the things of peace (τὰ τῆς εἰρήνης) may point to different issues in which Paul and his colleagues had to work to create unity and harmony. Apparently, it also indicates Paul's accommodation of different people of different status ('all things to all people' [1 Cor. 9.19-23]).

Jewett, *Tolerance*, 55.

83   Jewett, *Romans*, 884.

84   Murray, *Romans*, 2.194.

85   Dunn, *Romans 9–16*, 824. εἰρήνη has a corporate dimension rather than an individual dimension, since Paul is dealing with the issues relating to community; there is no peace with God in a divided community (v. 17). Elsewhere in Paul 'peace' is used in Rom. 15.13, 32; 2 Cor. 1.2, 24; 2.3; 7.13; 8.2; Gal. 5.22; Phil. 1.4, 25; 2.2, 29; 4.1, etc.

86   Käsemann, *Romans*, 377.

6.5.4. The 'up-building' metaphor (οἰκοδομή 14.19; 15.2)

Welcoming one another has its result in mutual up-building. The change from the third-person singular (v. 18) to first-person plural (v. 19) implies that Paul and his associates are examples for the weak and the strong to 'pursue' (διώκειν) so they can attain peace and edify others.

The expression 'to pursue peace' (14.19) has a corresponding expression τὰ τῆς οἰκοδομῆς 'the edification of one another', which amplifies the significance of the former statement 'pursue peace'. Cranfield suggests that this expression 'should probably be understood as serving more to fill out and clarify the significance which τὰ τῆς εἰρήνης has in this context'.[87] The use of οἰκοδομή is characteristic of Paul's language to denote congregational work (1 Cor. 3.9-10; 14.3, 5, 12, 26; 2 Cor. 10.8; 12.19; 13.10). In the LXX, the term is used to describe 'God's building of Israel' (Jer. 12.16; 38.4, 28; 40.7; 49.10; 45.4; 51.34). There are also parallels in the Qumran community such as, 'eternal planting of a holy house for Israel and a circle of the Most High' who witness to the truth of the law, and 'make atonement for the land and judge the helpless'.[88] Although the metaphor of building is the same, the context in the early Christian communities is different, and the task of up-building is broader than in the context of the Qumran community;[89] there are closer parallels to Paul's up-building of the community in Epicurean philosophical communities.[90] To build one another up requires that different groups, the weak and the strong, have to work for the other side. The ἀλλήλους formula (cf. 14.13) calls both groups to unite and work together for mutual edification. Jewett suggests, 'as each group supports the integrity of the other and encourages growth in others, a "mutually nurturing community" flourishes'.[91]

The double emphasis (εἰς τὸ ἀγαθὸν πρὸς οἰκοδομήν 15.2) to strive for good and mutual up-building by pleasing one's neighbour indicates that Paul is reinstating his earlier exhortations: 'love does not do evil to the neighbour' (13.10a), the quality of goodness versus evil that each believer should uphold (12.9), and the need to make every effort to overcome evil (12.21). If each

---

87   Cranfield, *Romans*, 2.721.

88   *IQS* 8.5–10

89   'οἰκοδομεῖν as a spiritual task in a community' in Otto Michel, οἰκοδομέω κτλ., *TDNT* 5 (1967), 140–42. 'Edification defines the unity and growth of the community as the task of every charismatic action of individuals.' Käsemann, *Romans*, 378.

90   There are 'four dimensions of Epicurean correction practice; one involving self-correction, another when a correction is administered by "others," thirdly, when members report errors to the teachers for them to correct, and finally, when the wise correct each other ... a network of social relations in which active participation of friends is presupposed in mutual edification, admonition and correction'. Glad, *Paul and Philodemus*, 132 (see also 124–32). 'Pauline communal psychagogy' in Romans 14–15 is different from 'Epicurean Communal Psychagogy' in which 'an asymmetrical relationship between the "weak" and "powerful" is assumed but Paul emphasizes the responsibility of the latter and the need of accommodation for both ... to teach members of his communities to implement a certain form of mutual psychagogy'. Glad, *Paul and Philodemus*, 214.

91   Jewett, *Romans*, 866; Jewett, *Tolerance*, 139.

believer, in contrast to the social norms of the day, seeks the good of his neighbour, the community will ultimately flourish. As Jewett rightly suggests, 'If each group seeks constructively to encourage the development of integrity and maturity in other groups, rather than trying to force them to conform to a single viewpoint, the ethnic and theological diversity in Rome would no longer be divisive and destructive.'[92] It seems that Paul reinstates the implications of the body metaphor here, since the body works for a common purpose in spite of the differences and diversities of its members (Romans 12). Similarly, οἰκοδομή calls forth unity in the purpose of the community to work for the edification of one another. As M. L. Reid rightly suggests, 'Paul's rhetoric of mutuality thus defines the social reciprocity that exemplifies acceptable and honourable community conduct.'[93]

6.6. The Pauline ethos of mutuality

It is very interesting to note the paradigm of mutuality, 'Pauline love-mutualism' as I refer to it, since love has an important role in leading towards mutual responsibilities. Paul envisages such mutuality in Romans as he instructs the two groups in Romans 14–15 in their dealings with one another. This is significantly different from the simple idea of reciprocity and mutualism because it requires being servants to one another without pleasing oneself. Each side has to give preference to the other in a continuous reciprocal manner.

The same pattern of mutualism that Paul depicts in Romans 12–13 can be seen in Romans 14, 15, and 16. Paul moves from the simple idea of interdependence to a new pattern of relationship: serving one another in mutualism based on love. Christ is emulated when the two groups emerge mutually edified and welcomed without any necessary change in their mutual identity. When the mutual exchange of joy, peace, righteousness, hope, truth, grace, promises, etc. takes place, the edification causes a chain reaction that is passed on from each member of the congregation. In this section we deal with the similarities and differences between the standard and Pauline approaches to reciprocity.

6.6.1. ἀλλήλους: two-way relationships

Paul's exhortation to love and care for one another is a crucial element of his instruction to the community. Paul's main aim is to encourage the believers to relate appropriately towards each other, which explains the emphasis he places on mutuality. As Paul encourages the two groups of Roman Christians

---

92   Jewett, *Romans*, 876.
93   M. L. Reid, 'Paul's Rhetoric of Mutuality: A Rhetorical Reading of Romans', in E. H. Lovering (ed.), *SBL Papers* (Atlanta: Scholars Press, 1995), 117–39, at 137. S. J. Stowers interprets the 'principle of faithfulness as adaptability to others'; S. J. Stowers, *A Re-reading of Romans: Justice, Jew, and Gentiles* (New Haven: Yale University Press, 1994), 318.

to practise mutual relations to each other, he carries the ἀλλήλους language into chs. 14 and 15 from 12 and 13. There are four 'one another' (ἀλλήλους) references in chs. 14–15.1-13.

1. Do not judge one another (14.13).
2. Let us pursue matters that lead to peace and to edification for one another (14.19).
3. May the God of endurance and of comfort give to you the power to think the same thing among one another according to Jesus Christ (15.5).
4. Welcome one another, therefore, as Christ has welcomed you, for the glory of God (15.7).

Paul's desire is to urge the need for unity and solidarity among the believers by developing mutual relations between them. Paul wants to emphasise this in the different dimensions of Christian life, i.e. it can be explicit in different forms of love such as affection, generosity, hospitality, identifying with, honouring and forgiving (chs. 12–13). The attitude of sober-mindedness (12.3) creates 'other'-mindedness, and as members of the 'one' body (in Christ) each one's task of welcoming, bearing, and edifying one another is significant; its implication to the community is also remarkable as each one is required to avoid judging that destroys the work of God and ruins the fellow brother/sister.

6.6.2. *Dynamic relationship*

The basic idea of reciprocity in antiquity is a dynamic two-way relationship that can be between individuals on equal or unequal grounds. However, the uniqueness of Pauline mutuality involves the reversal of culturally accepted norms and status. In Paul, receiving one another includes a repeated process of change in position that places others in balance. This type of relationship is sustained by becoming servants of one another, and by regarding others as a sibling.

Servants of one another: The Christological motivation for the dynamic process of behaviour in welcoming, bearing, pleasing, edifying, etc. is the fundamental mode of community relationships that leads to unity and harmony. Romans 15.1-3 is closely paralleled with Mk. 10.45: Jesus came to the world 'not to be served, but to serve'. Being servants of one another doesn't work unless one individual or group is ready to accept a lower state which automatically uplifts the opposite group. Selfish motives have to be surrendered for the sake of others. In turn, the recipient of the service intends to serve the donor by going through the same process.

The strong and the weak members of the community are like the diversities and differences that make up the body. The differences between the members help the community to follow Christ's examples through the act of welcoming others described in Romans 14, 15. If all the members are either weak or strong, how can the community exercise the character of other-mindedness?

The effectiveness of the Christ-like character could only be revealed if it is given an opportunity to be seen in action. Those who have greater strength are obliged to bear those who do not, thereby implying mutuality in the community by giving more honour to other members. The implications of being the body of Christ are expressed in receiving one another as Christ has received all. It seems that the gist of all that Paul has explained regarding being one body in Christ, and members of one another, is clearly implied in the action of mutual welcoming. The act of welcoming or receiving does imply the denial of one's own motives in order to promote others.

Brother/sister metaphor: It is striking that Paul brings up relationships between one another by introducing models from the practical realm. If the first metaphor he used in Romans 14–15 is the servant model (14.4), the second pattern of relationship is depicted as holding membership of one family (14.10, 13, 15, 21). It implies the belonging-togetherness of the members[94] and their effort for the common good in lifting up one another.

Working for the common good involves honouring others rather than oneself. As Aasgaard puts it, Paul's aim in the use of this metaphor 'is to make each party hold the other party in higher esteem than previously'.[95] The singular usage of the brother metaphor probably indicates individual responsibility towards others as well as to God (14.12), which, although all are ultimately working together as a group, is crucial for each individual to develop.

6.7. Conclusion

The paradigm of mutuality that Paul emphasises in Romans 14–15 is brought to life in mutual welcome. Judgemental and despising attitudes are hindrances to this mutuality. Genuine love for a brother or sister is shown by accepting him or her in their present state of existence. Even if one is undeserving of acceptance, they should still be accepted on the basis that Christ accepted all in their state of sin. The Christian φιλαδελφία (Rom. 12.10) and κοινωνία (Rom. 12.13) are expressed in the form of welcoming one another while still retaining one's respective identity. (Practically, this could include an individual's choice to keep observing Jewish practices.)

The eventual purpose of love mutualism is that it glorifies God (15.7). Love mutualism not only works between humans, but it begins with God bestowing grace through Christ to humans; humans pass on this grace to each other, and it ends in glorification and thanksgiving. Since grace is involved in love

---

94   See A. D. Clarke, 'Equality or Mutuality? Paul's Use of "Brother" Language', in P. J. Williams et al. (eds.), *The New Testament in its First Century Setting: Essays on Context and Background in Honour of B. W. Winter* (Grand Rapids: Eerdmans, 2004), 151–64, at 164; P. Arzt Grabner, 'Brothers and Sisters in Documentary Papyri and in Early Christianity', *Revista Biblica* 50 (2002), 187–202.

95   Aasgaard, *My Beloved Brothers*, 214.

mutualism it can work in both favourable and unfavourable conditions. Paul speaks about negative reciprocity (repaying evil for evil; Rom. 12.17) and positive reciprocity (repaying good for evil; Rom. 12.17). Love mutualism has the power to overcome evil with good by displaying love towards enemies (Rom. 12.21), which is based on the self-giving model of the cross.

It is probable that Paul wants to follow the same ethos of mutualism in the greetings (Rom. 16.1-16). It is not hard to see that Rom. 16.1-16 could be used by Paul to give the Romans a chance to practise love mutualism by extending greetings to other people who have exercised love mutualism towards him. In addition, Paul urges this love mutualism to work throughout all the diverse organs of the 'body in Christ'. Therefore, I will conclude this book by showing that greetings work as a significant model to enhance love mutualism, which also aims to acknowledge the hard work of some people towards Paul and the church, irrespective of gender.

CHAPTER 7

CONCLUSION: TOWARDS A THEOLOGY OF LOVE MUTUALISM

As stated in the introductory chapter, the three major issues discussed in this research are the leadership roles of women in the Pauline churches as specified in Romans 16, the disposition of the mutuality reflected in the greetings to men and women, and the way in which the greetings to men and women in Romans 16 relate to the ethos of mutualism in Romans 12–15. The Pauline ethos of mutuality embedded in the greetings (Rom. 16.1-16) seems to be a continuation of the exhortations to the Romans about how to relate to one another in the body of Christ by following the model of Christ (Romans 12–15); Paul's positive approach to the role of women in the Roman church, in spite of his prohibitions and restrictions to women's participation in the church and worship elsewhere, is especially striking.

7.1. A retrospect

In chapter 2, the form of greetings in the Pauline letters against the backdrop of Hellenistic letters' use of greetings was examined, and the significance of the specific form of the greetings in Rom. 16.1-16 was noted. The second-person plural of the greeting verb, used extensively in Romans 16, had the purpose of encouraging mutual relationships.

In chapter 3, study on the leadership of women in the Greco-Roman world revealed that some women with wealth, family, prestige, and social position exerted independence and freedom. It was noted, however, that one cannot make the general claim that all women had independence. The analysis showed that women's leadership roles in the Pauline churches were not counter-cultural, but a normal part of Greco-Roman culture.

Chapter 4 analysed the women mentioned by name (Rom. 16.1-16) and greeted with descriptive phrases, which indicated their leadership roles in the church and their relation to Paul. This drew attention to Paul's acknowledgement of some women who worked as his associates, and pointed to relationships of mutuality in the greetings.

Chapter 5 examined the implicit mutuality modelled in the body metaphor and the recurring 'ἀλλήλους/ ἀλλήλων' in Paul's exhortations (Romans

12, 13). The body metaphor pointed to the significance of being in Christ, which did not exclude individual difference, but respected difference as well as belonging-togetherness. The repeated term 'ἀλλήλους' signifies that Christian experience is not only an individual experience but also has social and ethical aspects which are derived from incorporation into the body of Christ.

Chapter 6 discussed the contextual application of mutuality in the community embodied in mutual welcoming and up-building (Romans 14–15). It seems that differences and diversity in a person's cultural practice might have hindered welcoming, which may be the reason why Paul strongly urges Roman Christians to bear with one another irrespective of position or status.

As I have already provided a summary of findings at the relevant junctures, I will now attempt to draw together the peculiarities of the Pauline ethos of mutuality that encourages the leadership of women in the closing greetings. A discussion on the significance of greetings (7.2) in Romans is followed by a discussion on women in leadership within the structures of mutualism (7.3). Third, 1 Cor. 11.1-16 is discussed briefly to understand whether hierarchy or relationality is the main emphasis (7.4). And fourth, a final remark is made on the Pauline ethos of mutuality in Romans and further scope for research is outlined (7.5).

7.2. *The impact of* ἀσπάσασθε

ἀσπάσασθε 'you greet' denotes an instruction to greet that forges a web of relationships. Paul's instruction to the Romans to greet the people named and mentioned with descriptive phrases works as an introduction to comprehend their actions with regard to each other as well as to himself. The instruction 'you greet' deepens and strengthens relationships between B (recipients of the letter) and C (the recipients of the greeting), thus establishing a mutual bond between A (Paul) and B, between B and C, and also between A and C.

The persons who do the greeting are not only acting as agents but also as recipients, thus there is a web of mutual interaction. Moreover, the descriptive phrases used to portray the actions of the people on behalf of the church and Paul provide strong commendation to the greetings, reinstating positive relations between Paul and the persons greeted. The relational character of the greetings is also significant as the persons are described in relation to Paul, Christ, and the church. The belonging-togetherness of the community is expressed in the phrase: 'in the Lord'. This phrase unifies and maintains the new identities of the believers in relation to Christ, irrespective of gender, status, and ethnicity.

Paul's instruction to greet ends in him exhorting the Romans to greet one another with a holy kiss (Rom. 16.16a), which covers all the individuals not specified by name and unifies the people with different perspectives and practices; this serves to hold the community together in mutual love, which is the focus of Romans (especially chs. 12–15). Relational mutuality in Romans transcends gender differences as Paul accepts and appreciates men and women for their toil for the church and him. Therefore, this type of greeting builds up mutual love among the Roman Christians in a way that repositions one another.

7.3. The women in leadership within the structures of mutualism

The women named and greeted with specific roles (Romans 16) are Phoebe, Prisca, Junia, Persis, Mary, Tryphaena and Tryphosa, Rufus' mother, Nereus' sister, and Julia. It is quite striking that some women clearly exercised leadership roles while others actively participated in the ministry of the church and Paul's mission (Rom. 16.1-16). Their leadership roles and participation are honoured as the same as that of men (or even over men), which seems to be well known and taken for granted by the Roman believers. The mutuality of leadership is a remarkable aspect, as men and women were primarily identified by their relation to the Lord. The leadership is gender blind and without any limitations on women. The practice of mutualism among the leaders serves as a demonstration for the rest of the community to follow.

Paul's appreciation of these women's roles drew attention to the fact that they held leadership roles. First, Phoebe, as the διάκονος, played an important and significant role in the church of Cenchreae. Her position is further emphasised in the title προστάτις, which revealed her benefaction of many Christians including Paul. Her expected role among the Roman church could not be limited to the Spanish mission, since πρᾶγμα is not a definite matter in the request for help. Moreover, the chiasm of the passage is woven in such a way as to show the aspect of reciprocity. Her action for others needs to be reciprocated, and she is a woman qualified to receive hospitality and help in whatever matter she needs. On the one hand, this gives an insight into Phoebe's contribution to the Pauline mission, and on the other it shows Paul's way of presenting her and his desire to reciprocate her actions.

Second, Paul's description of Prisca and Aquila as his associates (συνεργοί μου), and as having risked their lives for his sake, obviously states their relationship with Paul. But their action on behalf of Paul brought them thanksgiving (εὐχαριστῶ) not only from Paul, but also from all the churches of the Gentiles. Prisca was a co-worker of Paul and possibly acted as the leader of the church in her house, which consisted of a community of saints. Her contribution was profound as she was beneficial to all the churches of the Gentiles, including both men and women.

Third, Paul describes Junia (with Andronicus) as his relatives and fellow prisoners (συγγενεῖς μου, συναιχμάλωτοι), which implies their relationship to Paul and his co-workers. But the other two descriptions: prominent among the apostles (ἐπίσημοι ἐν τοῖς ἀποστολόις) and 'in Christ before me' (πρὸ ἐμοῦ γέγοναν ἐν Χριστῷ) explicitly state their relationship to the early Christian community and their significant contribution to the Christian mission. First, Junia is portrayed as an associate of Paul. She is not only an apostle (in the sense of a co-worker) but is prominent among them. The reason for her distinctiveness is not specific, but one can speculate that the reasons may include her toil (fellow prisoner) and missionary zeal (in Christ before Paul). Second, Paul's description of her as 'prominent among the apostles' seems to imply that Paul himself will get some benefit by sharing in the reputation of those who are associates with himself (cf. Rom. 16.3, 4). Third, it reveals the mutual obligation that comes about by being in Christ (cf. Rom. 12.5); and obligation that places all human relationships in a deeper context, i.e. all belong together because they are in Christ.

Mary, Persis, Tryphoena and Tryphosa were hardworking women and part of the appreciated and acknowledged team who had supported Paul and his mission by various means. Rufus' mother was a mother to Paul. Nereus' sister and Julia were possibly part of the leadership team of a tenement church. Paul's presentation of these women's roles in order to be greeted as well as appreciated by the Roman believers reinforces the Pauline ethos of mutuality.

These women were appreciated for their leadership roles alongside men, and the endorsement of women's roles elsewhere also gives evidence of Paul's positive attitude to women in ministry and leadership. Examples include: Apphia (our sister; Philemon 2); Nympha, greeted with the church in her house (Col. 4.15), and Euodia and Syntyche, co-workers of Paul, who shared his struggles (Phil. 4.2, 3).

7.4. 1 Corinthians 11.2-16: restriction or mutuality in gender roles?

Having explored Paul's positive approach to women and their roles in the church and to himself (Rom. 16.1-16), it is paradoxical to hear Paul's seemingly indifferent tone elsewhere in dealing with the roles of women in the church (1 Cor. 11.2-16; cf. 14.34f.;[1] 1 Tim. 2.13f.). First Corinthians 11.2-16 posits an apparent ambivalence with regard to gender relations: on the one hand, the text seems to affirm the subordination of women, especially with reference to the veiling of women in public worship. On the other, it seems to affirm mutuality between gender relations. I think that this passage significantly encourages mutuality in gender relations as in the greetings (Rom. 16.1-16).

In the first stage of Paul's argument, three parallel statements can be seen (v. 3): the head of every man is Christ, the head of every woman is man, and the head of Christ is God. κεφαλή has been rendered with different nuances, such as 'head' or 'chief', 'source' or 'origin', which indicates authority, supremacy, and leadership. Judith Gundry-Volf argues that neither merely 'egalitarian'

---

1   First Corinthians 14.34, 35 appears to contradict Paul's approval to pray and prophecy (11.5) and his affirmation that 'all are able to prophecy in turn' (14.31). I will leave 1 Cor. 14.34f. and 1 Tim 2.13f. without further discussion due to the limitation of space and reasons such as arguments on authorship.

nor merely 'hierarchical' interpretations do justice to the complexity of the theological issue for Paul.[2] In this verse, rather than a hierarchy, the relation between God and Christ shows order and differentiation as well as mutual and reciprocal relationships.[3] This is neither meant to show subordination nor inferiority, but rather, as Garland suggests, 'it establishes the need for loyalty to the head'.[4]

The second stage of argument is found in vv. 4-6, where the participation of men and women in the Christian assembly is explained. Every man who prays and prophesies with his head covered dishonours his head, whereas every woman who prays or prophesies with her head uncovered dishonours her head. As Hooker suggests, the man or woman who dishonours his or her own head in the literal sense brings dishonour also on his or her metaphorical head.[5]

Gundry-Volf observes that the characterisation of the Mediterranean world as a shame/honour society supplies the background for the shame/glory contrast in 1 Cor. 11.2-16.[6] Moxnes identifies the shame/glory category as: (1) a head covering, like that of Romans before their gods in public devotion, reduced his self-respect and shamed his own person and (2) this shames his head also in the sense of appearing to demean Christ or God as his Lord and head.[7] It seems that Paul wants to avoid the distractions in Christian worship from self-attention, which makes the person's head a source of shame.[8] Martin proposes that Paul is anxious about veiling for two reasons: order and sexuality; veiling situates women in their proper position in the ordered hierarchy of society, which also means that they are not intended to be passive

2   J. M. Gundry-Volf, 'Gender and Creation in 1 Cor. 11.2-16: A Study in Paul's Theological Method', in J. Adna, S. J. Hafeman, and O. Hofius (eds.), *Evangelium, Schriftauslegung, Kirche: Festschrift für P. Stuhlmacher* (Göttingen: Vandenhoeck & Ruprecht, 1997), 151–71. Økland (*Women in their Place*, 178) argues that these 'verses confirm gender difference on a cosmological level through the drawing of a hierarchy and a clear boundary between male and female'.

3   A. C. Thiselton, *The First Epistle to the Corinthians* (Carlisle: Paternoster Press), 803. In 1 Cor. 12.4-6, the one God, the one Lord, and the one Spirit shows mutuality, oneness, and distinctiveness.

4   D. E. Garland, *1 Corinthians* (BECNT; Grand Rapids: Baker Academic, 2003), 516. Garland agrees with Perriman who concludes: 'The point seems to be ... that the behaviour of the woman reflects upon the man who as her head is representative of her, the prominent partner in the relationship, or that the woman's status and value is summed up in the man.' A. C. Perrimann, 'The Head of a Woman: The Meaning of κεφαλή in 1 Cor. 11.3', *JTS* 45 (1994), 602–22, at 621.

5   M. D. Hooker, 'Authority on Her Head: An Examination of 1 Cor. 11.10', *NTS* 10 (1963–64), 410–16, at 411.

6   Gundry-Volf, 'Gender and Creation in 1 Cor. 11.2-16', 155. Wire (*The Corinthian Women Prophets*, 120) argues that 'Paul is not using "glory" to mean "copy" nor even "splendour" so much as honour in contrast to shame. If a woman is the glory of a man, her presence reflects honour on him and also makes the man vulnerable to shame through her.'

7   H. Moxnes, 'Honor, Shame and the Outside World in Paul's Letter to the Romans', in J. Neusner et al. (eds.), *The Social World of Formative Christianity and Judaism* (Philadelphia: Fortress, 1988), 208.

8   Thiselton, *First Epistle to the Corinthians*, 828.

but must participate in their covering. He states three reasons why he thinks Paul thought women should be veiled: 'the society worries about their social vulnerability; a woman's unveiled head constitutes a bodily defect; female sexuality and social order cannot be separated in veiling cultures'.[9]

Watson rightly argues that veiling is the symbol of woman's authority to speak rather than a symbol of division in the Christian congregation. It is agape and not eros that must rule in the public sphere of the congregation, and the veil is interposed as the condition of women's free speech and of men's respect of it.[10] For Watson, the real subject of the passage is togetherness of man and woman 'in the Lord', within the fellowship of agape.[11] In 1 Cor. 11.7, Paul asserts that man is the image and glory of God, the woman as the glory of man. Fee rightly asserts that Paul's use of glory in relation to image, and to the mutuality in v. 12, means that the existence of the one brings honour and praise to the other.[12] It is likely that Paul assumes man and woman are the glory of one another.

Mutual interdependence between man and woman in the Lord shows the character of relationality and mutuality in the new creation (v. 11). There could be no reciprocity or mutuality unless each was differentiated from the other. It is evident that the custom, which Paul is referring to here, concerns gender distinctions in public worship, and that Paul is addressing both men and women. He accepts the status of men and women in Christian worship as both are given the right to pray and prophesy without ignoring the gender distinctions. Judith Gundry-Volf in her discussion of 11.1-16 identifies three 'points of reference', 'lenses', or 'maps' in Pauline dialogue: the order of creation,

---

9   Martin, *Corinthian Body*, 245. He presents evidence in connection with physiology that the bodies of women are weaker, more vulnerable than men to desire, danger, and pollution, and all the more dangerous to the church's body (233). Therefore, the veil protected a women's body from dangers posed by external forces and protected the social body from dangers posed by the female body itself (248). Martin's attempt to present the different ideological expressions of body in the ancient times is interesting. But the question remains unanswered as to what extent we can ascertain that Paul was really influenced by the body ideology of the contemporary times. By contrast, Watson assumes that the appropriate criterion for judging the texts is only through the reality of agape. He argues that if agape is the beginning and the end of Christian faith and living, then it is agape that must provide the final criteria for Christian reflection on sexuality and gender. Watson, *Agape, Eros, Gender*, ix.

10   Watson, *Agape, Eros, Gender*, 41. See also E. H. Pagels, 'Paul and Women: A Response to Recent Discussion', *JAAR* 42 (1974), 538–49; R. Scroggs, 'Paul and the Eschatological Women', *JAAR* 41 (1972), 283–303, at 297–300.

11   I support the following arguments of Watson. (1) Divine love is the basis of human love and the Christian faith and living should be in accordance with it (p. 1); (2) In the new creation, eros is not at the centre of the relationship of man and woman. The sense of eros is not negated but not seen as the guiding factor in the Christian community (p. 68); (3) Respecting womanhood as 'belonging together' does not exclude difference. Belonging together acknowledges difference and difference as that of belonging together (p. 3); (4) He opposes the strands of feminism that seem to be at the opposite extreme of patriarchy, which either advocate or presuppose a self-definition apart from man (p. 5). For more discussion see, Watson, *Agape, Eros, Gender*, 1–89.

12   Fee, *The First Epistle to the Corinthians*, 514.

custom as propriety, and eschatology or the gospel. She bases her arguments on honour and shame on these points, and urges 'control over the head' and the relationship of mutuality, reciprocity, and gender distinctiveness.[13]

As Paul advises husbands and wives in 1 Cor. 7.3, 4, he gives mutual authority over each other's body, where we see neither a hierarchical pattern nor the pattern of equality, rather mutuality and reciprocity considering the will of the partner in the marital relationship. It is striking to note that Paul addresses both husband and wife, urging them to give 'themselves over to each other in their marital commitment'.[14] The basis of this relationship is Christian love that uproots selfish desires and upholds pleasing others and belonging-togetherness. Paul wants love to be the basis of mutual relationships in the family and community. Love does not divide, but rather it unites all in mutual relationship and also it governs gender issues in the community as a whole.

If one attempts to establish hierarchy in the man/woman relationship, there is a danger of missing out on what Christ has secured for humanity through the New Creation (Gal. 3.28). But on the other hand, if one intends to affirm an egalitarian view, there is an apparent danger of pressing homogeneity that excludes difference. A more viable way of reading the text should be with a view that combines sharing in the benefits of Christ's redemption by men and women and affirmation of mutuality in gender relations.

Therefore, 1 Cor. 11.11, which highlights the interdependence of man and woman 'in the Lord', serves as the hermeneutical key for understanding the text. I consider this text as significant in defining gender relations in the Lord, with its emphasis on the mutual relationship and interdependence of man and woman; hierarchy in one direction is reversed by the hierarchy in the other direction, which supports the Pauline ethos of mutuality in Romans 12–16.

7.5. 'Pauline love mutualism': a challenge to communitarian ethics

The model of mutuality which Paul wants to highlight in the greetings to men and women in the church seems to be the first practical step towards the fulfilment of the exhortations to the Roman community to practise love, welcome, and honour to one another (Romans 12–15).[15] The distinctive feature of the Pauline ethos of mutuality is that it is initiated by grace, mediated by love, and sustained by the Spirit. It avoids extremes of either an atomised

---

13   Gundry-Volf, 'Gender and Creation in 1 Cor. 11.2-16', 160, 162, 169.

14   Garland, *1 Corinthians*, 259. I agree with Garland as he suggests, 'Paul does not frame this relationship in terms of husband's rights and the wife's duties ... she is an equal partner ... neither can claim to have authority over his or her body and disavow further sexual relationship with the marriage partner' (*1 Corinthians*, 259–61). See also P. B. Payne, *Man and Woman, One in Christ: An Exegetical and Theological Study of Paul's Letters* (Grand Rapids: Zondervan, 2009), 107.

15   The theme of mutual encouragement is introduced by Paul in the beginning of Romans (1.11, 12): 'mutually encouraged by faith which is in one another, both yours and mine'.

individualistic approach or a blatant collectivism. Rather, it promotes a dialectics of person-in-community. An individual is an isolated being cut off from all external relationships, and as such, is the antithesis to authentic human existence; whereas to be human is to be a person whose existence is predicated within a web of relationships.

Paul makes it abundantly clear that the well-being of a person potentially leads to the well-being of the community. Persons with different gifts can up-build the community in the ethos of mutuality. In turn, this enhances the significance of the giftedness of each in the context of mutual affirmation. The believers form a close-knit family, who are committed to solidarity and mutual care, and mutuality is rooted in their belonging to Christ.

I call this model of mutuality 'Pauline love-mutualism' since love has an important role in leading to mutual relations, which is profound in Romans (12–16) and has a constructive impact on the community. Paul advises the Romans that their love should be genuine. He begins this ethos of mutualism with the body metaphor (12.3, 4), and tries to develop mutual relations (12.9-13) by describing different aspects (outdo one another in honouring, hospitality), and more clearly emphasises how love mutualism works between two groups (the strong and the weak). The uniqueness of Pauline mutuality is that there is a dynamism involved in the perpetual reversal of positions. The notion of hierarchy is also strange to this model as both parties would act in mutual interdependence. The hierarchical model is replaced by a mutuality model, where members act in unity and mutuality with no question of permanent inferiority or superiority.

Thus Paul alters the static hierarchical model of antiquity to that of equalisation via a constant process of promoting the other. This dynamic is modelled in the pattern of Christ's service (cf. Rom. 15.1-6) as the two groups come out as mutually edified and mutually welcomed (the strong and the weak). The edification passes on to others in a chain reaction since each member of the congregation is involved in this process.

The dynamics of mutualism we have explored here fit neither the label 'hierarchical' or 'egalitarian' as they are usually understood, since each suggests a static state rather than the dynamic and constantly reversible conditions we have identified. Nor is the label 'complementarian' quite appropriate, if that again suggests a permanent division of roles and powers. Rather, Paul seems to promote processes (not states) of reciprocal and constantly reversed asymmetry, in a dynamic trajectory which never stabilises into a permanent hierarchy or division of roles. The end result may be described as a kind of dynamic process of equalisation, since the tasks of mutual promotion are equally incumbent on all parties, but this is not quite identical to the more static models of egalitarianism which are characteristic of modernity.[16]

---

16   Within Evangelicalism, two key positions on the issue of gender are egalitarian and complementarian. For more discussion see Michael Lakey, *Image and Glory of God: 1 Cor. 11.2-16 As A Case Study in Bible, Gender and Hermeneutics* (LNTS; London: T&T Clark, 2010), 18, 19.

Paul asks his recipients to practise this love mutualism between them, where he introduces Phoebe and a number of people to be greeted (Rom. 16.1-16). He points to some people whom he knows well and whom he thinks special with regard to him and the Roman church. Greeting cannot be done without honouring, and the honouring is expected to move in both directions as the pendulum of a clock oscillates. Love cannot do wrong to a neighbour, but love is the fulfilment of the law (Rom. 13.10). Mutualism can be negative or positive (negative in the sense of judging one another and positive in the sense of welcoming without considering status): the strong and the weak. In order to sustain good relationships, one should not think highly of him or herself and not be of a haughty mind (Rom. 12.3, 16b). The attitude of the person who exercises love mutualism should be as if one is serving the Lord (12.11c) and serving Christ (14.18); δουλεύω means enslaved or serving as a slave. Every believer is enslaved to Christ in order to serve others with an attitude of serving Christ. That means, one who exercises love mutualism fulfils the law and serves Christ: A serves under B; B serves under A.

Divine initiative and grace are involved in love mutualism since grace is bestowed on humans to act in mutuality, which brings glorification to God at the end.[17] Humans participate with the divine in the transformative power of Christ to bring glory and honour to God, the Father. This is a challenge to communitarian ethics as it requires divine–human participation and it acts in a way to challenge negative with positive reciprocity. This helps to honour the least honourable in the community and uplift them to the main strata, irrespective of race, colour, sex, and status.

In sum, the leadership of women in the church is placed within the structures of mutuality in Romans. Mutuality is the model of relationship Paul wants to urge on Roman Christians and the ethical obligations are guided by the dynamic relationships of 'love mutualism'. Love mutualism works as mutual service to the other that works within the hierarchies by continually reversing them so that the superiority of x to y is continually subverted by the superiority of y to x.

There is clearly scope for further research along these lines, such as the place of grace in love mutualism and its transformative power in mutual service. Further analysis is needed concerning the reception of grace in serving Christ as his bond slave, and the manifestation of grace in serving a brother or sister as a bond slave, on the mode of working together through self-emptying, and also the empowering function of grace in believers.

---

17   For more discussion see, Harrison, *Paul's Language of Grace in its Greco-Roman Context*, 211–23; J. M. G. Barclay, 'Grace within and Beyond Reason: Philo and Paul in Dialogue', in P. Middleton, A. Paddison, and K. Wenell (eds.), *Paul, Grace and Freedom: Essays in Honour of J. K. Riches* (London, T&T Clark, 2009), 9–21.

BIBLIOGRAPHY

Aasgaard, R. '*My Beloved Brothers and Sisters!*': *Christian Siblingship in Paul.*
JSNTSup 265; London: T&T Clark, 2004.

Achtemeier, P. J. *Romans: Interpretation. A Bible Commentary for Teaching
and Preaching.* Atlanta: John Knox Press, 1985.

Althaus, P. *An die Römer übersetzt und erklärt.* NTD 6; Göttingen: Vandenhoeck
& Ruprecht, 1966.

Arichea, D. C. 'Who was Phoebe? Translating *Diakonos* in Romans 16:1', *BT*
39 (1988), 401–409.

Arlandson, J. M. *Women, Class, and Society in Early Christianity: Models from
Luke-Acts.* Peabody: Hendrickson, 1997.

Ascough, R. S. 'Voluntary Associations and the Formation of Pauline Christian
Communities: Overcoming the Objections'. In A. Gutsfeld and D.-A.
Koch (eds.), *Vereine, Synagogen und Gemeinden im kaiserzeitlichen
Kleinasien.* Studies and Texts in Antiquity and Christianity 25; Tübingen:
Mohr Siebeck, 2006, 149–83.

Badiou, A. *Saint Paul: The Foundation of Universalism.* Stanford: Stanford
University, 2003.

Banks, R. *Paul's Idea of Community: The House Churches in their Historic
Setting.* Exeter: Paternoster, 1980.

Barclay, J. M. G. 'Do we undermine the Law? A Study of Romans 14:1–15:6'.
In J. D. G. Dunn (ed.), *Paul and the Mosaic Law.* Tübingen: Mohr, 1996,
287–308.

—— 'Neither Jew Nor Greek: Multiculturalism and the New Perspective on
Paul'. In M. G. Brett (ed.), *Ethnicity and the Bible.* Leiden: Brill, 1996,
197–214.

—— 'Is it Good News that God is Impartial? A Response to Robert Jewett,
Romans: A Commentary', *JSNT* 31 (2008), 89–111.

—— 'Grace Within and Beyond Reason: Philo and Paul in Dialogue'. In P.
Middleton, A. Paddison, and K. Wenell (eds.), *Paul, Grace and Freedom:
Essays in Honour of J. K. Riches.* London, T&T Clark, 2009, 9–21.

Barnett, P. W. 'Apostle', *DPL* (1993), 45–51.

Barrett, C. K. *The First Epistle to the Corinthians.* London: Adam & Clark, 1968.

—— *The Signs of an Apostle.* London: Epworth, 1970.

—— *A Commentary on the Epistle to the Romans.* London: A&C Black, 1991.

Bartsch, H.-W. 'Die antisemitischen Gegner des Paulus im Römerbrief'. In P.
W. Eckert, N. P. Levinson, and M. Stöhr (eds.), *Anti judaismus im Neuen
Testament? Abhandlungen zum Christlich-jüdischen Dialog.* Munich:
Kaiser, 1967, 33–34.

Bassler, J. M. 'Phoebe'. In C. Meyers (ed.), *Women in Scripture*. Grand Rapids: Eerdmans, 2000, 134–35.

—— 'Prisca/Priscilla'. In C. Meyers (ed.), *Women in Scripture*. Grand Rapids: Eerdmans, 2000.

Bauckham, R. *The Gospel Women: Studies of the Named Women in the Gospels.* Grand Rapids: Eerdmans, 2002.

Bauer, W., W. F. Arndt, F. W. Gingrich, and F. W. Danker. *Greek–English Lexicon of the New Testament and Other Early Christian Literature.* 3rd edn. London: University of Chicago, 2000.

Bauman, R. A. *Women and Politics in Ancient Rome.* London: Routledge, 1992.

Beard, M. 'The Sexual Status of Vestal Virgins', *JRS* 70 (1980), 12–27.

Belleville, L. L. 'Continuity or Discontinuity: A Fresh look at 1 Corinthians in the Light of First Century Epistolary Forms and Conventions', *EvQ* 59 (1987), 15–37.

—— 'Ἰουνιαν...ἐπίσημοι ἐν τοῖς ἀποστόλοις: A Re-examination of Romans 16:7 in Light of Primary Source Materials', *NTS* 51 (2005), 231–49.

Benko, S. *Pagan Rome and the Early Christians.* Bloomington: Indiana University, 1969.

Bertram, G. and H. Seesemann. 'πατέω, κτλ.', *TDNT* 5 (1967), 544.

Best, E. *One Body in Christ: A Study of the Relationship of the Church to Christ in the Epistles of the Apostle Paul.* London: SPCK, 1955.

—— 'Bishops and Deacons: Phil 1:1', *SE* 4 (1968), 371–76.

Betz, H. D. 'Apostle', *ABD* 1 (1992), 309–11.

Beyer, H. W. 'διακονέω, διακονία, διάκονος', *TDNT* 2 (1964), 81–93.

Bieringer, R. 'Women and Leadership in Romans 16: The Leading Roles of Phoebe, Prisca, and Junia in Early Christianity: Part I', *East Asian Pastoral Review* 44 (2007), 221–37.

Bjerkelund, C. J. *Parakalo. Form, Function und Sinn der parakalo-Sätze in den paulinischen Briefen.* Bibliotheca Theologica Norvegica 1; Oslo, 1967.

Black, M. *Romans.* 2nd edn. NCBC; Grand Rapids: Eerdmans, 1989.

Boatwright, M. T. 'Plancia Magna of Perge: Women's Roles and Status in Roman Asia Minor'. In S. B. Pomeroy (ed.), *Women's History and Ancient History.* London: The University of North Carolina Press, 1991, 249–72.

Bonhoeffer, D. *The Communion of the Saints: A Dogmatic Inquiry into the Sociology of the Church.* Eng. trans., New York: Harper & Row, 1963.

—— *Ethics.* New York: Macmillan, 1965.

—— *Christology.* Eng. trans., London: SCM, 1978.

Bornkamm, G. 'The Letter to the Romans as Paul's Last Will and Testament'. In K. P. Donfried (ed.), *The Romans Debate.* Peabody: Hendrickson, 1991, 16–28.

Branick, V. *The House Church in the Writings of Paul.* Wilmington: Michael Glazier, 1989.

Brooten, B. J. *Women Leaders in the Ancient Synagogue: Inscriptional Evidence and Background Issues*. BJS 36; California: Scholars, 1982.

Bruyne, D. de. 'Les deux derniers chapitres de la lettre aux Romains', *RBen* 25 (1908), 423–30.

Burchard, C. 'Joseph and Aseneth'. In J. H. Charlesworth (ed.), *The Old Testament Pseudepigrapha* 2. London: Longman and Todd, 1985, 177–248.

Burer, M. H. and D. B. Wallace. 'Was Junia Really an Apostle? A Re-Examination of Rom 16:7', *NTS* 47 (2001), 76–91.

Byrne, B. *Romans*. Sacra Pagina Series 6. Collegeville: Liturgical, 1996.

Calvin, J. The *First Epistle of Paul the Apostle to the Corinthians*. Edinburgh: Oliver & Boyd, 1960.

—— *Commentaries on the Epistle of Paul to the Romans*. J. Owen (trans.). Vol. XIX; Grand Rapids: Baker House, 1993.

Cameron, A. 'Neither Male nor Female', *Greece and Rome* 27 (1980), 60–68.

Campbell, J. C. *Phoebe: Patron and Emissary. Paul's Social Network: Brothers and Sisters in Faith*. Minnesota: Liturgical, 2009.

Campbell, W. S. *Paul and the Creation of Christian Identity*. London: T&T Clark, 2006.

Cervin, R. S. 'A Note Regarding the Name "Junias" in Romans 16:7', *NTS* 40 (1994), 464–70.

Chapple, A. L. 'Local Leadership in the Pauline Churches: Theological and Social Factors in its Development. A Study based on 1 Thessalonians, 1 Corinthians and Philippians'. PhD Dissertation. University of Durham, 1984.

Chow, J. K. *Patronage and Power: A Study of Social Networks in Corinth*. JSNTSup 75; Sheffield: JSOT, 1992.

Clarke, A. D. *Secular and Christian Leadership in Corinth: A Socio-Historical & Exegetical Study of 1 Cor 1–6*. New York: Brill, 1993.

—— *Serve the Community of the Church: Christians as Leaders and Ministers*. Grand Rapids: Eerdmans, 2000.

—— 'Jew and Greek, Slave and Free, Male and Female: Paul's Theology of Ethnic, Racial and Gender Inclusiveness of Romans 16'. In P. Oakes (ed.), *Rome in the Bible and the Early Church*. Grand Rapids: Baker Academic, 2002, 103–25.

—— 'Equality or Mutuality? Paul's Use of "Brother" Language'. In P. J. Williams et al. (eds.), *The New Testament in its First Century Setting: Essays on Context and Background in Honour of B. W. Winter*. Grand Rapids: Eerdmans, 2004, 151–64.

Clemente, G. 'Il Patronato Nei Collegis Dell'Impero Romano', *Studi classici e orientali* 21 (1972), 142–229.

Coffee, D. M. 'The Function of Homeric Simile', *AJP* 78 (1957), 113–32.

Cohen, S. J. D. 'Women in the Synagogues of Antiquity', *Conservative Judaism* 34 (1980), 23–29.

Cohick, L. Y. *Women in the World of the Earliest Christians: Illuminating Ancient Ways of Life*. Grand Rapids: Baker Academic, 2009.

Collins, J. N. *Diakonia: Re-interpreting the Ancient Sources*. Oxford: Oxford University Press, 1990.

Collins, M. S. 'Money, Sex and Power: An Examination of the Role of Women as Patrons of the Ancient Synagogues'. In P. J. Hass (ed.), *Recovering the Role of Women: Power and Authority in Rabbinic Jewish Society*. Atlanta: Scholars Press, 1992, 7–22.

Collins, R. F. *First Corinthians*. Collegeville: Liturgical Press, 1999.

Corssen, P. 'Zur Überlieferungsgeschichte des Römerbriefes', *ZNW* 10 (1909), 1–45.

Cotter, W. 'Women's Authority Roles in Paul's Churches: Countercultural or Conventional?', *NovT* 36 (1994), 350–72.

Cranfield, C. E. B. *A Critical and Exegetical Commentary on the Epistle to the Romans*. 2 Vols. Edinburgh: T&T Clark, 1978.

Croft, S. 'Text Messages: The Ministry of Women and Romans 16', *Anvil* 21 (2004), 87–94.

Dautzenberg, G. 'Zur Stellung der Frauen in der paulinischen Gemeinden'. In *Die Frau im Urchristentum*. QD 95; Freiburg: Herder, 1983, 182–224.

Deissmann, A. *Light from the Ancient East*. L. R. M. Strachen (trans.). London: Hodder and Stoughton, 1910.

Delling. G. 'ἀρχηγός', *TDNT* 1 (1964), 487–88.

Dodd, C. H. *The Epistle of Paul to the Romans*. London: Collins, 1932.

Donfried, K. P. 'A Short Note on Romans 16'. In K. P. Donfreid (ed.), *The Romans Debate*. Peabody: Hendrickson, 1991, 44–52.

Doty, W. G. *Letters in Primitive Christianity*. Philadelphia: Fortress, 1973.

Dunn, J. D. G. *Romans 9–16*. WBC 2; Texas: Word Books, 1988.

—— 'Romans', *DPL* (1993), 838–46.

—— *The Epistle to the Colossians and to Philemon: A Commentary on the Greek Text*. Grand Rapids: Eerdmans, 1996.

—— *Theology of Paul the Apostle*. London: T&T Clark, 2003.

Edgar, C. C. *Annales du Service des Antiquités de l'Egypte* 22 (1922), 13.

Ehrensperger, K. *That We may be Mutually Encouraged: Feminism and the New Perspective in Pauline Studies*. London: T&T Clark, 2004.

Ellis, E. E. 'Paul and his Co-workers', *DPL* (1993), 183–89.

—— 'Paul and his Co-workers', *NTS* 17 (1977), 437–52.

Engberg-Pedersen, T. *Paul and the Stoics*. Edinburgh: T&T Clark, 2000.

—— 'The Relationship with Others: Similarities and Differences between Paul and the Stoics', *ZNW* 96 (2005), 35–60.

Epp, E. J. *Junia: The First Woman Apostle*. Minneapolis: Fortress Press, 2005.

Esler, P. F. *Conflict and Identity in Romans: The Social Setting of Paul's Letter*. Minneapolis: Fortress Press, 2003.

—— 'Paul and Stoicism: Romans 12 as a Test Case', *NTS* 50 (2004), 106–24.

Exler, F. X. J. *The Form of the Ancient Greek Letter: A Study in Greek Epistolography*. Washington, DC: Catholic University of America, 1923, 73–77.

Fàbrega, V. 'War Junia[s], der hervorragende Apostel [Röm. 16, 7], eine Frau?', *JAC* 27/28 (1984/85), 47–64.

Fee, G. D. The *First Epistle to the Corinthians*. Grand Rapids: Eerdmans, 1987.

—— *Paul's Letter to the Philippians*. Grand Rapids: Eerdmans, 1995.

Fiorenza, E. S. 'Missionaries, Apostles, Co-workers: Romans 16 and the Reconstruction of Women's Early Christian History', *WW* 6 (1986), 420–33.

—— *Discipleship of Equals: A Critical Feminist Ekklesia-logy of liberation*. New York: Cross Road, 1993.

—— *In Memory of Her: A Feminist Theological Reconstruction of Christian Origins*. London: SCM, 1995.

Fitzmyer, J. A. 'Some Notes on Aramaic Epistolography', *JBL* 93 (1974), 201–25.

—— *Paul and his Theology*. New Jersey: Prentice Hall, 1989.

—— *Romans: A New Translation with Introduction and Commentary*. AB; New York: Doubleday, 1992.

Francis, F. O. 'The Form and Function of the Opening and Closing Paragraphs of James and 1 John', *ZNW* 61 (1970), 110–26.

Friedrich, G. (ed.) 'πρᾶγμα', *TDNT* 6 (1968), 638–40.

Funk, W. *Language, Hermeneutic, and Word of God: The Problem of Language in the New Testament and Contemporary Theology*. New York: Harper & Row, 1966.

Furnish, V. P. *The Love Command in the New Testament*. London: SCM, 1973.

Gamble, H. *The Textual History of the Letter to the Romans: A Study in Textual and Literary Criticism*. Studies and Documents 42; Grand Rapids: Eerdmans, 1977.

Garland, D. E. *1 Corinthians*. BECNT; Grand Rapids: Baker Academic, 2003.

Garland, R. 'Priests and Power in Classical Athens'. In M. Beard and J. North (eds.), *Pagan Priests: Religion and Power in the Ancient World*. London: Duckworth, 1990, 73–91.

Gaston, L. 'Faith in Romans 12 in the Light of the Common Life of the Roman Church'. In J. V. Hills (ed.), *Common Life in the Early Church: Essays Honoring Graydon F. Snyder*. Harrisburg: Trinity Press International, 1998, 258–64.

Gehring, R. W. *House Church and Mission: The Importance of Household Structures in Early Christianity*. Peabody: Hendrickson, 2004.

Georgi, D. *The Opponents of Paul in Second Corinthians*. SNTW; Edinburgh: T&T Clark, 1987.

Gillman, F. M. *Women Who Knew Paul*. Zacchaeus Studies: New Testament. Collegeville: Liturgical Press, 1992.

Glad, C. E. *Paul and Philodemus: Adaptability in Epicurean and Early Christian Psychagogy*. NovTSup 81; New York: Brill, 1995.

Godet, F. L. *First Epistle to the Corinthians*. A. Cusin (trans.). Vol. 2 CFTL, New Series XXX; Edinburgh: T&T Clark, 1898.

—— *Commentary on the Epistle to the Romans*. Vol. 2. Edinburgh: T&T Clark, 1880.

Goodenough, E. *Jewish Symbols in the Greco-Roman Period.* Bollingen Series 37; 13 Vols. Princeton, Princeton University Press, 1953–68.

Goodspeed, E. J. 'Phoebe's Letter of Introduction', *HTR* 44 (1951), 56–57.

Grey, M. *Redeeming the Dream: Feminism Redemption and Christian Tradition.* London: SPCK, 1989.

Grubbs, J. E. *Women and the Law in the Roman Empire: A Sourcebook on Marriage, Divorce and Widowhood.* London: Routledge, 2002.

Gundry-Volf, J. M. 'Gender and Creation in 1 Cor 11:2-16: A Study in Paul's Theological Method'. In J. Adna, S. J. Hafeman, and O. Hofius (eds.), *Evangelium, Schriftauslegung, Kirche: Festschrift für P. Stuhlmacher.* Göttingen: Vandenhoeck & Ruprecht, 1997, 151–71.

Haacker, K. 'πλησίον', *EDNT* 3 (1993), 113.

Hannaford, R. 'The Representative and Relational Nature of Ministry and the Renewal of the Diaconate'. In *The Ministry of Deacon: Ecclesiological Explorations.* Uppsala: NEC, 2000.

Harland, P. A. *Associations, Synagogues and Congregations: Claiming a Place in Ancient Mediterranean Society.* Minneapolis: Fortress, 2003.

—— 'Familial Dimensions of Group Identity (II): Mothers and Fathers in Associations and Synagogues of the Greek World', *JSJ* 38 (2007), 57–79.

Harnack, A. von. 'κοπιᾶν (Οἱ Κοπιῶντες) im frühchristlichen Sprachgebrauch', *ZNW* 27 (1928), 1–10.

—— *The Mission and Expansion of Christianity in the First Three Centuries.* J. Moffatt (trans.). New York: Harper, 1962 [1908].

Harrison, J. H. *Paul's Language of Grace in its Greco-Roman Context.* Tübingen: Mohr Siebeck, 2003.

Hentschel, A. *Diakonia im Neuen Testament: Studien Zur Semantik unter besonderer Berücksichtigung der Rolle von Frauen.* Tübingen: Mohr Siebeck, 2007.

Heyward, C. *The Redemption of God: The Theology of Mutual Relation.* Washington, D.C.: University Press of America, 1982.

Hock, R. F. 'Paul's Tent-making and the Problem of his Social Class', *JBL* 97 (1978), 555–74.

Hodge, C. *Commentary on the Epistle to the Romans.* New York: Hodder and Stoughton, 1983.

Holmberg, B. *Paul and Power: The Structure of Authority in the Primitive Church as Reflected in the Pauline Epistles.* Philadelphia: Fortress, 1980.

Hooker, M. D. 'Authority on Her Head: An Examination of 1 Cor 11:10', *NTS* 10 (1963–64), 410–16.

Horrell, D. G. *The Social Ethos of the Corinthian Correspondence: Interest and Ideology from 1 Corinthians to 1 Clement.* Edinburgh: T&T Clark, 1996.

—— *Solidarity and Difference: A Contemporary Reading of Paul's Ethics.* London: T&T Clark, 2005.

Horsley, G. H. R. 'Maria the διάκονος', *NewDocs* 2 (1982), 193–95.

—— 'Giving Thanks to Artemis', *NewDocs* 4 (1987), 127–29.

Horst, J. 'μέλος', *TDNT* 4 (1967), 556, 562.

Horst, P. W. van der. 'The Jews of Ancient Crete', *JJS* 39 (1988), 183–200.

Hort, F. J. A. 'On the End of the Epistle of Romans', *Journal of Philology* 3 (1871), 51–80.

Hurtado, L.W. 'The Doxology at the End of Romans'. In E. P. Epp and G. D. Fee (eds.), *New Testament Textual Criticism: Its Significance for Exegesis. Essays in Honour of Bruce M. Metzger*. Oxford: Clarendon, 1981, 185–99.

Hutter, D. 'Did Paul Call Andronicus an Apostle in Romans 16:7?', *JETS* (2009), 747–78.

Jewett, R. *Paul's Anthropological Terms: A Study of Their Use in Conflict Situations*. AGJU10; Leiden: Brill, 1971.

—— *Christian Tolerance: Paul's Message to the Modern Church*. Philadelphia: Westminster, 1982.

—— 'Paul, Phoebe, and Spanish Mission'. In J. Neusner et al. (eds.), *The Social World of Formative Christianity and Judaism: Essays in Tribute to Howard Clark Kee*. Philadelphia: Fortress, 1988, 144–64.

—— 'Honour and Shame in the Argument of Romans'. In A. Brown, G. F. Snyder, and V. Wiles (eds.), *Putting Body and Soul Together: Essays in Honour of Robin Scroggs*. Valley Forge: Trinity Press International, 1997, 257–72.

—— *Romans*. Minneapolis: Fortress, 2007.

Judge, E. A. 'Cultural Conformity and Innovation in Paul: Some Clues from Contemporary Documents', *TynBul* 35 (1984), 3–24.

Karris, R. J. 'Romans 14:1–15:13 and the Occasion of Romans'. In K. P. Donfried (ed.), *Romans Debate*, revised and expanded edition. Peabody: Hendrickson, 1991, 65–84.

Käsemann, E. 'The Theological Problem Presented by the Motif of the Body of Christ'. In *Perspectives on Paul*. London: SCM, 1971, 102–21.

—— *Commentary on Romans*. Grand Rapids: Eerdmans, 1980.

Kearsley, R. A. 'Women in the Public East: Iunia Theodora, Claudia Metrodora and Phoebe, Benefactress of Paul', *TynBul* 50 (1999), 189–21.

Keck, L. E. *Romans*. Nashville: Abingdon, 2005.

Keener, C. S. *Paul, Women and Wives: Marriage and Women's Ministry in the Letters of Paul*. Peabody: Hendrickson, 1992.

Keyes, C. W. 'The Greek Letter of Introduction', *AJP* 56 (1935), 28–44.

Keil, J. 'Inschriften'. In *Forschungen in Ephesos* III (Vienna, 1923), 94–95.

Kim, C.-H. *The Form and Structure of the Familiar Greek Letter of Recommendation*. SBLDS 4; Missoula, MT: Scholars Press, 1972.

Kim, Y. S. *Christ's Body in Corinth: The Politics of a Metaphor*. Minneapolis: Fortress Press, 2008.

Kittel, G. 'συναιχμαλώτος', *TDNT* 1 (1964), 196–97.

Klassen, W. 'Kiss', *ABD* 4 (1992), 89–92.

—— '*Agape*', *ABD* 1 (1992), 381–396.

—— 'The Sacred Kiss in the New Testament: An Example of Social Boundary Lines', *NTS* 39 (1993), 122–35.

Klauck, H. J. *Hausgemeinde und Hauskirche im frühen Christendum*. Stuttgart: Katholisches Bibelwerk, 1981.

—— *Herrenmahl und Hellenistischer Kult. Eine religionsgeschichtliche Untersuchung zum ersten Korintherbrief*. Münster: Aschendorff, 1982, 281–83.

Kloppenborg, J. S. 'Collegia and Thiasoi: Issues in Function, Taxonomy and Membership'. In J. S. Kloppenborg and S. G. Wilson (eds.), *Voluntary Associations in the Graeco-Roman World*. London: Routledge, 1996, 16–30.

Koenig, J. *New Testament Hospitality: Partnership with Strangers as Promise and Mission*. Philadelphia: Fortress, 1985.

Koester, H. 'Ephesos in Early Christian Literature'. In H. Koester (ed.), *Ephesos: Metropolis of Asia*. Harrisburg: Trinity Press, 1995, 119–40.

Koskenniemi, H. *Studien zur Idee und Phraseologie des griechischen Briefes bis 400 n. Chr.* Helsinki: Akateeminen Kirjakauppa, 1956.

Kraemer, R. S. *Her Share of the Blessings: Women's Religions among Pagans, Jews, and Christians in the Greco-Roman World*. Oxford: Oxford University Press, 1992.

Krauss, S. *Synagogale Altertümer*. Berlin: Benjamin Harz, 1922.

Kümmel, W. G. *Introduction to the New Testament*. Nashville: Abingdon, 1975.

Kurek-Chomycz, D. A. 'Is there an "Anti-Priscan" Tendency in the Manuscripts? Some Textual Problems with Prisca and Aquila', *JBL* 125 (2006), 107–28.

La Piana, G. 'Foreign Groups at Rome', *HTR* 20 (1927), 183–403.

Lagrange, M.-J. *Saint Paul: Épître aux Romains*. Études Bibliques; Paris: Gabalda, 1931.

Lampe, P. 'Persis', *ABD* 5 (1992), 244.

—— 'Prisca', *ABD* 5 (1992), 467–68.

—— 'Julia', *ABD* 3 (1992), 1125.

—— 'Iunia/Iunias: Sklavenherkunft im Kreise der vorpaulinischen Apostel (Röm 16 7)', *ZNW* 76 (1985), 132–34.

—— 'The Roman Christians of Romans 16'. In K. P. Donfried (ed.), *The Romans Debate*, revised and expanded edition. Peabody: Hendrickson, 1991, 216–30.

—— *From Paul to Valentinus: Christians at Rome in the First Two Centuries*. Minneapolis: Fortress Press, 2003.

Lakey, M. *Image and Glory of God: 1 Cor. 11:2-16 as a Case Study in Bible, Gender and Hermeneutics*. LNTS; London: T&T Clark, 2010.

Leenhardt, F.-J. *The Epistle of St. Paul to the Romans: A Commentary*. London: Lutterworth, 1961.

Lefkowitz, M. R. and M. B. Kant, *Women's Life in Greece and Rome: A Source Book in Translation*. London: Duckworth, 1992.

Lenski, R. C. H. *The Interpretation of St. Paul's Epistle to the Romans.* Minneapolis: Augsburg, 1961.

Liddell, H. G., R. Scott, and H. S. Jones, *A Greek–English Lexicon.* 9th edn. with Revised Supplement. Oxford: Oxford University Press, 1996.

Lietzmann, H. *Kleine Schriften.* Kurt Aland (ed.). 3 vols. *Untersuchungen zur Geschichte der Altchristlichen Literatur* 67, 68, 74. Berlin: Akademie-Verlag, 1958–62.

Lightfoot, J. B. *St. Paul's Epistle to the Philippians.* London: Macmillan, 1894.

—— (ed.) *Biblical Essays.* New York: Macmillan, 1904.

Llewelyn, S. R. 'The Christian Letters of Recommendation', *NewDocs* 8, 170.

—— 'Changing the Legal Jurisdiction', *NewDocs* 9, 45–53.

Lohfink, G. 'Weibliche Diakone im Neuen Testament'. In J. Blank et al. (eds.), *Die Frau im Urchristentum.* QD 95; Freiburg: Herder, 1983, 320–38.

Lowe, S. D. 'Rethinking the Female Status/Function Question: The Jew/ Gentile Relationship as Paradigm', *JETS* 34 (1991), 59–75.

Luck, U. B. 'σωφρονέω κτλ.', *TDNT* 7 (1971), 1098–100.

Luther, M. *Early Theological Works.* J. Atkinson (trans. and ed.). London: SCM, 1962.

McDonald, J. I. H. 'Was Romans XVI a Separate Letter?', *NTS* 16 (1969–70), 369–72.

McLean, B. H. *An Introduction of Greek Epigraphy of the Hellenistic and Roman Periods from Alexander the Great down to the Reign of Constantine (323 B.C.–A.D. 337).* Michigan: The University of Michigan Press, 2002.

MacMullen, R. *Roman Social Relations.* London: Yale University Press, 1974.

—— 'Women in Public in the Roman Empire', *Historia* 29 (1980), 208–18.

Malina, B. *The New Testament World: Insights from Cultural Anthropology.* Louisville: John Knox Press, 2001.

Manson, T. W. 'St. Paul's Letter to the Romans – and Others'. In K. P. Donfried (ed.), *The Romans Debate*, revised and expanded edition. Peabody: Hendrickson, 1991, 3–15.

—— 'St. Paul's Letter to the Romans – and Others'. In M. Black (ed.), *Studies in the Gospels and Epistles.* Manchester, 1962, 225–41.

Marshall, I. H. and D. A. Hagner, *1 Corinthians.* Grand Rapids: Eerdmans, 2000.

Marshall, I. H. and P. H. Towner, *A Critical and Exegetical Commentary on The Pastoral Epistles.* Edinburgh: T&T Clark, 1999.

Martin, D. B. *Slavery as Salvation: The Metaphor of Slavery in Pauline Christianity.* London: Yale University Press, 1990.

—— 'Tongues of Angels and Other Status Indicators', *JAAR* 59 (1991), 547–89.

—— *The Corinthian Body.* New Haven: Yale University, 1995.

Meeks, W. A. *The First Urban Christians; The Social World of the Apostle Paul.* New Haven: Yale University Press, 1983.

—— 'Judgement and the Brother: Romans 14:1–15:13'. In G. F. Hawthorne with O. Betz (eds.), *Tradition and Interpretation in the New Testament*:

Essays in Honor of E. Earle Ellis for his 60th birthday. Grand Rapids: Eerdmans, 1987, 290–300.

Meggitt, J. *Paul, Poverty and Survival.* SNTW; Edinburgh: T&T Clark, 1998.

Metzger, B. M. *A Textual Commentary on the Greek New Testament.* 2nd edn. London: Deutsche Bibelgesellschaft/UBS, 1994.

Meyer, H. A. W. *Critical and Exegetical Handbook to the Epistle to the Romans.* J. C. Moore (trans.). Edinburgh: T&T Clark, 1876.

—— *Critical and Exegetical Handbook to the Epistles to the Corinthians: First Epistle.* Vol. 1; Edinburgh: T&T Clark, 1892.

Michel, O. 'οἰκοδομέω κτλ.', *TDNT* 5 (1967), 140–42.

—— *Der Brief an die Römer.* KEK, 4; Göttingen: Vandenhoeck & Ruprecht, 1978.

Michelis, W. 'συγγενής, συγγένεια', *TDNT* 7 (1971), 742.

Minear, P. S. *The Obedience of Faith; The Purposes of Paul in the Epistle to the Romans.* SBT 2/19; London: SCM, 1971.

Mitchell, M. M. *Paul and the Rhetoric of Reconciliation: An Exegetical Investigation of the Language and Composition of 1 Corinthians.* Tübingen: Mohr, 1991.

Moffatt, J. *Introduction to the Literature of the New Testament.* 3rd edn. New York: Charles Scribner's Sons, 1918.

Moo, D. J. The *Epistle to the Romans.* Grand Rapids: Eerdmans, 1996.

Morris, L. The *Epistle to the Romans.* Grand Rapids: Eerdmans, 1988.

Moulton, J. H. and G. Milligan. *The Vocabulary of the Greek Testament: Illustrated from the Papyri and Other Non-literary Sources.* London: Hodder and Stoughton, 1914–29.

Moulton, W. F. and G. S. Geden. *Concordance to the Greek New Testament.* I. H. Marshall (ed.). Edinburgh: T&T Clark, 2002.

Moxnes, H. 'Honour and Righteousness', *JSNT* 32 (1988), 61–77.

—— 'Honour, Shame and the Outside World in Paul's Letter to the Romans'. In J. Neusner et al. (eds.), *The Social World of Formative Christianity and Judaism.* Philadelphia: Fortress, 1988, 208.

—— The Quest for Honour and the Unity of the Community in Romans 12 and in the Orations of Dio Chrysostom'. In T. Engberg-Pederson (ed.), *Paul in his Hellenistic Context.* Edinburgh: T&T Clark, 1994, 203–30.

Mullins, T. Y. 'Greeting as a New Testament Form', *JBL* 87 (1968), 418–26.

Murphy-O'Connor, J. 'Prisca and Aquila: Travelling Tentmakers and Church Builders', *BRev* 8 (1992), 40–51.

Murray, J. *The Epistle to the Romans.* NICNT Vol. 2. Grand Rapids: Eerdmans, 1965.

Ng, E.Y. 'Phoebe as *Prostatis*', *TJ* 25 (2004), 3–13.

Noy, D. *Jewish Inscriptions of Western Europe.* 2 vols. Cambridge: Cambridge University Press, 1993.

Nygren, A. *Commentary on Romans.* C. C. Rasmuussen (trans). Philadelphia: Fortress Press, 1975.

Oakes, P. *Reading Romans in Pompeii: Paul's Letter at Ground Level.* Minneapolis: Fortress Press, 2009.

O'Brien, P.T. *The Epistle to the Philippians: A Commentary on the Greek Text.* Grand Rapids: Eerdmans, 1991.

—— 'Letters, Letter Forms', *DPL* (1993), 550–53.

Økland, J. *Women in their Place: Paul and the Corinthian Discourse of Gender and Sanctuary Space.* JSNTSup 269; London: T&T Clark, 2004.

Ollrog, W.-H. *Paulus und seine Mitarbeiter.* WMANT 50; Neurkirchen: Neukirchener, 1979.

Omanson, R. L. 'Who's Who in Romans 16? Identifying Men and Women among the People Paul Sent Greetings to', *BT* 49 (1998), 430–36.

Osiek, C. '*Diakonos* and *Prostatis*: Women's Patronage in Early Christianity', *HTS* 61 (2005), 347–70.

Osiek, C. and D. L. Balch, *Families in the New Testament World: Households and House Churches.* Louisville: Westminster John Knox, 1997.

Osiek, C. and M. Y. MacDonald, *A Woman's Place: House Churches in Earliest Christianity.* Minneapolis: Fortress, 2006.

Oster, R. E. 'Congregations of the Gentiles (Rom 16:4): A Culture-based Ecclesiology in the Letters of Paul', *RestorQuart* 40 (1998), 39–52.

Pagels, E. H. 'Paul and Women: A Response to Recent Discussion', *JAAR* 42 (1974), 538–49.

Pallas, D. I., S. Charitonidis, and J. Venencie. 'Inscriptions lyciennes trouvées à Solômos près de Corinthe', *Bulletin de Correspondance héllenique* 83 (1959), 496–508.

Payne, P. B. *Man and Woman, One in Christ: An Exegetical and Theological Study of Paul's Letters.* Grand Rapids: Zondervan, 2009.

Pederson, S. 'Agape – der eschatologische Hauptbegriff bei Paulus'. In S. Pederson (ed.). *Die Paulinische Literatur und Theologie.* Anlässlich der 50 jähringen Gründungs-Feier der Universität Aarhus. Göttingen: Vandenhoeck & Ruprecht, 1980, 159–86.

Peristiany, J. G. *Honour and Shame: The Values of Mediterranean Society.* London: Weidenfeld and Nicolson, 1965.

Perrimann, A. C. 'The Head of a Woman: The Meaning of κεφαλή in 1 Cor 11:3', *JTS* 45 (1994), 602–22.

Peterson, J. M. 'House-Churches in Rome', *VC* 23 (1969), 264–72.

Philsy, Sr. 'Diakonia of Women in the New Testament', *IJT* 32 (1983), 110–18.

Piper, J. *Love your Enemies: Jesus' Love Command in the Synoptic Gospels and the Early Christian Paraenesis.* SNTSMS 38; Cambridge: Cambridge University Press, 1979.

Piper, J. and W. Grudem (eds.). *Recovering Biblical Manhood and Womanhood: A Response to Evangelical Feminism.* Wheaton, IL: Crossway, 1991.

Plisch, U.-K. 'Die Apostelin Junia: Das Exegetische Problem in Röm 16:7 im Licht von Nestle–Aland und der Sahidischen Überlieferung', *NTS* 42 (1996), 477–78.

Poland, F. *Geschichte des griechischen Vereinswesens.* Leipzig: Teubner, 1909.

Reasoner, M. *The Strong and the Weak: Romans 14:1–15:13 in Context.* SNTSMS 103; Cambridge: Cambridge University Press, 1999.

Reid, M. L. 'Paul's Rhetoric of Mutuality: A Rhetorical Reading of Romans'. In E. H. Lovering (ed.), *SBL Papers*. Atlanta: Scholars Press, 1995, 117–39.

Reike, B. 'προΐστημι', *TDNT* 6 (1968), 700–703.

Rengstorf, K. H. 'ἐπίσημος', *TDNT* 7 (1971), 267.

Reynolds, J. M. and R. Tannenbaum. *Jews and God Fearers at Aphrodisias: Greek Inscriptions with Commentary*. PCPSSV 12; Cambridge Philological Society, 1987.

Ridderbos, H. *Paul: An Outline of his Theology*. J. R. De Witt (trans.). London: SPCK, 1977.

Riggenbach, E. 'Die Textgeschichte der Doxologie Röm. 16, 25-27 im Zusammenhang mit den übrigen, den Schluss des Römerbriefs betreffenden, textkritischen Fragen', *Neue Jahrbüchen für deutsche Theologie* 1 (1892), 526–605.

Rives, J. 'Civic and Religious Life'. In J. Bodel (ed.), *Epigraphic Evidence: Ancient History from Inscriptions*. London: Routledge, 2001, 118–36.

Robert, J. and L. Robert. 'Bulletin épigraphique', *Revue der études grecques* 69 (1956), 152–53.

Robert, L. 'Inscriptiones de Chios du Ier siècle de notre ère'. In *Études épigraphiques et philologiques*. Paris: Champion, 1938, 133–34.

Robertson, A. and A. Plummer. *A Critical and Exegetical Commentary on the First Epistle of Paul to the Corinthians*. ICC; Edinburgh: T&T Clark, 1914.

Roetzel, C. J. *Judgment in the Community: A Study of the Relationship between Eschatology and Ecclesiology in Paul*. Leiden: Brill, 1972.

Roller, O. *Das Formular der paulinischen Briefe; ein Beitrag zur Lehre vom antiken Briefe*. BWANT 4/6 (58); Stuttgart: Kohlhammer, 1933, 481–82.

Romaniuk, K. 'Was Phoebe in Romans 16,1 a Deaconess?', *ZNW* 81 (1990), 132–34.

Saller, R. P. *Personal Patronage under the Early Empire*. Cambridge: Cambridge University Press, 1982.

Sampley, J. P. 'The Weak and the Strong: Paul's Careful and Crafty Rhetorical Strategy in Romans 14:1–15:3'. In L. M. White and O. L. Yarbrough (eds.), *The Social World of the First Christians: Essays in Honour of Wayne A. Meeks*. Minneapolis: Fortress, 1995, 40–52.

Sanday, W. and A. C. Headlam. *A Critical and Exegetical Commentary to the Epistle to the Romans*. Edinburgh: T&T Clark, 1902.

Sanders, E. P. *Jewish Law from Jesus to the Mishnah*. London: SCM Press, 1990.

Schlatter, A. *Der Römerbrief*. HThKNT 6; Freiburg: Herder, 1977.

—— *Romans: The Righteousness of God*. Peabody: Hendrickson, 1995.

Schlier, H. *Der Römerbrief*. HThKNT, 6. Freiburg: Herder, 1970.

Schmidt, H. W. *Der Brief des Paulus an die Römer*. THKNT, 6; Berlin: Evangelische Verlagsanstalt, 1963.

Schmithals, W. *Der Römerbrief: Ein Kommentar*. Gütersloh: Mohn, 1988.

Schneider, J. 'τιμή κτλ.', *TDNT* 8 (1972), 169–80.

—— 'ὄνειδος κτλ.', *TDNT* 5 (1967), 238.

Schotroff, L. *Lydia's Impatient Sisters: A Feminist Social History of Early Christianity*. B. and M. Rumscheidt (trans). Louisville: John Knox Press, 1995.

Schreiber, S. 'Arbeit mit der Gemeinde (Rom16:6, 12). Zur versunkenen Möglichkeit der Gemeindeleitung durch Frauen', *NTS* 46 (2000), 204–26.

Schreiner, T. R. *Romans*. Grand Rapids: Baker Academic, 1998.

Schubert, P. *Form and Function of the Pauline Thanksgivings*. Berlin: A.Töpelmann, 1939.

Schulz, R. R. 'Junia or Junias?', *ExpT* 98 (1987), 108–10.

—— 'A Case for "President" Phoebe in Romans 16:2', *LTJ* 24 (1990), 124–27.

Schumacher, R. 'Aquila und Priscilla', *TGI* 12 (1920), 89–99.

Schürer, E. *History of the Jewish People in the Age of Jesus Christ*. Geza Vermes, Fergus Millar, Matthew Black, and Pamela Vermes (rev. and ed.). 2 vols. Edinburgh: T&T Clark, 1973–79.

Schweizer, E. 'σῶμα κτλ.', *TDNT* 7 (1971), 1041.

Scroggs, R. 'Paul and the Eschatological Women', *JAAR* 41 (1972), 283–303.

Segal, A. F. *Paul the Convert: The Apostolate and Apostasy of Saul the Pharisee*. New Haven: Yale University Press, 1986.

Sevenster, J. N. *Paul and Seneca*. NovTSup 4; Leiden: Brill, 1961.

Sigountos J. G. and M. Shank. 'Public Roles for Women in the Pauline Church: A Reappraisal of the Evidence', *JETS* 26 (1983), 283–95.

Silva, M. *Philippians*. Grand Rapids: Baker Academic, 2005.

Soards, M. L. *1 Corinthians*. NIBC; Peabody: Hendrickson, 1999.

Soden, H. F. von. 'ἀδελφός κτλ.', *TDNT* 1 (1964), 145.

Söding, T. *Das Liebesgebot bei Paulus: Die Mahnung zur Agape im Rahmen der paulinischen Ethik*. NTAbh 26; Münster: Aschendorff, 1995.

Spicq, C. *Agape dans le Nouveau Testament. Analyse des Textes*. EBib 1, 2; Paris: Gabalda, 1958–59.

Stählin, G. 'ἀσθενέω κτλ.', *TDNT* 1 (1964), 490–93.

—— 'σκάνδαλον, σκανδαλίζω', *TDNT* 7 (1971), 339.

Stauffer, E. 'ἀγαπάω, ἀγάπη, ἀγαπητός', *TDNT* 1 (1964), 21–55.

Stowers, S. K. *The Diatribe and Paul's Letter to the Romans*. SBLDS 57; Chicago: Scholars Press, 1981.

—— *Letter Writing in Greco-Roman Antiquity*. Library of Early Christianity, 265; Philadelphia: Westminster Press, 1986.

—— *A Re-reading of Romans: Justice, Jew, and Gentiles*. New Haven: Yale University Press, 1994.

Stuhlmacher, P. 'The Theme of Romans'. In K. P. Donfried (ed.), *The Romans Debate*, revised and expanded edition. Peabody: Hendrickson, 1991, 333–45.

—— *Paul's Letter to the Romans: A Commentary*. S. J. Hafemann (trans.) Westminster: John Knox, 1994.

Theissen, G. *The Social Setting of Pauline Christianity: Essays on Corinth*. Edinburgh: T&T Clark, 1982.

Thiselton, A. C. *The First Epistle to the Corinthians*. Carlisle: Paternoster Press, 2000.

Thomas, W. D. 'Phoebe: A Helper of Many', *ExpTim* 95 (1984), 336–37.

Thorley, J. 'Junia, A Woman Apostle', *NovT* 38 (1996), 18–26.

Thorsteinsson, R. M. 'Paul and Roman Stoicism: Romans 12 and Contemporary Stoic Ethics', *JSNT* 29 (2006), 139–61.

Thraede, K. 'Ursprünge und Formen des "heiligen Kusses" im frühen Christentum', *JAC* 11/12 (1967–68), 124–80.

Tobin, T. H. *Paul's Rhetoric in its Contexts: The Argument of Romans*. Peabody: Hendrickson, 2004.

Tomson, P. J. *Paul and the Jewish Law: Halakha in the Letters of the Apostle to the Gentiles*. CRINT Vol. 1; Minneapolis: Fortress Press, 1990.

Trebilco, P. R. *Jewish Communities in Asia Minor*. Cambridge: Cambridge University Press, 1991.

Tromp, J. (trans.). *The Assumption of Moses: A Critical Edition with Commentary*. Leiden: Brill, 1993.

Verner, D. C. *The Household of God: The Social World of the Pastoral Epistles*. SBLDS 71; Chicago: Scholars Press, 1983.

Vouga, F. 'L' Epître aux Romains comme document ecclésiologique (Rom 12–15)', *ETR* 61 (1986), 489–91.

Waltzing, J. P. *Etude historique sur les corporations professionnelles chez les Romains depuis les origines jusqu'à la chute de l'Empire d'Occident*, 4 vols. Louvain: Georg Olms, 1970, 1.348–49.

Wannenwetsch, B. '"Members of One Another": *Charis*, Ministry and Representation: A Politico-Ecclesial Reading of Romans 12'. In C. Bartholomew et al., *A Royal Priesthood? A Use of the Bible Ethically and Politically: A Dialogue with Oliver O'Donovan*. The Scripture and Hermeneutics Series, vol. 3; Grand Rapids, Michigan: Zondervan, 2002, 197–220.

Warnach, V. *Agape. Die Liebe als Grundmotiv der neutestamentlichen Theologie*. Düsseldorf: Patmos, 1951.

Watson, F. *Paul, Judaism and the Gentiles*. SNTSMS 56; Cambridge: Cambridge University Press, 1986.

—— 'The Two Roman Congregations Rom 14:1–15:13'. In K. P. Donfried (ed.), *The Romans Debate*, revised and expanded edition. Peabody: Hendrickson, 1991, 203–15.

—— *Agape, Eros, Gender: Towards a Pauline Sexual Ethic*. Cambridge: Cambridge University Press, 2000.

Wedderburn, A. J. M. 'Some Observations on Paul's Use of the Phrases in Christ and with Christ', *JSNT* 25 (1985), 83–97.

—— *The Reasons for Romans*. Edinburgh: T&T Clark, 1988.

Weima, J. A. D. *Neglected Endings: The Significance of the Pauline Letter Closings*. JSNTSup 101; Sheffield: Sheffield Academic Press, 1994.

Weiser, A. 'Der Rolle der Frau in der urchristlichen Mission'. In G. Dautzenberg (ed.). *Die Frau im Urchristentum*. QD 95; Freiburg: Herder, 1983, 158–81.

Whelan, C. F. 'Amica Pauli: The Role of Phoebe in the Early Church', *JSNT* 49 (1993), 67–85.

White, J. L. 'Epistolary Formulas and Clichés in Greek Papyrus Letters'. In *SBL Seminar Papers 2*. Missoula, MT: Scholars, 1978, 289–319.

—— 'The Greek Documentary Letter Tradition: Third Century BCE to Third Century CE', *Semeia* 22 (1981), 92–95.

—— 'Saint Paul and the Apostolic Letter Tradition', *CBQ* 45 (1983), 433–44.

—— 'New Testament Epistolary Literature in the Framework of Ancient Epistolography'. In *Aufstieg und Niedergang der römischen Welt*, II, 25.2. Berlin: de Gruyter, 1984, 1730–56.

—— *Light from Ancient Letters*. Philadelphia: Fortress Press, 1986.

Windisch, K. H. 'ἀσπάζομαι', *TDNT* 1 (1964), 496–502.

Wilckens, U. 'ὑποκρίνομαι κτλ.', *TDNT* 8 (1972), 559–71.

—— *Der Brief an die Römer*. Vol. 3. EKKNT, 6. Neukirchen-Vluyn: Neukirchener Verlag, 1978–82.

Wilson, F. V. 'The Significance of the Early House Churches', *JBL* 58 (1939), 105–12.

Wilson, W. T. *Love without Pretense: Romans 12:9-11 and Hellenistic-Jewish Wisdom Literature*. Tübingen: Mohr, 1991.

Winter, B. W. *Roman Wives, Roman Widows: The Appearance of New Women and the Pauline Communities*. Grand Rapids: Eerdmans, 2003.

—— 'Roman Law and Society in Romans 12–15'. In P. Oakes (ed.), *Rome in the Bible and the Early Church*. Carlisle: Paternoster Press, 2002, 67–102.

Wire, A. *The Corinthian Women Prophets: A Reconstruction through Paul's Rhetoric*. Minneapolis: Fortress Press, 1990.

Witherington, B. *Conflict and Community in Corinth: A Socio-Rhetorical Commentary on 1 and 2 Corinthians*. Grand Rapids: Eerdmans, 1995.

Yorke, G. L. O. R. *The Church as the Body of Christ: A Re-examination*. Lanham: University Press of America, 1991.

Zahn, T. *Der Brief des Paulus an die Römer*. Kommentar zum Neuen Testament 6; Leipzig: Deichert, 1910.

Ziemann, F. *De Epistularum Graecarum Formulis Sollemnibus Quaestiones Selectae*. Berlin: Haas, 1912.

Ziesler, J. *Paul's Letter to the Romans*. TPI; London: SCM, 1989.

Zmijewski, J. 'ἀσθενής κτλ.', *EDNT* 1 (1990), 171.

Index of Biblical and Other Ancient Sources

INDEX OF AUTHORS